GENDER IN HISTORY

Series editors:
Pam Sharpe, Patricia Skinner and Penny Summerfield

The expansion of research into the history of women and gender since the 1970s has changed the face of history. Using the insights of feminist theory and of historians of women, gender historians have explored the configuration in the past of gender identities and relations between the sexes. They have also investigated the history of sexuality and family relations, and analysed ideas and ideals of masculinity and femininity. Yet gender history has not abandoned the original, inspirational project of women's history: to recover and reveal the lived experience of women in the past and the present.

The series Gender in History provides a forum for these developments. Its historical coverage extends from the medieval to the modern period, and its geographical scope encompasses not only Europe and North America but all corners of the globe. The series aims to investigate the social and cultural constructions of gender in historical sources, as well as the gendering of historical discourse itself. It embraces both detailed case studies of specific regions or periods, and broader treatments of major themes. Gender in History titles are designed to meet the needs of both scholars and students working in this dynamic area of historical research.

The shadow of marriage

MANCHESTER
1824

Manchester University Press

+━━━━+

Gender, myth and materiality in an island community:
Shetland, 1800–2000
Lynn Abrams

'The truest form of patriotism':
pacifist feminism in Britain, 1870–1902
Heloise Brown

Masculinities in politics and war: gendering modern history
Stefan Dudink, Karen Hagemann and John Tosh (eds)

Noblewomen, aristocracy and power
in the twelfth-century Anglo-Norman realm
Susan Johns

The business of everyday life:
gender, practice and social politics in England, c. 1600–1700
Beverly Lemire

The independent man:
citizenship and gender politics in Georgian England
Matthew McCormack

THE SHADOW OF MARRIAGE
SINGLENESS IN ENGLAND, 1914–60

━━━━━━━━━━━━━━━━━━━━━━━━━━━

━ Katherine Holden ━

Manchester University Press
Manchester and New York

distributed exclusively in the USA by Palgrave

Published by Manchester University Press
Oxford Road, Manchester M13 9NR, UK
and Room 400, 175 Fifth Avenue, New York, NY 10010, USA
www.manchesteruniversitypress.co.uk

Distributed exclusively in the USA by Palgrave
175 Fifth Avenue, New York,
NY 10010, USA

Distributed exclusively in Canada by UBC Press
University of British Columbia, 2029 West Mall,
Vancouver, BC, Canada V6T 1Z2

British Library Cataloguing-in-Publication Data
A catalogue record for this book is available from the British Library

Library of Congress Cataloging-in-Publication Data applied for

ISBN   978 0 7190 6892 8 *hardback*

First published 2007

16 15 14 13 12 11 10 09 08 07   10 9 8 7 6 5 4 3 2 1

Typeset in Minion with Scala Sans display
by Koinonia, Bury
Printed in Great Britain
by Antony Rowe Ltd, Chippenham, Wiltshire

For the men and women who shared their life histories
with me.
In memory of Norah Lea-Wilson 1886–1976
and Derek Shuttleworth 1910–97

Contents

Acknowledgements

This book has a long history. It was conceived during an undergraduate feminist theory class on motherhood in 1990 (where as a single, childless woman I felt my experiences were being ignored) and has been growing ever since, moving from an extended essay into BA and then MA dissertations, a PhD thesis and finally a book. During my journey over the last sixteen years so many people have offered me advice, references, illuminating discussions and feedback that it would be impossible to name them all without risking leaving some out. I would therefore like to offer collective thanks to the many friends, family members, archivists, librarians, colleagues and acquaintances with whom my theme struck a chord for variously giving me access to research materials, helping to expand and change my thinking, saving me from errors and most importantly offering me encouragement to keep going, especially when times were hard. Equally important are the unmarried women and men I interviewed, many of whom have since died, whose stories are central to the book and to whom I owe a profound debt of gratitude.

Thanks are due to the school of history at the University of the West of England, which supported my academic work throughout this period. I was fortunate also in receiving funding from the Economic and Social Research Council for my MA studies and PhD research at the University of Essex (1991-5), bursaries from the Hall School Trust (Wincanton) (1994-6), a Wingate Foundation scholarship (1996-7), and an honorarium from Rutgers Center for Historical Analysis at Rutgers University, where I spent a month in 2004 as a visiting research fellow. A research leave grant from the Arts and Humanities Research Council (2005-6) was invaluable, enabling me to complete the final manuscript. My grateful thanks go to each of these organisations.

A few individuals have stood by me throughout the vicissitudes of my journey. My parents, Hyla and Joan Holden, my uncle, Tom Davis, and my aunts, Ursula Holden and Lesley Davis, gave financial and practical help and moral support over the years as well as enabling me to grasp the significance of single women within my own family. Ursula's belief in me as a writer is an enduring legacy. Moira Martin encouraged me in my first attempt to write about the history of single women and has remained a wise critic and counsellor ever since. June Hannam supervised my BA dissertation and has been an ongoing source of encouragement. Leonore Davidoff was an exemplary PhD supervisor. Without her support in many different ways, this project would never have come to fruition. As members of the BCI research group, Leonore, Janet Fink and Megan Doolittle were my principal academic advisers, giving astute critical feedback on countless chapter drafts. Janet read the entire final draft and saved me from many errors. Without their help, this would be a much poorer book.

My biggest thanks are to my dear friend and companion Helen Kendall, who since 1992 has shared my life and home, has endured my obsession with singleness and knows me in some ways better than I know myself. She has commented helpfully on drafts of almost everything I've ever written, ensured that I face up to the conflicts as well as the pleasures of being single and given me the courage to say what I really believe at the end of this book.

Abbreviations

BRO	Bristol Record Office
FLOP	Family Life of Old People (survey)
FLOP	Peter Townsend, *The Family Life of Old People*, 1957 (Harmondsworth: Penguin, 1963) (published version of FLOP)
GFS	Girls' Friendly Society
KH	Katherine Holden
MO	Mass Observation
MSP	Marie Stopes Papers
MWC	Moral Welfare Council
NA	National Archive
NCH	National Children's Home
NCUMC	National Council for the Unmarried Mother and her Child
NSLLL	New Survey of London Life and Labour
NSLLL	London School of Economics and Political Science, *The New Survey of London Life and Labour*, 9 vols (London: P. S. King and Son, 1930–5) (pubished version of NSLLL)
NSPA	National Spinsters' Pension Association
NSPCC	National Society for the Prevention of Cruelty to Children
NUSEC	National Union of Societies for Equal Citizenship
NUWT	National Union of Women Teachers
YWCA	Young Women's Christian Association

1

Introduction:
'the prince may yet come'

'It has always been a mystery to me why people marry' said Mr Prender-gast. 'I can't see the smallest reason for it. Quite happy normal people ... I don't believe ... that people would ever fall in love or want to be married if they hadn't been told about it. It's like abroad: no one would want to go there if they hadn't been told it existed.'[1]

Miss Bousie: 'There is enough misery in the world without getting married. And they are all so young that they will change their minds quickly and then it will be too late.'[2]

The consolations of spinsterhood are mainly negative ... [but] the greatest is this – that out of the dim and uncertain future, perchance in the guise of a divorced man or a widower with four children, the Prince may yet come.[3]

I N THIS BOOK, I argue that marital status is a vital but largely unexam-ined analytical category for historians, which offers new challenges to historical scholarship. The institution of marriage, and the political, economic, social and cultural structures which support it, have created relations of power, authority and subordination in which every member of society has been implicated, but these have often been taken as given rather than subjected to any sustained historical analysis. The unmarried state is generally viewed as a stage or stages in the lifecycle preceding or following marriage, with never-married people seen as exceptions to a norm. Thus, while scholars have paid attention to power relations surrounding workers, women, homosexuals, colonial subjects and people of colour, few similar analyses have been made of marital status from the perspective of single people.[4]

The main purpose of the book is to gain a better understanding of the married/single divide, and in particular to examine the impact of continuities and change in marital beliefs and practices on men and women who never married in early and mid-twentieth-century England. These were years in which, despite the rising divorce rate and family dislocation brought about by the two world wars, marriage and the nuclear family were in a dominant position as social structures, deriving their authority from both church and state.[5] But what has been insufficiently recognised is the part single men and women living in the shadow of marriage played in maintaining the power base of marriage. Whether or not individual men and women may have actually subscribed to the belief that it should be the goal of every normal person, the life-paths and economic opportunities of those living outside its boundaries were still influenced by it. Even men and women living outside the family, either alone or in same-sex environments, were doing so from a position which was always marginal when set against models of marriage and the nuclear family.

As a childless, single woman, these exclusions have a bearing on my own adult life, but they also haunted my middle-class childhood in the 1950s and 1960s as they did the early life of my parents and their siblings before and after the Second World War. It is therefore not coincidental that I have chosen this period for my analysis or used my own family's experiences as a basis from which to launch this study. My family stories demonstrate the difficulties of creating clear conceptual boundaries between marriage and singleness and show the intersections between marital status and other categories such as parenthood, class, gender and age. They also raise questions that will be pursued further in this introduction and in subsequent chapters.

Colonial childhoods

Unmarried women were an important presence in my parents' young lives. As in most colonial upper- and middle-class families, the nuclear ideal did not match the system they subscribed to, in which child care was often delegated to others. Elizabeth Buettner's sensitive exploration of British white colonial families in India, *Empire Families*, suggests how common it was for school-age children to spend substantial periods of time apart from their parents in Britain, cared for by governesses, teachers and matrons during term time and in the school holidays by nannies or housekeepers, by members of their own extended families or by family friends.[6] Many of those who undertook this work were childless, unmarried women (and in boys' boarding schools also often unmarried men), but while accounts by children cared for in this way are beginning to emerge, we have very little evidence of the long-term effects of this system on the carers.

My mother and her siblings, aged between six and nine, were left in boarding schools in England for three years between 1929 and 1932 when their parents returned to their missionary work in India. In the school holidays, these children were cared for by their much-loved unmarried aunt Lilla and her companion Nona. My father and his sisters were in a similar position, spending much of their time at home with an unmarried governess (who later became a housekeeper) while their parents were abroad in the Egyptian civil service. She gave them a sense of security described by one sister as 'beyond price', yet was still dismissed when she was no longer needed.[7] In both these cases there is a curious role reversal which allowed middle- and upper-class married couples to act as freely as single people who did not have families, while unmarried women were temporarily tied to married people's children as substitute mothers. The psychic cost of these triangular relationships between mothers, children and unmarried carers is a key theme explored in Chapters 6–9 through the medium of fiction, film, memoirs, autobiographies and oral history and drawing upon feminist and psychoanalytic theory.

This was not, however, the only face of female singleness to which my mother and aunts were exposed in their younger lives. Lilla's elder sister, Norah (born 1886), was vegetarian, a theosophist, and decidedly eccentric. Thanks to a legacy from her sister who died in the mid-1930s, she was also a traveller, journeying alone through China and India. She had a flat in London where her nieces as young adults could take refuge from the eyes of judgemental parents and, although she herself appeared to be celibate, she never asked awkward questions about their romantic affairs. Later she supported several of her nieces and nephews financially, providing my mother with a small income when she was particularly in need of help as a young adult.[8]

This kind of gendered narrative of freedom, escape and financial power has more often been attached to single men, but could also be linked to middle- and upper-class unmarried women who chose to live independent lives apart from their families, and aspects of this image have been heavily drawn upon by historians in accounts of single women particularly in late nineteenth- and early twentieth-century western societies.[9] Like the previous stories, it rests upon implicit contrasts with married people, but here the power relations are reversed. By the late 1930s, my mother's mother was back in England in the traditional role of a vicar's wife looking after her family, while her unmarried sister-in-law sent home letters telling of her adventures abroad. As an unmarried, childless woman Norah could also make choices about how much financial support she gave her nieces and nephews, and in this respect had more freedom than many parents who felt obligated to provide for their children.

Yet the shadow of marriage made it hard for Norah to maintain this image in the longer term. She used her professional expertise as a trained 'Truby King'[10] nurse to advise her married relatives about how they should bring up children, advice which was often welcomed but also at times resented as interfering. As she grew older, she felt increasingly sad about her exclusion from marriage and motherhood and could no longer sustain an independent lifestyle. When she became in need of physical care, she was rejected by the Theosophists who had taken much of her money and in the late 1960s came to live with my family. As a teenager, I thought of her as an archetypal spinster and had ambivalent feelings about her gifts to me. Although I appreciated the crate of oranges at Christmas and was touched when she gave me her parents' engagement rings, I did not want to associate too closely with an unhappy old woman who had been labelled by my family as sexually frustrated. Maybe I feared I might become like her.

This image of Norah as a sad, unwanted, frustrated old maid is another familiar stereotype, originating in the late seventeenth century,[11] which has been drawn upon extensively by historians, and it could be applied equally to her sister Lilla's companion Nona in old age. She had described her relationship with Lilla as being like 'husband and wife' but, because they were not married, after her partner died she could not claim to be a widow nor did she have any children of her own who might have supported her. Left alone in the house, she wrote pathetic letters to my mother, hungering for any scraps of affection and reminiscing about the past: 'I don't think I shall ever get over Lilla and all she meant to me ... I often think of those *lovely* Christmases we had when you were here. Do you remember the excitement of choosing the tree from the drive? And what fun it all was – The house seems so big and empty but I can't bring myself to leave.'[12]

These contradictory images of spinsterhood which have emerged in telling my own family history may be familiar to many of my readers. I have discussed them here not because I think my family were exceptional but rather because they were not. Indeed, in introducing this subject to almost any English man or woman over the age of forty, it is unusual to find a family who did not have unmarried aunts, teachers, governesses, servants or family friends as significant figures in their younger lives And while the stories told about these women vary in term of class, age, region, occupation and familial composition, the central characteristics that are associated with spinsterhood are remarkably similar. One of the main aims of this book is to cast light on how and why this is the case.

Gender and the politics of singleness

My study initially concentrated solely on women like Norah, Lilla and Nona, and on their working-class counterparts who performed similar roles within families and most commonly worked as nannies and domestic servants, or in shops and factories. However, as I progressed, it became increasingly important to compare men and women in my analysis, not least because of the gap between popular understandings of bachelorhood and spinsterhood. Yet the more necessary it seemed to bring bachelors as well as spinsters into the daylight, the more invisible bachelors appeared to be. As Howard Chudacoff points out in his study of American bachelorhood, single men have been largely excluded from family and social history and regarded as inhabiting 'the edges of family life'.[13] Not only were accounts of bachelors much less common in families, but they were also more difficult to identify in my sources. Because men do not change their title when they change their marital status, they are concealed within many documents, for example in lists of members and officers of organisations or of witnesses for parliamentary commissions, both of which identify unmarried women. Advice books on the problems of singleness, common for women throughout the period, also rarely focused on unmarried males. Men who wrote autobiographies often neglected to mention marriage or family in the text, leaving their marital status unknown or, if they had married, identifiable only in a dedication or acknowledgement.[14] While these problems have not been insurmountable, they have skewed the amount of research material in favour of unmarried women, and left bachelors often as shadowy figures whose significance is discussed as much in terms of invisibility and absence as of their presence.

To make sense of these gender differences we need to consider first the difficulties in separating singleness and marriage as discrete categories. This can be better understood by considering the approach one of the few other published books on singleness which includes men and women, a sociological study carried out in the USA and England by Margaret Adams in the 1970s. In *Single Blessedness: Observations on the Single Status in Married Society* (1977), a study of single women and men without family ties or responsibilities, Adams attempted to move away from seeing the single state either as marginal or as an antecedent to marriage by conceptualising it as 'a social status or situation that is complete in its own right and possessing its own intrinsic characteristics distinct from those that regulate the thinking and lives of people who are married'.[15]

However, there is a tension present within Adams' separatist stance. Her memory of the single women from her childhood in the 1920s as 'an accepted feature of normal society's fabric', receiving respect and support, seems at odds with her recognition of what lies behind the question commonly asked of single women: why they had not married. This question, Adams argues, implies that 'to be unmarried ... is such an affront to social norms as to absolve the interrogator from normal restraint and standards of good behaviour'.[16] These contradictory views of single women as both an 'accepted feature of normal society' *and* 'an affront to social norms' cannot simply be explained by historical change in views about marital status, since representations of single women in the 1920s frequently adopt the latter viewpoint. They can, however, be illuminated by a body of theory developed in the 1980s unavailable to Adams.[17]

Drawing upon the insights of poststructuralist theory, Joan Scott has shown how the meaning of any category is derived through explicit or implicit contrasts, with positive definitions resting always on the negation or repression of something represented as antithetical to them. Apparently fixed oppositions are not uncontested, but always open to challenge. They are also interdependent, in that they 'derive their meaning from internally established contrast rather than some inherent or pure antithesis'.[18] Thus, the meanings of singleness are in a dialogue with the meanings of marriage, with each category shifting in relation to the other in response to wider societal change.

Looked at in this light, singleness and marriage can be viewed not as discrete but rather as relational categories whose characteristics are understood in terms of one another. The positive aspects of the dominant category 'married' are established in relation to the negative aspects of the subordinate category 'single'. In this way, both the difficulties and ambiguities within marriage for women, such as dependence and confinement, and the possibilities of freedom and independence a single life could represent for them are suppressed. However, since these categories have no fixed meanings, they are always open to the possibility of contest and for their seemingly natural status to be challenged, allowing the oppositional meanings of singleness to emerge.

An understanding of the ways in which gender works through language to encode oppositional traits as either masculine or feminine is also important here. The connotations within the term 'single' of autonomy and independence favour the masculine pole and are in direct opposition to dependence, a core attribute of femininity. Because marriage has been both the institution and symbol of women's dependence and containment,[19] being single and male appears normal and even desirable while for females it appears inherently contradictory, with the term 'single woman' almost an oxymoron.

If we see discourses on singleness and marriage as being two sides of the same coin, the 'otherness' of the unmarried state becomes more explicable. The perceived necessity to separate them is indicative of the extent to which they are bound together and implicated in each other's characteristics.[20] The loss of freedom which women experienced in marriage could be mediated both by projecting a sense of loss on to unmarried women, and through envy of their apparent independence and capability of acting 'selfishly'. For men, female singleness could be equally disturbing because of the possibility it represented of women competing with or living apart from men. The idea that a woman might not want a husband and wish to be independent is latent within representations of the spinster and the old maid, and explains the malevolent power with which these images can be invested.

Yet the contradictions inherent within the single/married dichotomy for women are more complex than the above account allows and are not all of the same order. Attributes commonly assigned to unmarried women are inconsistent. They could be silly, gossipy, affected, sentimental, foolish, fussy and eccentric; or downtrodden, pathetic and spineless. But they might equally be dominating, severe and gaunt, or rigid, bitter and frustrated. This list is by no means exhaustive, nor does it necessarily present a coherent image. This is because the figures of old maids and spinsters are a location for personality traits widely believed to be unattractive and by implication unmarriageable in women. Their negative stereotypes define the limits of normative feminine behaviour.[21]

The importance for women of being physically attractive to men, heightened through the influence of cinema and images of glamorous Hollywood stars, was signalled by a woman's apparent powerlessness to choose her own marital destiny. The necessity of waiting to be chosen in marriage increased women's fears of spinsterhood and the misery of being 'left on the shelf'. Polarised negative images of singleness sent strong messages to women that only marriage and motherhood could give them a completely fulfilled life. Yet these messages could also lead to other kinds of contradictions not confined to the levels of discourse or representation. Women's expectations of living 'happily ever after' have often been held in common with their knowledge of difficulties in friends' and families' marriages, such as sexual incompatibility or abuse, material inequalities between husband and wife, the pain and risks of childbirth or the burden of children. Some girls' and young women's understanding of the lives of older single women of their acquaintance may equally have conflicted with dominant images of spinsters and with the expectation that all women should marry, enabling them in particular circumstances to challenge these norms.

The sexual double standard operated as another primary area of contradiction. Unmarried women's knowledge that they could only gain sexual satisfaction respectably within marriage conflicted with what they knew was acceptable for unmarried men. Young men's propensity to 'sow wild oats' has been regarded as healthy, normal and excusable, while women were expected to control male sexuality in order to prevent pregnancy. Those that failed could be conflated with prostitutes, perceived as victims of male lust or as unfairly trying to trap men into marriage and therefore the cause of men's lack of sexual self-control. In the late nineteenth and early twentieth century, marriage was perceived to be a containing force for 'the beast' in men,[22] yet concerns about the spread of venereal disease to wives and children suggest that it had limited success in this respect.

Middle-class unmarried women were at the forefront of efforts to change male sexual behaviour at this time. Drawing on the language of sexual and social purity and the dominant Victorian ideology of women as passionless, they used their celibacy as a source of power and were at the centre of campaigns to give women more power within marriage. The married state was likened to prostitution and denounced as sexual and economic slavery.[23] A postcard sent by a woman to an unmarried friend or relative in 1906 is, however, indicative of some ambiguity in this conception of marriage. A photo of a lioness in a cage with the accompanying caption 'waiting for hubby',[24] suggests that while women might be trapped in marriage, they were also wild beasts and therefore it was female as much as male sexuality that was to be feared.

Similar kinds of contradictions can be found in the term 'bachelor', which has a long tradition of association with sexual libertarianism, economic freedom and choice, of a man without the responsibilities of marriage and children.[25] Nevertheless, bachelors could also be perceived as selfish, fussy and crusty, or as 'milksops' tied to their mothers, not quite proper men, images which belied the idea that their bachelorhood really had been freely chosen. And while the secondary meaning of the term 'celibacy' (whose primary dictionary definition is 'the state of being unmarried') has in most western societies come to be 'abstaining from sex',[26] it was harder for bachelors than for spinsters to make this a positive claim unless they were in holy orders, since it raised questions about their masculinity and virility. However, as we shall see in chapter 4, celibacy for both sexes became a particularly pressing concern after the First World War, as sexology and psychoanalytic theories stressing the importance of the sex drive for physical and emotional health entered more widely into the public domain.

Bachelorhood was also associated with youth and irresponsibility. The commonly held view of marriage as a trap for a man was held in tandem with the knowledge that it was also a rite of passage into the adult world and in particular into breadwinning and family responsibilities. Michael Roper's interviews with middle managers who married in the 1940s and 1950s showed them establishing their ties to the domestic domain through children and to their wives through the role of mother. These responsibilities could also give their career ambitions a new lease of life as they sought 'to maximise their income and social standing for the family'.[27] Although bachelors could also see the lack of family responsibilities as offering them the freedom to develop their careers, their relationship to the domestic sphere was more problematic. The idealisation of motherhood left them in the position of either having to reject maternal and familial ties or be seen as mothers' boys who had never grown up.

A more fundamental separation between single men and women, which may explain the relative invisibility of bachelorhood, derives from the view that single men are not fundamentally different from their married peers. As Adams argued, this creates the paradox that while bachelors are in demand and desirable for social events, spinsters are 'socially superfluous and slightly comic, if not pathetic'. Thus the identity of a bachelor is less clearly delineated from that of husband than that of a spinster from a wife.[28] Indeed the very fact that they do not declare a change of name or title suggests that for men the passage from singleness into marriage carries a less significant change in their status than it does for women.

This difference can be related to the links between 'man' and 'individual' which suggest that whatever his current burden of responsibilities within marriage, a man is always single. These associations were strengthened in the nineteenth century through Enlightenment discourses which emphasised masculine independence and freedom, and the sexual division of labour within capitalist modes of production. As Davidoff notes, 'In popular mythology as well as legal conception, the single, individualistic and self-generated entrepreneur came to embody the man of property … His supporting network of female kin, their labour and the contribution of their property were obliterated.'[29] Thus, the apparent independence of both husbands and bachelors was illusory because their freedom depended upon invisible but essential domestic support from women.

By contrast, the links between 'woman' and 'dependence' position the spinster not as single and independent but as potentially married, ready to give service to men, and imply that spinsterhood was never a choice. Thus it was harder for women to see singleness as signifying freedom and marriage as a trap than it was for men, and the terms 'spinster' and 'old maid' have carried a more negative load of cultural baggage than that of 'bachelor'.

Categorising marital status

The discussion so far has placed singleness and marriage in dialogue and shown how these concepts are fractured by gender. The term 'single' is, however, slippery and elusive, encompassing a range of different meanings both in law and in popular understanding, changing in significance over time and also in relation to age as well as gender. Chudacoff argues that to define singleness as a marital status creates a contradiction in terms and that 'the most common characteristic of single people is that literally they do not have marital status'.[30] Yet while the primary meaning of 'single' may be the state of not being married, this is far from a unified category, frequently referring both to those who have never married (spinsters and bachelors), and to those whose marriages have ended through either widowhood or divorce. This blurring of categories is apparent in the British census, which has been an important source for this study. While the term 'single' generally referred to never-married people, they were not always distinguishable from those in other categories of singleness. Some census tables used the term 'marriageable' to include widows and divorcees, while others counted married workers by age without giving a similar breakdown for single, widowed or divorced workers. Equally, before the 1921 census, because divorce was relatively rare, divorcees were not even included as an official category and it is unclear whether they were counted among the widowed, married or single population.[31]

This lack of clarity, also apparent in other sources, has led to a problem with terminology, resolved by using 'never married', 'unmarried', 'spinster' or 'bachelor' in cases where there is little or no ambiguity of status, and 'single' in cases where widowed, separated and divorced people are (or are likely to have been) included. It also makes a demographic analysis of never-married people harder to sustain. Nevertheless, I attempt this task in chapter 2 in order to assess the gap between the popularly held belief that marriage was the normal adult condition and the reality that for much of our period, nearly half the adult population was single, and well over a third had never married. The changes that occurred over the period 1914 to 1960 in the numbers of unmarried women and men in the population as a whole, and in particular age groups and occupations, are related both to the ways in which these groups were represented and to the material conditions in which they worked and lived.

The purpose of this demographic work is not simply to discover the proportions of unmarried men and women of different ages and in different contexts. Equally important are the ways in which popular knowledge and beliefs about these statistics coloured the lives of unmarried people. Making this link is particularly important in this period because of the major disjuncture in the lives of young men and women affected by the First World War. Unprecedented casualties amongst soldiers led to a belief in a 'lost generation' of men, who either had died or were left with long-term physical and mental disabilities, and an accompanying surplus of young women who would never be able to marry and were often portrayed in similar terms to widows.[32]

Demographic historians have gone to some lengths to point out the misleading implications of these beliefs and to play down their importance by showing that the short-term effects of the war disguise long-term trends.[33] There had been a substantial surplus of women in the population throughout the late nineteenth and early twentieth centuries and concern about women's marriage prospects was not a new phenomenon;[34] yet as Jay Winter pointed out, celibacy rates did not rise in the interwar period, and he applauded 'the apparent success of British women in finding marriage partners despite the carnage of war',[35] confirming the dominant ideology of the period of a society where universal marriage was the norm. Women continued to marry at a later age than was the case after the Second World War and would have to reach the age of at least forty-five before they could judge whether or not they would be likely to remain unmarried.[36] During the 1930s, this sense of it never being too late is suggested in sympathetic fictional portraits of older single women which indicate their marriage potential, alongside others which show spinsters as failures or as threatening to marriage.

Although I cannot dispute Winter's statistical accuracy, the problem with the picture he presented is that it reinforces the assumption that, given the choice, women would necessarily want to marry.[37] His description of interwar Britain as a society where the trend was towards universal marriage has the effect of making unmarried women disappear as a significant category. They are reduced in his analysis to a few 'aged spinsters' who 'point to the war as a catastrophe which sealed their fate'.[38] It is worth noting also here that while acknowledging the genuine sense of loss and bereavement felt by a nation in mourning for its young men, Winter was also recreating a familiar spinster stereotype, by marginalizing and dismissing these women's claims. But most importantly, he failed to take into account how the idea of a lost generation of men might have influenced women's views of marriage in a variety of ways and encouraged some women actively to seek alternatives. Thus if one follows the fortunes both of this particular cohort of men and women (many of whom never did marry), and of their successors (whose chances were considerably improved), in terms both of attitudes and of opportunities available to them, wider social and economic trends are illuminated.

For example, it has been suggested that the very fact that the vote was denied to women under thirty in 1918 is indicative of fears not simply that women would out-vote men, but that the excess numbers would be 'flappers', predominantly young single women out of direct male control.[39] The decline of this image after universal suffrage was finally achieved in 1928, and the increasingly vicious attacks upon spinsters in the 1930s, 1940s and 1950s (the last of these often linked by historians to the greater public visibility of lesbians after the notorious *Well of Loneliness* trial in 1928)[40] may also reflect the fact that this cohort was reaching the age when their marriage prospects were perceived to be growing ever worse in a society in which the trend was moving gradually towards younger marriage. The ageing of the lost-generation cohort of women seems to parallel a change in the dominant image of female singleness from youth and sexual availability to sexual frustration. This reached a peak in the 1950s as marriage became ever more strongly reinforced as a norm. Literature and film from this period suggest that the danger older single women represented was their unfortunate influence on a younger generation who might be turned against marriage,[41] a generation whose chances of marriage with the increased numbers of men in the population had significantly improved.

Beliefs about bachelorhood were similarly affected. During the 1920s, the links between bachelorhood, sexual liberation and freedom sat uncomfortably with the knowledge that many of the men who had not married had been mentally or physically disabled or traumatised by war.[42] Cultural historians have noted the popularity of desert romances and novels with Mediterranean heroes in this decade, believed by editors to be "hotter" than British heroes.[43] As I show in chapter 4, the idea that there were thousands of women in the population desperate to marry, intensified concerns about male sexuality and the damaging effects of either remaining celibate or using prostitutes.[44] Yet the image of higher-status bachelors as liberated, urbane and sophisticated still remained in currency, and in women's magazines and fiction this image was also linked to urban working women, in the shape of the bachelor girl who lived independently from her family and who, like the flapper, symbolised youth and modernity.

In the post-war years however, as the proportion of young unmarried women in the population declined and remaining unmarried became increasingly unacceptable, the bachelor girl was represented as less glamorous and more pragmatic. Despite the fact that career opportunities for women were expanding, particularly in the caring professions, and more women moving into paid employment, the bachelor girl's working life was often portrayed primarily as a preparation for marriage. In popular women's novels the skills and training of professional women tended to be played down and presented as naturalised feminine assets, and paid work was often represented as an option for women 'who were undesirable and therefore unmarriageable'.[45]

By contrast, in the late 1950s, full employment, increasing affluence and leisure (especially among young male urban white-collar and professional workers), the greater sexual availability of women outside marriage (although not publicly sanctioned), and the shift in the sex ratio in favour of youthful unmarried men can be connected with a heightening of the playboy image of swinging bachelorhood and a more misogynistic, aggressively heterosexual, masculinity. This culture had its roots in post-war America and was imported into Britain through Hollywood movies featuring hedonistic, carefree bachelors, with stars such as Bob Hope and Cary Grant, and the men's lifestyle magazines *Playboy* and *Men Only*, surfacing also in light, humorous books telling men how to avoid marriage.[46]

The links between popular beliefs about single people and gendered hierarchies created through the use of marital categories is not confined to the demography of sex ratios but can also be read in the concept of the household. The household model generally used in social surveys to count the numbers of the population living in poverty (which also applied to the ways in which state welfare benefits were calculated in the interwar years) assumed a married couple with the husband as head as the norm, with other household members treated as secondary wage earners or dependants.[47] While wives could easily be identified within this structure, single people who lived with their families were much harder to count, since they were categorised in relation to the head rather than as individuals in their own right and their marital status was often not given. The implications of this system and its effects on the familial social and economic relationships are discussed in chapter 3.

Another definitional problem relating to households is that the primary designation of singleness as a marital status could be clouded by secondary meanings which refer principally to living alone. Thus while people who were legally single could be subsumed within families and their marital status ignored, separated married people living alone could be viewed as single, and unmarried cohabitants treated as if they were married. In early and mid-twentieth-century England, when divorce was still relatively difficult to obtain, cohabitants often posed as married couples, usually because one of them was married to someone else and often harboured this as a guilty secret. Yet for same-sex partnerships, the reverse was true. Because lesbianism was stigmatised, homosexuality illegal and marriage the official container only for heterosexual relationships, women who shared their lives with other women or men with men were in an anomalous position, neither married nor single. As was the case with my great-aunt Lilla and her friend Nona, these relationships were many respects like that of a husband and wife. Yet as we shall see in chapter 4, until 2005 such partnerships were never recognised in law, and fear of being labelled perverted or deviant led many in this position to reaffirm their single status and to conceal emotional and/or sexual aspects of their relationships. The silence and secrecy around these living arrangements is one reason why some historians have associated, and sometimes unhelpfully conflated, the categories of spinster and lesbian,[48] although more recent work in this area has pointed to the difficulties of categorising these relationships and of imposing modern sexual categories and terminology.[49]

Motherhood, fatherhood and marital status

Cohabiting couples who pretended to be married were also often avoiding stigma, particularly necessary when they had children. Historian Carolyn Steedman's parents were in this position. Her father had a wife and child elsewhere and was never divorced, and her mother went to great lengths to conceal her children's illegitimacy, including lying to the registrar. Living in the shadow of marriage had a profound effect on Steedman's childhood. Her parents appeared to be married, but her mother acted like and was in law a single mother. And, although Steedman did not know this as a child, because it was marriage rather than the act of insemination that legitimated fatherhood, her father's legal status was 'putative', which meant he had no rights over his children even though he remained living with the family. The dynamics of this particular relationship were such that although he paid her mother housekeeping money, he had no authority in the family and was treated almost like a single man. Indeed,

Steedman compared her father with the 'sad long-term men' who shared their house as paying guests, and he is said to have described himself as 'the other lodger'.[50]

The relationship between the state and unmarried fathers and mothers and how it affected their children has received remarkably little attention from historians, despite much anecdotal evidence and discoveries by genealogists that in almost every family until very recently illegitimacy was hidden as a shameful secret.[51] I address this neglected area in chapter 5 and examine the consequences not simply for the women, who were often shamed by their children's existence, but also for the men, who were excluded from the rights and responsibilities of fatherhood. Steedman described her childhood self as an object of exchange. In a society in which motherhood was held out as a 'natural' driving force to all women irrespective of marital status, yet which condemned sexual relationships outside marriage, Steedman's mother took a gamble in having children. Her hope that their father would bring her inside the law was never fulfilled, yet she still saw her children as an insurance policy for the future.[52]

This view can be linked not only to the social and economic exclusions of Steedman's mother's gender and class position, but also to the major investment in childbearing and motherhood that was attached to women. It was an investment that had a peculiar power in late 1940s and 1950s Britain, as in the popular imagination marriage was being refashioned as a companionate partnership central to the nation's wellbeing and particularly to the health and welfare of its children as citizens of the future. It can also be connected to the perceived importance of rebuilding the family in the wake of widespread damage and dislocation. This involved a stress on the importance of the maternal relationship within marriage by psychologists and psychoanalysts, principally John Bowlby, Donald Winnicott and Anna Freud. Although the number of young unmarried women in the population had fallen to a new low, the regulation of female sexuality after the supposed sexual excesses of the Second World War still appeared necessary and working-class unmarried mothers were increasingly portrayed as disturbed and delinquent.

Yet, paradoxically, greater stress was also laid on the links between spinsterhood, maternal frustration and the damaging effects of the denial of motherhood, particularly on middle-class women. Such a climate of opinion (which in many respects was not new and has relevance for unmarried women throughout our period) intensified many women's sense of desperation to find a husband. But for those who could not or would not marry, it encouraged them to satisfy or sublimate their maternal desires in other contexts, through the care of children either unpaid within their families, through fostering and adoption, or in jobs such as midwifery, health visiting, teaching and nursery nursing, and as house mothers, matrons and nannies. Thus representations of the despised old maid or of frustrated spinsters disguise the extent to which the meanings we attach to 'family' have actually been shaped and perpetuated as much by the single as the married woman. As we shall see, single women's agency within cultural discourses and practices which gave priority to marriage lay less in a rejection of or exclusion from the conjugal or the familial than in a reworking of terms to allow them a place and voice. For a high proportion of single women, service in the cause of the family became a primary focus for their life's work.

The amount of space in the book that has been allocated to these kinds of relationships reflects not only unmarried women's pivotal position in relation to child care, but also their invisibility in the historical literature both on singleness and on children. Unmarried women have been studied much more often as workers who, unlike married women, did not have the dual burden of caring for children. Or, viewed through the lens of sexuality, they have been seen as forging primary emotional (and sometimes physical) relationships with other women because their lives were not dominated by the demands of marriage and motherhood.[53] Their important role supporting and caring for parents and other elderly relatives has also been highlighted,[54] but there has been very little discussion except in anecdotal form or in biographies of individual women of the key roles that women of all classes played in the emotional and physical care and education of children, at both practical and policy-making levels.

The predominance of single women in child-related occupations before the Second World War reflects not only the demographic surplus of women over men, particularly in older age groups, but also the low rates of participation of married women in the workforce, even in working-class families, compared with the post-war years. From the late 1940s, higher marriage rates and the need for women workers to make up for the post-war labour shortage increased the numbers of married women in all these occupations. Yet there were still large numbers of young and older single women in the labour force in these positions in schools, hospitals, nurseries and children's homes during the 1950s and even into the 1960s.

Equally important throughout our period are the roles played in making, influencing and implementing policy in relation to children: women such as Ellen Wilkinson, minister of education in the immediate post-war years, who had the major task of implementing the 1944 Education Act; Eleanor

Rathbone, who campaigned tirelessly throughout the interwar period for the introduction of family allowances; Myra Curtis, whose 1945 'Care of Children Committee Report' gave shape to the 1948 Children's Act; and Anna Freud, whose work in wartime nurseries showed the importance of continuity of care for young children. It has been impossible to do sufficient justice in this book to the work of these and other high-profile unmarried women in different policy contexts, but this is an area which deserves closer investigation.

The picture for unmarried men in relation to children seems on one level to be very different. There was little expectation that unmarried men should become involved with the care of young children, although the juxtaposition of a bachelor and a baby was sometimes used in popular fiction in similar ways to that in the 1980s' film *Three Men and a Baby*,[55] as a device to stimulate maternal or paternal feelings in the hero and/or heroine and to expedite their marriage.[56] Perhaps partly because men can become fathers at any age and have no biological clock to consider, the imperative to be identified with mothering was much stronger for single women than was the call to take on the responsibilities of fathering for single men, a burden which 'gay' bachelors were usually deemed lucky to have escaped. Yet, as with single women, the education of boys and young men was not infrequently undertaken by bachelors, particularly in schools or colleges run by religious orders, where monks or Catholic priests were barred from marrying. Unmarried men also often worked in boys' clubs, scouts and other youth organisations in a voluntary capacity. And although child care was an area in which they were much less likely to be visible than women, some evidence of their relationships with children can be found in autobiographies and oral histories. Perhaps most significantly, as we shall see in chapter 7, they make frequent appearances as uncles or avuncular figures in children's fiction.

Sources and methods

Unmarried women and men are undoubtedly a neglected group, but I am not trying to portray them simply as unsung heroes. At the level of individual beliefs and behaviour, the contradictions and stereotypes produced through dividing people by marital status do not always make comfortable reading. Psychic conflicts are particularly obvious in the area of motherhood and child care, perhaps because, as Lyndall Roper points out, attachment and conflict between those in maternal positions and children are 'pretty fundamental to human existence, but the form those conflicts may take and the attitudes societies may adopt to them may change'. The conflicts between mothers and childless women assisting with childbirth in the mid-twentieth century are reminiscent of Roper's account of mothers and their lying-in maids in Reformation Augsburg who drew upon the idea of diabolic possession if their child failed to thrive, projecting their fear and anxieties onto older, infertile women who had taken on maternal roles.[57]

Following Roper, I have drawn upon Melanie Klein's concept of splitting, in which a baby's helplessness, frustration and dependency on a seemingly omnipotent mother or mother figure are resolved by dividing her into two internal objects: the baby experiences both 'good' and 'bad' feelings towards its mother but dissociates the two sets of feelings from one another. The value of this idea is not simply to gain a greater understanding of the feelings of babies towards maternal figures. It is also helpful in understanding relationships in childhood and adult life in which these kinds of splits can recur, particularly those which invoke feelings of dependency or provoke anxiety and contradictory or ambivalent feelings. In an adult context, splitting off and repressing aspects of oneself felt to be shameful, unbearable and intolerable often arises in intimate relationships and is used unconsciously to deal with external situations experienced as ambiguous or threatening. In such situations negative feelings towards a loved one are projected into someone else who is demonised, while the loved object is idealised and remains untarnished by feelings of hatred, envy, anger or aggression.[58]

These ideas can throw light on the complexities of the triangular relationship between birth mothers, their children and childless women who advised or gave hands-on care to children, but it has been important not to pathologise them. Rather I locate them historically in the context of mid-twentieth-century theories of childrearing and patterns of child care, and also within specific sets of economic and class relationships. The work of Pateman and Davidoff has been helpful in pointing to ways in which care unsettles the boundaries of paid and unpaid work and creates the kind of ambiguous situations in which splitting often occurs.[59] Pateman argues that in the unwritten terms of the marriage contract, wives have been defined as economic dependants, expected to provide domestic labour including child care for their husbands.[60] When middle- and upper-class wives have subcontracted this labour to unmarried women, it is possible to see similarities in the terms of that subcontract with the contract wives had with their husbands. Carers' low wages, paid mainly as board and keep, parallel the housekeeping allowance. Equally, the freedom from responsibility for the day-to-day care of children middle-class wives gained can be compared to that of a husband. It is important therefore to see tensions in mothering created by unmarried women's participation in this area of work as related not simply to marital status but also to class (and in the case of carers from other ethnicities also sometimes 'racialised') divisions.

For many single women involvement with children represented an important source of love and fulfilment, but in circumstances of this kind, it could also involve anxiety, frustration and pain. This was also the case with single men's relationships with children, which may have been neglected by historians partly through fear of discovering paedophilia and abuse.[61] One of the ways to gain perspective on these more troubling features of single-ness, as well as the other more positive aspects, is to move between public and private viewpoints and between structural and individual levels. To achieve this I have drawn upon a variety of sources within each chapter including oral history, auto/biography, social survey and census data and reports, organisational records, parliamentary debates and reports, advice literature, novels, films and children's stories. Where no source is cited, the material is from the interviewees in my own study; see appendices for interviewee profiles.

Moving between these sources and levels shows how, for example, changes in sex ratios, family size and structure, attitudes to sex and repro-duction, and patterns of employment and leisure impacted upon single men's and women's behaviour, decisions and choices (or lack of choices). Equally, we can see how household and marital categories adopted by the census and social surveys often obscured the significance of single people's position and importance both within and outside their families.

Unmarried men and women's own accounts offer different perspec-tives, showing both a belief in their central position within many families and their feelings of marginality in the face of an aggressively 'married' world. Yet these oral and autobiographical accounts are also mediated. Summerfield argued in her study of wartime women that personal narra-tives are 'the product of a relationship between discourse and subjec-tivity', and that narrators draw upon the generalised subject available in discourse to construct their own personal subjectivities.[62] My analysis takes account of the many and varied discourses in both the past and present which contribute towards the reconstruction of a life. It shows how, in life-story work, different cultural beliefs and ideas both from the past and in the present are drawn upon and reworked by individuals to explain their marital status and to present a particular version of their lives. And it suggests how in certain circumstances single people have engaged both with cultural discourses and with material constraints to become active agents of change.

Fictional discourses are present throughout the book but have been particularly important in later chapters. Here they illustrate not only the variety of ways in which writers and filmmakers imagined relationships between unmarried adults and children, but also how these imaginings could be in dialogue with lived experience and offer both adults and children ways of understanding and telling their own stories. Children's fiction is a particularly important source for studying singleness, and not simply for the ways in which it offers child readers particular views of marital status. Like fairy tales and nursery rhymes, these stories draw upon well-recognised archetypes and narratives which are engaged with by grownups as well as children and have remained active in many adults' memories. Juxtaposing novels and autobiographical sources also brings out contrasts as well as similarities between often stereotypical fictional accounts and more complex personal narratives which represent lived experience.

I begin my analysis, however, on a broader canvas in the next chapter by setting unmarried men and women's lives in the context of wider social, demographic and economic conditions in early and mid-twentieth-century England.

Notes

1 Evelyn Waugh, *Decline and Fall*, 1928 (Harmondsworth: Penguin, 1965), p. 103.
2 Diary of Miss Eileen Potter, in Simon Garfield (ed.), *We Are at War: The Diaries of Five Ordinary People in Extraordinary Times* (London: Ebury Press, 2005), p. 22.
3 Myrtle Reed, *The Spinster Book* (London: G. P. Putnam's Sons, 1911), pp. 215 and 217. This book was reprinted eighteen times between 1901 and 1911.
4 Important exceptions to this for the early modern period are Amy M. Froide, *Never Married: Singlewomen in Early Modern England* (Oxford: Oxford University Press, 2005), and Judith M. Bennett and Amy M. Froide (eds), *Singlewomen in the European Past* (Philadelphia, PA: University of Pennsylvania Press, 1999).
5 See John Gillis, *For Better, for Worse: British Marriages 1600 to the Present* (Oxford: Oxford University Press, 1985), for a discussion of the changing nature of marriage over the past 400 years.
6 Elizabeth Buettner, *Empire Families: Britons and Late Imperial India* (Oxford: Oxford University Press, 2004), ch. 3.
7 Ursula Holden, unpublished autobiography (c. 1996).
8 Letter from Norah Lea-Wilson to Joan Holden, 10 April 1950.
9 Dea Birkett, *Spinsters Abroad: Victorian Lady Explorers* (London: Gollancz, 1991); Martha Vicinus, *Independent Women: Work and Community for Single Women 1850–1920* (London: Virago, 1985); Trisha Franzen, *Spinsters and Lesbians: Independent Womanhood in the United States* (New York: New York University Press, 1996); Catriona Elder, 'The Question of the Unmarried: Some Meanings of being single in Australia in the 1920s and 1930s', *Australian Feminist Studies*, 18:2 (1993).
10 See chapter 8 for a discussion of Truby King's influence.

11 For example Bridget Hill, *Women Alone: Spinsters in England* (London: Yale University Press, 2002). See Froide, *Never Married*, pp. 175–81, for a useful discussion of the origins of this term.

12 Letter from Nona to Joan Holden, 31 December 1955.

13 Howard Chudacoff, *The Age of the Bachelor: Creating an American Subculture* (Princeton, NJ: Princeton University Press, 1999), pp. 4–5.

14 Donna Loftus, 'The Self in Society: Middle Class Men and Autobiography' in David Amigoni (ed.), *Life Writing, Gender, and Class Identity Formation in Victorian Culture* (Aldershot: Ashgate, 2004). Michael Roper found it hard to ascertain whether his middle-manager interviewees were married or not. Roper, *Masculinity and the British Organisational Man since 1945* (Oxford: Oxford University Press, 1994), p. 167.

15 Margaret Adams, *Single Blessedness: Observations on the Single Status in Married Society* (London: Heinemann, 1977), p. 15.

16 *Ibid.*, pp. 31 and 61. See also Nancy Peterson, *Our Lives for Ourselves: Women Who Have Never Married* (New York: G. P. Putnam and Sons, 1981), p. 258.

17 Writing in the 1970s, Adams suggested that society might be in a transitional stage with singleness about to emerge as the dominant social pattern.

18 Joan Scott, *Gender and the Politics of History* (New York: Columbia Press, 1988), p. 7.

19 Leonore Davidoff and Catherine Hall, *Family Fortunes: Men and Women of the English Middle Class, 1780–1850* (London: Hutchinson Education, 1987), p. 491.

20 Ludmilla Jordanova, *Sexual Visions: Images of Gender in Science and Medicine between the Eighteenth and Twentieth Centuries* (Brighton: Harvester Wheatsheaf, 1989), p. 14.

21 Rosalind Urbach Moss, 'Reinventing Spinsterhood: Competing Images of "Womanhood" in American Culture, 1880–1960', unpublished PhD thesis, University of Minnesota, 1988, p. 15.

22 See Lucy Bland, *Banishing the Beast: English Feminism and Sexual Morality 1885–1914* (Harmondsworth: Penguin, 1995).

23 *Ibid.* See also Sheila Jeffreys, *The Spinster and her Enemies: Feminism and Sexuality 1880–1930* (London: Pandora, 1985); Margaret Jackson, *The Real Facts of Life: Feminism and the Politics of Sexuality 1850–1940* (London: Taylor and Francis, 1994); Susan Kingsley Kent, *Sex and Suffrage in Britain 1860–1914* (Princeton, NJ: Princeton University Press, 1987); Cicely Hamilton, *Marriage as a Trade*, 1909 (London: Women's Press, 1981).

24 Postcard sent to Miss L. M. Morris by a friend signing herself as Ratz, sent 10 June 1906. Real Silverprint Photograph Series, Rapid Photo Printing Co., Ltd, Barbican, London E.C.

25 This was the original meaning of the term 'gay bachelor', but the fact that many bachelors were actually homosexual offers one explanation for its changed meaning since the 1960s. The term 'bachelor' has denoted unmarried status in men since the fourteenth century. Its associations with youth are suggested in alternative, now obsolete meanings such as a 'junior or inferior member of a trade-guild or City Company' (1390). Similarly a bachelor of arts, defined as 'one who has taken the first or lowest degree at a university who is not yet a master of arts' (first recorded 1362), suggests a man at the beginning of his career. *Oxford English Dictionary* (second edition, 1989), 1, p. 855.

26 Chudacoff, *The Age of the Bachelor*, p. 9.

27 Roper, *Masculinity*, pp. 167–8.

28 Adams, *Single Blessedness*, p. 24.
29 Leonore Davidoff, "'Adam Spoke First and Named the Orders of the World": Masculine and Feminine Domains in History and Sociology' in Helen Corr and Lynn Jamieson (eds), *The Politics of Everyday Life: Continuity and Change in Politics, Work and the Family* (London: Macmillan, 1990), p. 240.
30 Chudacoff, *The Age of the Bachelor*, p. 9.
31 I used selected tables relating chiefly to marital status within the General Reports and Occupational Tables for all censuses between 1921 and 1961.
32 Katherine Holden, 'Imaginary Widows: Spinsters, Marriage and the Lost Generation in Britain after the Great War', *Journal of Family History*, 30:4 (2005).
33 See for example J. M. Winter, The Great War and the British People (London: Macmillan, 1985), pp. 255–6; Michael Anderson, 'The Social Implications of Demographic Change', in F. M. L. Thompson (ed.), *The Cambridge Social History of Britain*, II (Cambridge: Cambridge University Press, 1990), p. 29.
34 See J. Worsnop, 'A Reevaluation of "the Problem of Surplus Women" in Nineteenth-Century England: The Case of the 1851 Census', *Women's Studies International Forum*, 13:1/2 (1990), pp. 21–31. John Holt Schooling used demographic data in his article 'A Woman's Chance of Marriage', *Strand Magazine*, 15 (1898), to show the relative sex ratios of spinsters to bachelors in different parts of the country.
35 His explanations for the increased marriage rate include 'cohort raiding' through increased social and geographical mobility, a tendency to earlier marriage (the proportion of women aged twenty to twenty-four who were married rose from about 24 per cent in 1911 to 34.45 in 1934), and a reverse trend in male immigration. Winter, *The Great War*, pp. 255–73.
36 Michael Anderson points out the radical difference between post-Second World War marriage patterns and those characteristic of the nineteenth and early twentieth centuries. 'The Emergence of the Modern Lifecycle', *Social History*, 10 (1985).
37 For a discussion of this issue in relation to professional women, see Alison Mackinnon, *Love and Freedom: Professional Women and the Reshaping of Personal Life* (Cambridge: Cambridge University Press, 1997).
38 Winter, *The Great War*, p. 255.
39 Martin Pugh, *Women and the Women's Movement, 1900–1950* (London: Macmillan, 1992), pp. 42–3.
40 See chapter 4.
41 For example, the psychologist Mary Chadwick takes this view in *Adolescent Girlhood* (London: George Allen and Unwin, 1932), pp. 237–8 and 255–6.
42 For a discussion of the legacy of war for disabled service men, see Joanna Bourke, *Dismembering the Male: Men's Bodies, Britain and the Great War* (London: Reaktion Books, 1996), and Peter Barham, *Forgotten Lunatics of the Great War* (London: Yale University Press, 2004).
43 Jay Dixon, *The Romantic Fiction of Mills and Boon, 1909–1990s* (London: UCL Press: 1999) p. 51. See also Billie Melman, *Women and the Popular Imagination in the 1920s: Flappers and Nymphs* (London: Macmillan, 1988), ch. 6.
44 This is explored in more depth in Katherine Holden, '"Nature takes no Notice of Morality". Singleness and *Married Love* in Interwar Britain', *Women's Historical Review*, 11 (2002).
45 Deborah Philips and Iyan Haywood, *Brave New Causes: Women in British Postwar*

Fiction (Leicester: Leicester University Press, 1998), ch. 6; Estella Tincknell, 'Jane or Prudence? Barbara Pym's Single Women, Female Fulfilment and Career Choices in the "Age Of Marriage"', *Critical Survey*, 18:1 (2006).

46 Bill Osgerby, '"Bachelors in Paradise": Masculinity, Lifestyle and Men's Magazines in Post-War America', in John Horne (ed.), *Masculinities: Leisure Cultures, Indentities and Consumption*, LSA Publication 69 (Eastbourne: 2000), pp. 51–80; Herald Froy, *How to Avoid Matrimony* (London: Frederick Muller, 1957).

47 The two main surveys used in this study are 'The New Survey of London Life and Labour', directed by Sir Hubert Llewellyn Smith (from 1928), published as London School of Economics and Political Science, *The New Survey of London Life and Labour*, 9 vols (London: P. S. King and Son, 1930–5) (hereafter *NSLLL*) and Peter Townsend's 'The Family Life of Old People (1954–5), published as Peter Townsend, *The Family Life of Old People*, 1957 (Harmondsworth: Penguin, 1963) (hereafter *FLOP*). In the latter survey, the household model is critiqued.

48 Jeffreys, *The Spinster and her Enemies*, is particularly guilty of this.

49 See for example Martha Vicinus, *Intimate Friends: Women who Loved Women 1887–1928* (London: University of Chicago Press, 2004); Catherine Clay, *British Women Writers, 1914–1945: Professional Work and Friendship* (London: Ashgate, 2006).

50 Carolyn Steedman, *Landscape for a Good Woman: A Story of Two Lives* (London: Virago, 1985), p. 58.

51 See Leonore Davidoff, Megan Doolittle, Janet Fink and Katherine Holden, *The Family Story: Blood Contract and Intimacy, 1830–1960* (London: Longman, 1999), ch. 9; Kathleen Kiernan, Hilary Land and Jane Lewis, *Lone Motherhood in Twentieth Century Britain: From Footnote to Front Page* (Oxford: Clarendon Press, 1998), is focused mainly on policy, privileges the late twentieth century and does not discuss men.

52 Steedman, *Landscape*, p. 70.

53 See Jeffreys, *The Spinster and her Enemies*; Vicinus, *Independent Women*; Vicinus, *Intimate Friends*; Alison Oram, *Women Teachers and Feminist Politics, 1900–39*, Manchester University Press, 1996). While Oram's main emphasis is on their professional lives and feminist politics, she does place women teachers in the context of family and marriage and gives an illuminating discussion of the complexities of marital status.

54 For example, Katherine R. Allan, *Single Women, Family Ties: Life Histories of Older Women* (Newbury Park, CA: Sage, 1989); Diana Gittins, 'Marital Status, Work and Kinship 1850–1930' in Jane Lewis (ed.), *Labour and Love: Women's Experience of Home and Family, 1850–1940* (Oxford: Blackwell, 1986).

55 *Three Men and a Baby* (Touchstone/Silver Screen: 1987).

56 On two novels that used this device, *A Bachelor's Baby* (1920) and *The Bachelor's Baby* (1958), see chapter 6.

57 Lyndall Roper, *Oedipus and the Devil: Witchcraft, Sexuality and Religion in Early Modern Europe* (London: Routledge, 1994), p. 218.

58 Katherine Holden, 'Personal Costs and Personal Pleasures: Care and the Unmarried Woman' in Janet Fink (ed.), *Care: Personal Lives and Social Policy* (Bristol: Policy Press, 2004), pp. 67–8.

59 Leonore Davidoff, *Worlds Between: Historical Perspectives on Gender and Class* (Cambridge: Polity, 1995) chs 1, 3 and 4. See also Davidoff *et al.*, *The Family Story*, chs 6 and 8.

60 Carol Pateman, *The Sexual Contract* (Cambridge: Polity, 1988).

61 This has also had the effect of making it more difficult to access institutional records, which can be withdrawn if an institution is currently under investigation.

62 Penny Summerfield, *Reconstructing Women's Wartime Lives: Discourses and Subjectivity in Oral Histories of the Second World War* (Manchester: Manchester University Press, 1998), p. 16.

2

'Consider her palaces':
work, housing and lifestyles

What's the use o' me going to the Borough to ask for a room. I havna' a job and I havna' reference. A've kept masel' since I was twelve years of age an' always paid ma' way, but now the work's not regular for my eyes are bad, and I cannot see the black stuff. If I had a room about 6s a week I could manage, but I'm that afraid o' bugs, I'd drown masel' sooner nor go in the slums. I've had it hard at times but I still had the little room and it was somewhere to go, and when I give it up, I'll have nothing.[1]

I tell you one thing about that, we used to have very good food when we was in lodgings. We only paid a pound a week for lodgings, and we used to get three meals a day, board and lodgings and, er, room; we used to sleep with their sons you know, two or three of us in one room. It was only a cottage you see. I was there for 5 years in the end ... Landlord was a bit strict ... he wouldn't let you drink ... he knew if you'd been drinking, come in drunk. He was a very particular man to live with. His wife was alright. I got on well with his wife. But they were strict in those days. (Interview with Fred)

Introduction

N 1934, IN THE MIDST of the Depression, a group of middle-class women set up a rest room for women who were out of work in central London. Within a few months it had become the Fitzroy Club and recruited more than a thousand members, and the Over Thirty Association was formed, a campaigning group set up to combat the serious problems caused by the widespread unemployment and lack of housing for older working women, many of whom were living in dismal bed-sitting rooms. Its housing report carried a number of extracts from interviews with single women like the one above who longed for homes of their own. The second quotation, from an interview with a lifelong bachelor, shows a very different face of working-class singleness in the interwar years.

Son of a Devonshire farm labourer, as a young man Fred (born 1903) had travelled around the south of England looking for jobs and also had an uneven work history, frequently changing employment and with long periods 'on the dole'. Yet his memories of living in lodgings are in stark contrast with those of the migrant Irish woman. For him it meant sharing a bedroom and meals with the sons of the family and being subjected to similar filial disciplines and restraints.

These contrasting narratives complicate popular beliefs that unmarried men were loners, while unmarried women were primarily dependent upon and living within families. They also show the necessity of locating single lifestyles in relation to gender, ethnicity and age as well as to class and marital status. This chapter situates unmarried people from different social backgrounds and age groups within a range of working and living situations between 1914 and 1960, and considers what employment and housing opportunities were available to them during their lives in this turbulent period of two world wars, a major economic depression and post-war reconstruction. Higher-status single men and women's work in the fields of health, social welfare and other professional and industrial work, and their lifestyles and community networks, are fully acknowledged. But attention is also paid to the often invisible majority, including those who did not work, who lived in lodgings, boarding houses or institutions or who had no permanent home. My main focus will be on unmarried people living apart from their own families, since familial relationships are discussed in chapter 3.

Attempting to set the lives of this disparate group within the English[2] population in demographic, economic, residential and cultural contexts and to show changes over time is not easy. I have adopted a cohort approach, which traces a range of possible life and work pathways for lifelong unmarried men and women born in or around 1890 and compares them with those of younger generations. The importance of looking at cohorts is evident if we take some broad demographic snapshots at different census dates showing the proportions of unmarried men and women in the population. Cultural norms for both men and women in English society assume that most men and women marry at some point during their lives, for women ideally during childbearing years. Yet at each census date from 1891 until 1931 only just over half the adults over fifteen at any one time were actually married, and well over a third had never married. It appears from this that marriage could hardly be regarded as a normal condition for the adult population as a whole. During the post-war years, however, a rather different pattern emerges. Rapidly rising marriage rates diminished the proportion of never-mar-

Table 2.1 Single (unmarried) women and men in the population by age in thousands, 1911–51

	1911				1921			
Age	Men	Women	Single men	Single women	Men	Women	Single men	Single women
20–4	1502	1673	1288	1266	1448	1703	1191	1237
25–34	1822	3125	1091	1109	1621	3140	894	1058
35–44	2336	2509	394	493	2496	2850	375	548
45–54	2073	1834	205	290	2133	2287	256	375
55–64	1085	1213	107	160	1383	1530	143	234
65+	849	1070	65	127	980	1311	84	180

	1931				1951			
Age	Men	Women	Single men	Single Women	Men	Women	Single Men	Single Women
20–4	1699	1795	1463	1322	1427	1500	1088	777
25–34	3062	3350	1079	1105	3140	3219	854	587
35–44	2512	2954	315	573	3291	3397	397	467
45–54	2303	2633	250	431	2874	3123	266	471
55–64	1766	1960	181	306	2028	2538	158	394
65+	1272	1690	110	261	1972	2853	162	453

Source: Census: England and Wales, 1911, 1921, 1931, 1951

ried men and women in the population to around one quarter, with a low point for women in 1961 showing only one in five never having married. In this era of marriage, then, both spinsterhood and bachelorhood were markedly less common. In 1951 just over a quarter of men and only 18 per cent of women aged twenty-five to thirty-four remained unmarried compared with one third of the women and more than half the men in this age group thirty years earlier (table 2.1).[3]

Regional variations are also significant and show the need for more local studies, since to be unmarried was much more common in some parts of the country than in others. For example, the 1931 census shows 7–8 per cent more unmarried women over the age of twenty in all age groups in the south east of England, where female unemployment was well below the national average, than in the north east where it was high and where the sex ratios were almost exactly equal. These figures suggest north–south migration by unmarried women from depressed industrial areas to find employment, most of which was in domestic service.[4] The largest surplus of women over men was in Bath and in wealthy London boroughs with a high proportion of servants, suggesting that inward migration of single women was common in these areas.[5]

Age is also an important variable. The 1951 census showed one fifth more unmarried men living in rural than in urban districts in all age groups over twenty, with the highest proportion aged forty-five to sixty-four. Yet the higher numbers of women than men in these older age groups meant the difference between the sexes would have appeared insignificant. By contrast, there were a quarter of a million more men than women aged twenty to thirty-five, which meant that the higher numbers of unmarried men in rural districts (partly a result of National Service camps) would have been more noticeable. Thus, young rural women in the 1950s had a greater choice of marriage partners than did urban women.[6]

The shadow of war: 1914–30

Women and men born in 1890 were in a very different position from later generations, having lived most of their adult lives in the shadow of the Great War. But their knowledge and understanding of the significance of that war was also deeply divided by gender. The war experience of young bachelors depended partly on their willingness to enlist as soldiers. Their lack of a dependent family made this harder to avoid than if they had been married. But they were also more vulnerable to criticism, with letters in *The Times* claiming that single men were only enlisting because 'their occupation as cricket bat manufacturers was at a standstill' and that their 'devotion to football had overpowered their sense of patriotism'.[7] In 1915, Kitchener's need for fighting men led to an announcement that all men between the ages of nineteen and forty-one must attest that they would be willing to serve. But young, fit bachelors who did not enjoy occupational exemption shunned attestation forms, believing that they would be the first to be recruited, while married men signed up on the grounds that they would be immune from immediate call-up.[8] After January 1916, bachelors were, however, forced towards the front by a Military Service Bill which conscripted all unmarried men. Many of those who survived the war spent the next two or three years watching their fellow soldiers being wounded or killed, and those lucky enough to emerge without physical scars were still often left in shock, mourning for lost comrades and alienated from potential marriage partners.

Unmarried women born in or around 1890 had a very different war. The diaries, journalism and autobiography of Vera Britain (born 1893) speak poignantly of the pain and alienation she experienced as she watched her generation of men, including her brother, fiancé and close friends, being decimated on the battlefields of Flanders.[9] Many women like her were prompted to join the nursing services or the Voluntary Aid Detachment and work alongside men near the battle front, while others learned new skills and gained financial independence in civilian or munitions work normally done by men. Though such work was often hard and could be dangerous, pay rates were considerably higher than in the usual female occupations. Thus, some felt anger or disappointment when the men returned and they were dismissed from their jobs and pushed back into the home or domestic service.[10]

By the time the census statistics were published in 1921, this newly enfranchised cohort of women were thirty-one years old, the flurry of marriages delayed by the war had subsided, and they were faced with the widely publicised belief that there were one or (by some accounts) two million surplus women in the population unable to marry.[11] Similar statistics had been used to raise alarm about earlier generations of unmarried women, but the war rekindled this debate. The lack of men was particularly noticeable in this age group, with 1,158,000 marriageable (unmarried, widowed or divorced) women and only 919,000 marriageable men aged twenty-five to thirty-four, a shortfall of 239,000.[12] The implications of these figures for these women's marriage chances cannot simply be dismissed as scaremongering since half of all unmarried women in their late twenties had still not married a decade later.[13] However, with a third in their age group also unmarried, they were likely to have known many others in a similar situation and would have been prepared for the possibility that they would never marry. Testimony from two women born around the turn of the century suggests that young women from middle-class backgrounds were warned in schools and universities about the shortage of men and that some made their career decisions with this advice in mind.[14]

Popular novels and journalism were divided in the ways in which they represented this generation of men and women during the 1920s. Marriage as an institution was strongly reinforced, and spinsters were often viewed as either imaginary widows bereaved by the war or a disruptive force without husbands to control them.[15] But although the labour-market gains made by women during the war were not sustained, some single women writing to the popular press disputed the view that they were surplus because they had no husbands, pointing out that 'we have a glorious freedom of our own' and that 'marriage is not the only thing in life open to women.[16]

Melman argues that fear of these independent women, who were perceived as beyond the control of men, and the alienation of ex-service men from post-war society, are reflected in popular novels about returning soldiers during the 1920s which give a pessimistic view of relations between the sexes. Both marriage and extramarital liaisons were seen as inferior substitutes for comradeship between men. Women were charac-terised as 'subsidiary and in some cases dispensable', but also as competing with men in social and economic spheres and therefore degrading and emasculating, making the non-marital bonds of the 'fraternity of men at arms' seem more attractive.[17]

Another ubiquitous fantasy of modern bachelorhood in popular fiction and film offered men unlimited sexual access to women outside marriage. Here English men were depicted as asexual pals or companions and displaced by powerful, virile, 'oriental' men. This 'desert romance' narrative was pioneered by Edith Hull in her novel *The Sheik*, first published at the end of the war, whose sales surpassed all other contem-porary best-sellers put together. It had many imitators and was made into a hugely popular film starring Rudolph Valentino.[18]

The Sheik masters the frigid white English woman who had rejected marriage both through his sexual magnetism and through physical force and keeps her living with him in the desert. Yet all is not as it seems, and the eventual discovery that he has European origins made their long-term relationship more acceptable to a British readership. Melman argues that rather than simply dismissing this story as a racist, sadomasochistic tale of male sexual aggression, it needs to be understood as a female escapist fantasy in which the oversexed Arab male is transformed into a white English hero.[19] This was a very different image from the older Victorian ideal of chaste, muscular Christianity embodied in the imperial bachelor heroes of pre-war Britain such as Lord Kitchener or Cecil Rhodes.[20] Rather, it was modelled on the romantic legend of Lawrence of Arabia, which offered a new version of the soldier hero as a fantasy of omnipo-tent British manhood in authority over both Arabs and Turks.[21] With two and a half million British men mentally traumatised and/or physi-cally mutilated by war, such images also reflect a society where many marriages were not living up to expectations and where marriageable English bachelors in their twenties and thirties were no longer perceived as strong, virile men.

Working-class employment in the interwar years

Conditions for this generation of bachelors were not improved by the employment situation, which was affected by the restructuring of British industry during the interwar years. Those in work and living alone had a considerable advantage over married men, since they were paid the same wages but had no families to support. But the older heavy industries such as marine engineering and coal mining, employing mainly men, were in decline, while the new light industries like engineering, metal and food were increasingly taking on young single women workers at the expense of men because their wages were lower and they were regarded as more suitable for assembly-line work.[22] Furthermore, when women were ejected from their jobs at the end of the war, the excuse given was generally that a married man needed the work because he had a family to keep. Many bachelors were hit by unemployment and, because it was easier for them to be mobile, some travelled widely to find work. Fred was in this position. He had worked in so many different unskilled, un-unionised jobs (including farm labourer, stable lad, kitchen porter, and on boats and the railways) that he could not count them all, but had also spent long periods unemployed in the 1920s and remembered queuing at the labour exchange with thousands of others and having his money stopped if he refused a job,, however, low the wages.

In the 1930s, bachelors of the 1890 cohort were disproportionately represented in both agriculture and mining, each containing more than one in five male unmarried workers aged thirty-five to forty-four, as against one in seven of all men of a similar age. And for younger men in agriculture the discrepancy was even larger. Nearly half the workforce aged twenty-five to thirty-four was single, compared with just over one third of the same cohort overall. Most agricultural workers were employed as farm labourers on low wages in a modernising industry that was shedding manpower but still the main source of rural employment. For an unmarried man, however, prospects were limited. Jack Lawley (born 1905) described long hours in his job as a herdsman during the 1930s, with handicaps such as an attack of sickness which would take all his small savings, and the pressure he was under to return to work before he was well. He finally achieved his ambition to run his own farm by buying into a partnership after the Second World War. However, despite having an uncle's help and his mother as housekeeper, after a few years he gave it up. Jack's story shows how both gender and marital status structured this kind of work. His business partner died and when his elderly mother's burden of worries became too great, Jack was forced to acknowledge the impossibility of running 'a family farm … without a family'.[23]

In heavy industrial occupations during the 1930s, unemployment was the main hazard. While the 1931 census shows unemployment rates in agriculture to be only one in seventeen,[24] mining (which employed just over one in ten of the single men aged thirty-five to forty-four) was one of the principal industries hit by the slump, with a third of coal miners out of work in 1932. Age was a critical determinant of long-term unemployment, with the chances of being out of work for over a year increasing with advancing years and chances of re-employment diminishing, particularly after the age of fifty.[25] And with so many men with long-term injuries after the war, the 1890 cohort were additionally disadvantaged in containing an unusually high number with a physical or mental disability, many of whom remained unmarried. Joanna Bourke has argued that disabled men were discouraged from marrying after the war. Those who did could be considered improvident and some people believed their children might be born with disabilities.[26] Although they received pensions according to the severity of their injuries,[27] the sums were often too small to live on and the men still had to seek work. But, despite pressure on employers to take them, this marginal group of shabby, dispirited older workers was less attractive to employers than younger, physically fitter men who had spent less time out of work.[28]

Although the numbers of unemployed older single women in the workforce were lower, age discrimination hit men and women alike. Women from a respectable lower-middle-class or working-class urban background often aspired to enter retail or clerical work, which employed nearly a quarter of all occupied unmarried women. However, both these areas of work were considered suitable for younger, more attractive women, with 75–80 per cent of workers in these groups under the age of thirty. Unemployment rates were noticeably higher for women over thirty in these occupations and few women moved into higher grades or management positions.

Some younger women also failed to find jobs in these occupations. Ruby (born 1907) and Pearl (born 1910) had envied other women the glamour of shop work and dressmaking but had been forced to settle for jobs in a chocolate factory and a wholesale grocer, where they remained for most of their working lives. Their testimony typifies the discourse of missed opportunity that pervaded interviews with women who left school during and after the war, whose career and educational aspirations had been dashed by the necessity of going into service or other low-paid work. A certificate of character issued to Meg (born 1902) on leaving her Wesleyan elementary school in 1916, confirms these low expectations. No mention was made of any knowledge or skills acquired in the six years she had been there, but her regular attendance, punctuality, diligence and conduct were commended as very good or excellent and she was described as 'careful, quiet, industrious, painstaking and thoroughly dependable'.[29]

The long-term effects of these low educational expectations and marginalisation at work are suggested in Miriam Glucksmann's interviews with married women workers in the Peak Frean's biscuit factory. Her interviewees talked of antagonistic behaviour from older single women, whom they described as jealous 'old maids' without men to sleep with. This antagonism, they believed, stemmed from the spinsters' belief that as wives they must have men to keep them so did not really need the work.[30] Alice Kessler-Harris has argued in the context of 1930s America that in times of job shortages hostilities of this kind should be viewed in terms of social justice, with women who could claim to be providers being regarded as more deserving of jobs than those who could not.[31] Such hostilities must also, however, be understood in the context of a gendered labour market where older single women were in powerless positions, 'subservient to men with decades less experience',[32] and needed to find another way of asserting their authority as workers.

The Over Thirty Association offered support for urban women in these situations, some of whom were forced out of work and compelled to enter domestic service, where wage rates were even lower. Personal service was still by far the largest employer for single women in the 1930s and over half a million of the workforce (47 per cent of all women servants) were over thirty. The high numbers of older unmarried women in service may reflect the greater difficulty for domestic servants of getting married. Anti-social hours and a high degree of personal surveillance by employers, who generally discouraged male followers, were partly responsible for low marriage rates and the fact that, although declining in popularity, 'living in' was still common for unmarried women, particularly amongst migrant workers.[33] Yet it was hardly the most desirable option for older women who longed for homes of their own.

Pension campaigns, housing and homelessness in the 1930s

Interviews for the Over Thirty Association report *Consider her Palaces* (1936) with low-waged workers, including servants, show the discrimination faced by women of (or older than) the 1890 cohort. Male boarders were given the services usually offered by a wife, including laundry, mending, cleaning and cooking. Women, often paying the same rent, rarely had these services included and were generally viewed with suspicion by landladies, who claimed their tenants were in too much, always poking about, doing bits of washing, had no money and were more trouble.[34] Women interviewees testified variously that:

'All the women seem to pay higher than the men, but for the men she washes and mends and takes messages. For us she blows up a speaking tube and then says we are out. It is all the same if the call was about a job' ... 'I don't ask for anything, and cannot even invite a friend to tea but what she's up to see what I am doing! I have to carry my own coal from the basement to the top of the house' ... 'I was given a Valor Perfection oil stove which is much cheaper than gas ... this year she said I must use the gas, as they are not doing well and she gets a rebate. When I said I could not afford it, she took away my stove to the basement in case I should use it ... I used to go out and buy fish and chips, and I never put the light on until 4 pm., however, she said I should pay her 1/-a day for a dinner at night, and when I said I could not, she said she wanted my room.'[35]

Male boarders appear in a more advantageous position. Yet my inter-viewee Fred had not always found the familial style of lodging described earlier to be without problems. His landlord, a building contractor, was out at work all day and Fred had 'got on well with his wife', but 'had to get away' as soon as the quarrelling started. This story recalls Davidoff's analysis of the tensions embedded in the landlady/lodger relationship, in which semi-licit domestic, emotional and sometimes also sexual services were rendered for cash by an older woman to a younger man.[36]

Although widely ignored, single women's pleas for homes of their own did not go completely unanswered. Failing in their attempt to get government subsidies to build one-room flats, by 1938, the Over Thirty Association had secured the co-operation of Lambeth Housing associa-tion to supply some low-cost housing and was seeking support through donations or loans from graduate and professional women in return for the right to name a flat.[37]

A second campaigning group supporting older unmarried women was set up by Florence White (1886–1961), who in 1935 formed the National Spinsters' Pension Association (NSPA) to battle for a change in the 1925 contributory state retirement scheme which would allow never-married women to receive the state pensions at fifty-five rather than sixty-five. Its target group were single women workers who, in times of severe economic depression, were losing their right to a contributory pension because their records were incomplete through unemployment, illness or giving up paid work to look after parents.[38] Women in this position were forced to rely on the household means-tested public assistance or a means-tested pension after the age of seventy. The NSPA represented themselves as war spinsters who should have been married but for the accident of war and claimed equality with widows, who from 1931 could receive pensions from the age of fifty-five.[39]

At its height in 1938, the NSPA, with a mainly working-class member-ship, was the largest women's reform movement of the 1930s. It had around ninety-two branches, held demonstrations of up to 10,000 and handed in a petition to Parliament of nearly a million signatures.[40] The Lequesne Committee was set up by Parliament in 1938 to inquire into the spinsters' case, holding a public inquiry at which a variety of witnesses testified. The disadvantages of the single woman worker compared with the male worker were stressed: their physical weakness and lower wages, which meant they had less chance of being in insured employment until sixty-five, could not afford to take time off when they were ill and therefore were at risk of declining into chronic ill-health; and the extra expenses that men did not have of maintaining an attractive, youthful appearance.[41]

Not all spinsters, however, supported the scheme. Professional women with occupational pension schemes feared that it might be used to force early retirement, while the National Association of Civil Servants (claiming to represent 7,000 unmarried women) opposed it on the grounds that it would undermine the equal pay campaign, restrict employment oppor-tunities, reduce wages and force women out of employment.[42] Yet for a working-class woman in low-paid, sex-segregated employment offering little job satisfaction, without pension prospects and with insufficient income to pay for domestic support in times of sickness or family need, the prospect of equality with men may have seemed irrelevant, whereas to claim equality with married women appeared much more desirable. Thus, they claimed a victory when a compromise position was reached, and in 1940, the government reduced the retirement age for all women to sixty.

Bachelors had no political organisation to support their interests. Those in work and earning a family wage without a family to support were often objects of envy, particularly in occupations where men with families were unemployed. But older, unemployed single men were less fortunate. Too old to be drafted into government-sponsored Training and Instructional Centres aiming to improve the employment prospects of young single men,[43] they were more vulnerable than women to destitu-tion. In February 1931, over ten times more men than women in London were homeless or found in shelters, common lodging houses and casual wards. In the NSLLL (1932), a follow-up of Charles Booth's more famous turn-of-the-century study of poverty in London, 'destitute wayfarers' who used the casual wards were seen as belonging to the lowest social grade of the poor, and it was estimated that between four and five thousand visited these wards at some time during the year. Like the 750 sandwich-board men on the London streets, the great majority in casual wards were older, unmarried men. A sample from the Borough of Southwark found that out of thirty-four men, twenty-seven were bachelors and twenty-six were over the age of thirty. One third of these men were classified as mentally abnormal, mostly in the category 'feeble-minded', and links between vagrancy and mental deficiency were suggested, though it was acknowledged that some still suffered from shell-shock or other effects of the war. The absence of men over sixty-five suggested a short life expectancy.[44]

The number of destitute spinsters was lower, representing only half of the twenty-two women in Southwark's casual ward for women, but their higher incidence of 'mental abnormality' (with insanity and psycho-neurosis predominating)[45] made it appear that leaving their families and becoming homeless caused women more problems than it did men. The dangers of such a lifestyle had already been publicised in Mrs Cecil Chesterton's survey of women in London's public lodging houses, *In Darkest London* (1926), which called attention to the lack of facilities for homeless women. And while the London County Council refuted her allegations, the Ministry of Health was concerned that the absence of suitable accommodation for women in this position might be a cause of prostitution.[46]

Middle-class housing and lifestyles in the interwar years

Although Chesterton's main concern was with homeless women, she cast her net wider in her assertion that: 'for the single woman well onto middle age, to live alone is to court the desolation of spirit that saps vitality'. Many women during the 1930s would, however, have roundly rejected her view that middle-class women who lived alone had nothing to do but oppress their friends and relations. Some were inspired by Virginia Woolf's rallying cry that in order to fulfil her creative potential a woman must have £500 a year and a room of her own,[47] yet the tide of opinion seems on the whole to have been against the lone woman whatever her class. Even Marjorie Hillis' humorous advice book, *Live Alone and Like It* (1936), which offered suggestions as to how to make the best of a solitary life, opens with an announcement that 'this book is no brief in favour of living alone'. Her belief that 'five of the ten people who do so can't help themselves, and at least three of the others are irritatingly selfish', would hardly have been encouraging to the independent woman.[48] The pioneer doctor and feminist Dame Mary Scharlieb's account of the problems besetting the bachelor woman who lived alone was similarly pessimistic, alluding to her 'low habits', such as resorting to alcohol or opium because she lacked the comforts every worker deserved, having no one 'whose joy and duty it is to provide dressing gown and slippers, a cheering fire, and an easy chair'.[49]

The idea that spinsterhood meant loneliness would also have been refuted by those who had found companionship with other women. As well as in live-in partnerships (discussed in chapter 4), single women gained companionship and often lifelong friendships in boarding schools, colleges, convents and women's hostels or residential clubs, while details of clubs for women of all classes were featured in women's magazines and journals.[50] An advertisement in the British Federation of University Women's Newsletter in July 1932 for one such club in Liverpool offered at a weekly rate for dinner, bed and breakfast of £2 2s a week, with 'attractively furnished, Bed-Sitting Rooms with fires, good Common Rooms and Gardens. The residents include University Women and others engaged in Social Services, Business and other Professions'. Some hostel accommodation was also available to working-class women, promoted chiefly on moral grounds by organisations such as the Salvation Army, the Girls' Friendly Society (GFS) and the YWCA as 'their greatest safeguard from the Abyss'. Still, most of the approved hostels listed by the National Council of Women in 1923 were for professional women, and required references. Of the hostels on the London list, 75 per cent were for professional women, students, or the higher class of business woman, and about four fifths were in the wealthier districts.[51]

The opportunity they offered middle-class women to move away from home into an approved and safe environment, and to live alongside others engaged in similar kinds of work, may have helped to foster the development of the Federation of Professional and Business Women's Clubs during the late 1930s, whose aims were 'to weave a bond about business and professional women, uniting them in service and fellowship'. An entry in Eileen Potter's Mass Observation (MO) diary in October 1939 describing a branch meeting suggests that it offered a valuable forum for debate, partly because its members came from disparate political and economic backgrounds.[52]

Middle-class men had similar options: to live alone in their own houses or flats, share with friends or live in clubs, hotels or lodgings. However, their higher earnings made it easier to get domestic support. Middle-class records in the NSLLL show four bachelors and five spinsters aged thirty to thirty-seven living alone in Hampstead with the women earning on average two thirds of the men's income, while paying broadly similar rents. These differences in income in relation to expenditure and different gendered expectations about housework and cooking may explain why none of the women was recorded as having servants or taking meals from landladies (although some were tenants living in the same houses as bachelors who did receive meals), while two of the men received partial board and one had a woman to do his housework and had all his meals at restaurants.[53]

The advantages of a single lifestyle were made clear in the *London Opinion*, which carried the message that bachelors would remain sexually attractive and available whatever their age. This was one of the few lifestyle magazines aimed at, though not explicitly inviting, a general male readership (albeit a mainly middle-class urban one), carrying light humorous editorials, cartoons, gossip and fiction written from a man's viewpoint. By the 1930s, it also included financial, motoring, gardening and advice columns. The paper lampooned marriage in a 1930 edition where married men were 'distinguished by their habit of looking round anxiously for ash trays' (presumably because smoking calmed their nerves) and the 16,350 people married by a retired registrar were described as 'victims' who bore no grudges. In 1939, it went even further by depicting married men in revolt, with a cartoon showing members of the 'downtrodden husband society' doing a version of the Nazi salute.[54]

In contrast, a series of advertisements for Players 'Bachelor' cigarettes displayed images of well-groomed young and older men and announced that 'bachelors are different' and 'bachelors are always popular', while the sex appeal of the term was made even more obvious in a third image of a young woman smoking, with the caption: 'There is pleasurable anticipation in waiting for a bachelor.'[55] It is hard to imagine anyone being attracted by a 'spinster' cigarette, and as if to underline this point, the absurdity of spinsters trying to hide their age and adopt the habits of a bachelor was displayed in a front page cartoon depicting a stereotypical elderly spinster caught speeding in an open-top car, with the caption: 'Constable: (making a note of it) "Miss Olivia Twiddlefick, 73 Carlton Avenue – well over thirty-five." Speedy Lady: "Certainly not; twenty nine next month."'[56]

Middle-class employment in the interwar years

An important factor in examining employment opportunities for the 1890 cohort was the increasing gap between the sexes. By 1931 twice as many unmarried women as men were in the thirty-five to forty-four age band,[57] and, with a higher casualty rate in the war among the officer classes, the discrepancy would have been even greater amongst the middle and upper classes. The necessity of establishing a professional identity as an alternative to marriage was therefore particularly important for this generation of women. A precedent had already been set by advances in women's higher education and the expansion of teaching and nursing as careers for middle-class women during the late nineteenth and early twentieth century, leading to the recruitment of a significant body of professional unmarried women (including around 70 per cent of women students from Oxford University before the First World War).[58]

But while many of these women were dedicated professionals, they were less inspiring to the next generation than were their predecessors. Attracted by a range of new female occupations in career books, school-girl fiction, and girls' and women's magazines, younger women in the 1930s were drawn to glamorous images of the independent 'bachelor girl', particularly as, in the context of high male unemployment, these publications showed the feminine aspects of work and played down the idea that women were in competition with men for jobs.[59] Girls' and young women's views of older single working women were also influenced by the more limited range of occupations that were on offer in reality and by their knowledge that with marriage bars in most professions, they would ultimately have to choose between marriage and a career. The promotion of marriage and motherhood as a woman's most desirable future and the frequent denigration of spinsters made it harder for this younger generation to see singleness as a positive choice.

Teaching remained by far the most popular career, a predominantly female occupation particularly in elementary schools, which offered a route to social mobility for clever working-class and lower middle-class girls, and where during the interwar years three quarters of staff were women.[60] In 1931, over half of single professional women aged thirty-five to forty-four were teachers, representing one in eleven of all single women of comparable ages in employment. Health and welfare work was also an important area of work, employing well over a third of all professional single women in this age group. The great majority were trained sick nurses, with others working as social welfare workers, midwives or mental attendants or in subordinate medical services such as physiotherapy, massage and optometry.[61] But, although the Sex Disqualification (Removal) Act of 1919 declared the general principle that 'a person shall not be exempted by sex or marriage from the exercise of any public function, the holding of civil or judicial office, or the carrying on of any civil profession or from membership of any incorporated society',[62] the glass ceiling for women remained in place, with little job expansion in the higher professions.[63] Although women doctors had more than doubled in number since 1911, four out of five were men and only 226 single women aged thirty-five to forty qualified in 1931.[64]

Formal and informal marriage bars in the teaching and nursing professions, as well as gender and status divisions between male and female jobs, meant that although headmasters or male doctors were usually in overall charge, most workers were unmarried women. Those promoted to hospital matron or head teacher of a single-sex secondary school or women's college enjoyed both female friendships and some measure of power. Such pleasures were recalled by the headmistress of a girls' grammar school (Maud born 1907), who spoke of the 'camaraderie in the classroom' and the delights of the headmistress community where 'we were all women who had succeeded'.

However, a study of women civil servants born between 1905 and 1915 shows the difficulties of another popular career for middle-class girls. Promotional opportunities in the Civil Service, which also operated a marriage bar, were few and the career ladder blocked by older women, making the 'dowry' payment given to all women who left to marry a more attractive proposition than staying single and remaining in a low grade.[65] Hilda Martindale, a pioneer civil servant from an earlier generation, was concerned that between 1927 and 1936 only eighty-eight women entered the open competition for the Administrative Class, with just eight succeeding. When invited to speak at women's colleges and organisations, she tried to inspire more women from universities and women's colleges to enter the field:

> In my addresses, I tried to draw pictures of the work women were doing in these highest posts in connection, for example with town planning, slum clearance, commercial relations and negotiating trade agreements, the electricity industries, light railways, road safety, employment and training, and care of criminals, as well as acting as private secretaries to Under Secretaries of State and Ministers, as I hoped to stimulate the students to try and do likewise.[66]

Her efforts seem to have been partially successful, with more women being appointed to higher grades in the late 1930s, although still only a handful compared with men.

Whatever their profession, single women earned between 60–80 per cent of the wages of men in comparable jobs,[67] and a sense of unfairness at not having the same pay or promotion prospects prompted some into feminist politics during the 1920s and 1930s. Older members of the feminist National Union of Women Teachers (NUWT) and the National Union of Women Civil Servants generally followed in the footsteps of earlier generations in their fight for equality, eschewing the politics of difference embraced by some younger colleagues and which characterised the NSPA campaign discussed above. But by the 1930s, when attacks on older spinsters claiming they were leading abnormal lives became more common, they were forced into a defensive position. In 1934 a letter to the journal *The Woman Teacher* claimed that 'concerns about the rights and needs of married women' meant that 'the bachelor woman and her welfare and dignity as a worker' were being ignored or disparaged. The following year another, younger NUWT official wrote an article for a popular newspaper objecting to the marriage bar on the grounds that enforced spinsterhood was denying teachers 'the love and companionship that means a fuller, deeper life'.[68] These kinds of attacks may have prompted women, who during the interwar period for the first time were able to make careers in parliamentary politics, to represent themselves as 'married to their work'. In 1932 Labour MP Ellen Wilkinson (1891–1947) described herself as pouring the 'creative energy which other women have given to husband and children' into her work for the socialist movement.[69]

Although fewer in number, middle-class, middle-aged bachelors' commonest professional occupation was also teaching, occupying a third of all professional single men aged thirty-five to forty-four in 1931. Since elementary schools were mainly staffed by women, these men more often taught in boys' grammar or boarding schools, the latter option being particularly favoured because it offered board and keep and the companionship of other men. The quality of these largely unregulated institutions varied greatly, with some schools taking on staff with few qualifications or little aptitude for teaching. Evelyn Waugh's novel *Decline and Fall* (1928) caricatured such a fourth-rate boys' boarding school, but it also showed comradeship between the unmarried male staff and called into question the desirability of them changing their marital status. Thus, the master who married the headmaster's daughter was driven to suicide, while, as we have seen (chapter 1), Mr Prendergast, another older bachelor teacher, denounced marriage as a flight from normality.

Prendergast had been in holy orders before going into teaching, another profession lampooned by Waugh which, despite the decline in church attendance, remained a popular choice for professional single men. Nearly a quarter of professional bachelors aged thirty-five to forty-four had a religious vocation, with 30 per cent of Anglican clergy in this cohort remaining single. The numbers were particularly high because the celibacy rule meant that no Catholic priests and monks were married and this was the one arena where to be single was the normal status for older men. For priests at least, this also put them in a position of authority over their married peers.

This was less likely in a commercial business or trade, which middle-class boys in the 1920s were encouraged to consider as offering more scope for a career and better pay than the professions.[70] In areas such as banking, progression could be dependent on marriage, with proportionately fewer older unmarried men in senior positions.[71] Some younger men at this time delayed or abstained from marriage because they believed they were not earning enough to support a wife. David (born 1910) explained: 'Well I was rather put off getting married because one of these, a house master ... said you needed to give your wife two thousand a year. Now this was in 1930ish ... it impressed me no end and I didn't really consider marriage cos I thought I was never going to be able to give my wife a two thousand dowry'.

Finally, the army was another profession that offered accommodation, domestic support and companionship with other men. In 1931, nearly one in five commissioned officers aged thirty-five to forty-four were unmarried (most of whom had probably joined during the First World War), compared with one in seven unmarried men in this cohort as a whole.[72] However, the social composition of this group remained fairly narrow. Although the loss of so many officers had ensured more middle-class men received commissions during the war, men entering this profession during the interwar years were still almost entirely drawn from the upper and upper middle classes with a public school background. The necessity for a second lieutenant in an average regiment to have a private income of between £60 and £100 a year ensured that few others would be able to afford an officer's lifestyle. The retirement age of officers, which in 1938 was set at forty-seven for majors and fifty for lieutenant-colonels,[73] also shows the limited longer-term prospects of this profession which required men to be strong and physically fit. In her autobiography, Penelope Lively described a British expatriate soldier in this position who lived with her family in Egypt during the 1930s and was employed as a caretaker. She saw this man as living in limbo and interpreted his frustration, loneliness and xenophobia as arising from social insecurity.[74]

Work, housing and lifestyles in the 1940s and 1950s

By the advent of the Second World War, the 1890 cohort would have been around fifty, too old to have been conscripted into the forces or other war work which required them to be posted abroad or move away from home, although as urban teachers or social workers they might have been evacuated with pupils to the country. This was the case for an unmarried London probation officer who thought that she had been posted in Somerset because the Home Office might have thought 'it was a good thing for someone to be around who was conversant with [London children's] idiom'.[75]

With so many young men in the forces, unemployment was no longer such a problem for older bachelors, particularly in areas with labour shortages where the middle aged were often specifically targeted in recruitment drives.[76] Young bachelors' war experience was, however, more diverse, depending on eligibility to serve in the forces on health grounds, and whether they were posted abroad and saw active service or remained in Britain leading a more sedentary existence in camps or depots across the country.[77] For example, Sid (born 1925), who worked as a miner in the Durham coalfields after the war, had joined the Fusiliers with his school friends at the age of sixteen and was later captured by the Germans. As a prisoner of war, he was sent down the mines and watched all but three of his mates die. His wartime experiences had little in common with those of Jim (born 1921), another Durham bachelor, who hadn't been fit to join army, so carried on working in the building trade.

For unmarried women, age prejudice continued, particularly for those over forty. This was a result partly of the residual married identity attached to all older women and the assumption that they must have a man to support them. For Irish women emigrants, whose numbers were high throughout our period and who filled many of the vacancies in domestic and personal service, it was further compounded by their ethnicity, which branded them as both unreliable and immoral. The unchanging proportion of women workers aged over forty-four (16 per cent in both 1931 and 1943) suggests the reluctance of employers to take on older women, until in autumn 1943 they were put under pressure by official direction.[78]

Older unmarried men and women often went into civil defence and other voluntary work in the Home Guard, as ARP wardens (which in Bristol had recruited 3,756 men and 1,582 women by the end of the war, most of whom were aged over forty), or through the Women's Voluntary Service, which became an auxiliary of over twenty government departments during the war years.[79] My aunt Norah, who had trained as a nurse in 1927, was in this position. She had only ever practised private nursing and described her great fear that she would be forced back into hospital nursing with the expectation that she would become a sister or a staff nurse. Instead, she spent time in night shelters during the London Blitz looking after people on a voluntary basis.

While this experience enabled her to identify with the belief that 'we were all in it together', she did not see this as transforming her life in the ways remembered by some younger working women who were sent away from their families.[80] Rather, as a middle-class women of independent means, her sense of freedom and escape came earlier in the war during a journey through Japan, China, Manchuria and India, where for the first time in her life on board ship she found herself 'hobnobbing naturally with all the men … even getting as far as the bar', and feeling 'a much freer individual'.[81]

Norah's account of her wartime travels can be related to a discourse of modernisation in which 'the idea of the emergence of women from seclusion in the home' was a central element. Summerfield argues that ex-service women were especially likely to draw upon this narrative, seeing their wartime experience as opening new horizons, enabling them to escape from parental discipline and make new friends. She also found that all four of the unmarried women she interviewed offered such 'heroic' accounts of the war as being of great personal significance.[82] However, Sue Bruley's analysis of a diary written by two older unmarried women who worked in an aircraft components factory offers a much bleaker picture of entrapment and demoralisation, which suggests that some 'heroic' accounts may have been given with hindsight.[83]

My interviewee Betty (born 1921) told this kind of celebratory story. She had never been shown much affection from the grandmother who had brought her up, and she had felt unattractive and quite possessive of the few friends she had made at school. But after she joined the Wrens to 'see more of the world', she made many new friends from different backgrounds and was introduced to alcohol for the first time by a sailor. With so many 'kind decent helpful men' and little female competition, she enjoyed an active social life, and became engaged to be married.

But Betty was also able to draw upon this narrative of freedom and independence to explain her eventual deviance from social norms. After demobilisation she decided to break her engagement because she knew it wouldn't have worked, and with hindsight saw herself as 'ahead of her time'. It was 'quite an unusual stance in those days … you were on the shelf and that sort of thing … You definitely got married – you were a little bit beyond the pale if you didn't marry – sort of taken for granted that you weren't attractive to men, or nobody wanted you, or you weren't pleasant to live with – oh very much that way.'

It seems to have been harder for women in Betty's age cohort to contemplate lifelong spinsterhood than it had been for the preceding generation. A 1944 MO report found older unmarried women in factory work resigned to their circumstances. One fifty-year-old commented: 'I've been here twenty five years this very month. I hope I'll stay on after the war. You get used to your one job, and I don't think I'd like to do any other. I'm still on the shelf – most likely I'll be coming with my cloak and bonnet on.'[84]

With fewer than one in five of women aged twenty-five to thirty-four and one in seven aged thirty-five to forty-four still unmarried in 1951, it is hardly surprising that Maggie Blount, a freelance writer and publicity officer in a metal factory in her mid-thirties who lived alone with her cats, had felt estranged from her married peers after the war. In her diary she described a cousin with whom she had little in common as 'like a frustrated school mistress' and reflected gloomily: 'Yet now I have more in common with her than any of my other cousins who have long since married and been lost to me in the concerns of their families. J and I are the two old Maids of our generation.'[85]

While young men were also being encouraged to marry, their higher numbers compared to unmarried women left them less isolated and more able, in a period of full employment, rising wages and increased prosperity, to relate to an increasingly misogynistic, anti-marriage discourse in the 1950s. The increasing popularity of the playboy image led to the appearance of a genre of humorous books, like Cadwallader and Nudnick's *The Little Black Book: A Manual for Bachelors,* and *How to Avoid Matrimony* (1957) by the journalist and novelist Keith Waterhouse and actor Guy Deghy (writing together under the pseudonym Herald Froy),[86] which has no parallel for women. The latter book, which went through three impressions in two years, described married men as 'the greatest slave force in human history, and called for the formation of a 'marriage avoidance council'.[87]

Unmarried men were also still more likely than women to be looked after by families in lodgings or invited for meals because they were perceived as needing domestic services. Lionel (born 1929), who taught in a secondary school on the south coast in the early 1950s, remembered being treated like a 'surrogate son' by the childless couple with whom he lodged, while Elizabeth (born 1947) described a succession of bachelors being regularly asked to lunch during her 1950s childhood. These men were either army officers from the nearby military camp or curates and had been previously unknown to her family, yet she remembered no single women in a similar position being offered this kind of hospitality. An interview for *FLOP*, Peter Townsend's study of old age in Bethnal Green, with a bachelor who had been a merchant seaman in his youth, showed that the downstairs neighbours who shared his lodgings were more significant to him than his own family, with whom he had almost completely lost touch. But these kinds of relationships also had their boundaries. While he was willing to lend his neighbours money, both the man's age and single status made him reluctant to get too close to them, and he commented: 'you don't like putting your foot in the affairs of husband and wife'.[88]

Although professional opportunities for women in the new welfare state improved, the lifting of marriage bars at the end of the war meant that employment areas such as teaching and nursing were beginning to recruit married women, leaving spinsters even more vulnerable to attacks on their femininity and more defensive of their position. Within older age groups, single women were, however, still in the majority over single men. In 1951, the per centage of never-married women aged fifty-five to sixty-four was one in seven, but if widows and divorcees are included it was still more than a third of the adult female population in this cohort, compared with one in twelve bachelors and one in fourteen widowed or divorced adult men. By this date women born in 1890, who had been in continuous professional paid employment, would have been eligible to retire with pensions that gave them more long-term financial security than was enjoyed by many married women, whose retirement income was tied to their husband's occupational pension and national insurance contributions.[89] Although men had to wait until they were sixty-five to receive their pensions, those in senior business or management positions or the professions without wives to support were even more comfortable, and well able to pay for domestic help in their old age.

For unmarried men and women who had been in casual jobs or had periods of unemployment, however, the picture was much less rosy. Under the Beveridge Plan, which gave shape to the National Insurance Act of 1946, a social insurance system was instituted based upon contributory benefits, leaving those with insufficient contributions reliant on a means-tested National Assistance fund. This was often associated by older people with the pre-war Public Assistance and regarded as shameful.[90] Interviews for *FLOP* offer glimpses of the lives of elderly unmarried men and women in the mid-1950s dependent on the state. 'Miss Paley' (born 1886–7) and 'Mr Fortune' (born 1879) both lived alone in cold, dirty, poorly furnished rooms with shared toilets and no bath or water supply. They survived on non-contributory pensions and National Assistance and both had given up work before retirement on the grounds of ill-health. Mr Fortune had occasional contact with a sister-in-law and nephews and nieces and had been offered a home help for two hours a week, but Miss Paley was even more isolated, with no family or domestic help. Her overriding concern was that she was 'under the government' and she saw this as a reason as for cutting off all social contact. [91]

The 1957 Rent Act, which removed restrictions from some 800,000 rent-controlled houses,[92] made it even harder for women in Miss Paley's situation to survive, as revealed in an account of a seventy-one-year-old spinster forced out of her home and compelled to apply for admission to a Home:

She had received an eviction order which she showed to us. She was a victim of the Rent Act. She had no friends or relatives, just the daughter of a friend living nearby who did her shopping. The welfare officer showed no interests in asking about alternative accommodation. Slowly she answered questions about her pension and small amount of savings – these items accounting for half the welfare officer's questions. He sighed to me as he left. 'You see how difficult it is to work fast on this job.' This was after an interview lasting fourteen minutes flat.[93]

Townsend found the ten most isolated people out of a survey of 203 people over retirement age were all single or childless,[94] but not all low-waged unmarried people without families were in rented or council accommodation. More than 20,000 men and women over sixty lived as resident guests in larger boarding houses and hotels, with more than twice as many women as men. Only a quarter of female resident guests were married, and the Registrar-General's report described the dominant type as the unmarried female over sixty.[95] While these figures do not of themselves indicate neglect or poverty, the rent charged by landladies in boarding houses was too high for some unmarried women to survive without hardship. A study of 550 institutional cases in 1952 suggests that women admitted into institutional care from lodgings had often been housekeepers or hotel maids or in other residential work, and that after paying rent from their pension they often did not have enough to eat.[96] For such women institutional care in one of the small local authority Homes opened since the 1948 National Assistance Act often seemed a better alternative.[97] One woman forced onto the streets during the day by an uncaring landlady was greatly relieved when told about a Cottage Home by a stranger she met on a park bench.[98]

The numbers of unmarried people in institutional care are disturbing nevertheless, particularly as 'two-thirds of all the residents in the several institutions were fit to look after themselves in all respects [and] forty per cent of the old persons, many of whom had been resident in the institutions for years, were fit for some work.'[99] By 1961, the unmarried population over the age of sixty-five in institutions was nearly a quarter of women and 18 per cent of men situated in NHS hospitals, around a third of both sexes in Homes for the elderly, and four out of ten women and nearly half the men in psychiatric hospitals in this age group.[100] Townsend's survey in the late 1950s of institutions and Homes for the elderly found the numbers in residential Homes to be even higher, with half the female and two fifths of male residents in voluntary homes unmarried and 57 per cent in local authority Homes unmarried and/or childless.[101] He offers a grim picture of these institutions, which generally did not 'meet the physical, psychological and social needs of the elderly people living in them'.[102] One of the chief failings was lack of sensitivity in staff (many of whom were themselves middle aged or elderly spinsters and bachelors 'without complex family ties') to the residents' needs. Although these 'old reliables' had 'given a life time of service and often acted with sympathy and good humour in a depressing environment ... their horizons were limited by their experience and by the lack of opportunities for further training... and a few among them ... provoked resentment and even terror among infirm people'.[103]

The lack of sensitivity displayed by some unmarried institutional staff without families may have stemmed partly from their own anxieties and a wish to deny that they might themselves end up in a similar position. Yet, while childless unmarried men and women were undoubtedly more vulnerable to this fate, this does not mean that living outside the family was a typical lifestyle for single people, even in old age. As we shall see in the next chapter, many unmarried men's and women's lives were deeply embedded in a complex web of family ties, and it is to these relationships that we now turn.

Notes

1 Irish emigrant tailoress, aged fifty-seven quoted in Rosamund Tweedy, 'Consider Her Palaces': A Study of the Housing Problems of Lower Paid Single Women Workers in London (London: Over Thirty Association, 1936), p. 23.
2 Note that census tables do not separate England and Wales but my study does not include any specifically Welsh material.
3 1961 Census Summary Tables (London: HMSO, 1966), tables 5, 6 and 7.
4 Miriam Glucksmann, Women Assemble: Women Workers and the New Industries in Interwar Britain (London: Routledge, 1990), p. 36.
5 1931 Census General Report (London: HMSO, 1950), p. 76 and table 3.
6 1951 General Report (London: HMSO, 1958), p. 95 and table 45.
7 Evelyn Hubbard, 'The Voluntary System', The Times (26 November, 1914), p. 9; Charles Bright, 'Individual Responsibility', The Times, letter page (1 June 1915), p. 10.
8 R. J. Q. Adams, 'Asquith's Choice: The May Coalition and the Coming of Conscription, 1915–1916', Journal of British Studies, 25:3 (1986), pp. 243–63.
9 Vera Brittain, Chronicle of Youth: Great War Diary 1913–1917, ed. Alan Bishop (London: Phoenix Press, 1981); Vera Brittain, Testament of Youth, 1933 (London: Virago, 1978).
10 Gail Braybon, Women Workers in World War One (London: Croom Helm, 1981), chs 7 and 8.
11 The 1921 census shows totals of 19,811 women and 18,075 men: 1921 Census General Report (London: HMSO, 1927), p. 81, table 39.
12 1921 General Report.
13 Jane Lewis, Women in England: Sexual Divisions and Social Change 1870–1950

(Brighton: Wheatsheaf, 1984), p. 4.

14 Rosamund Essex, *Woman in a Man's World* (London: Sheldon Press, 1977); Phyllis Wilmott, *A Singular Woman: The Life of Geraldine Aves* (London: Whiting and Birch, 1992).

15 Holden, 'Imaginary Widows'.

16 Adrian Bingham, *Gender, Modernity and the Popular Press in Interwar Britain* (Oxford: Oxford University Press, 2004), p. 54.

17 Melman, *Women and the Popular Imagination*, ch. 3.

18 E. M. Hull, *The Sheik*, 19 (London: Virago Press, 1996).

19 Melman, *Women and the Popular Imagination*, p. 104.

20 For a discussion of bachelorhood in this pre-war context see John Tosh, 'Domesticity and Manliness in the Victorian Middle Class: The Family of Edward Benson' in Michael Roper and John Tosh (eds), *Manful Assertions: Masculinities in Britain since 1800* (London: Routledge, 1991), p. 67.

21 Graham Dawson, 'The Blonde Bedouin: Lawrence of Arabia, Imperial Adventure and the Imaginings of English-British Masculinity', in Roper and Tosh, *Manful Assertions*, pp. 136–7.

22 The numbers of women employed in the electrical industries more than doubled between 1921 and 1931 and rose by 43,300 in the food industries between 1923 and 1938: Glucksmann, *Women Assemble*, p. 50.

23 Jack Lawley, *Memories of a Herdsman* (Ilfracombe: Arthur H. Stockwell, 1961), p. 93.

24 *1931 Census: Occupation Tables* (London: HMSO, 1934), table 1, occupations of males and females aged over fourteen and over with an analysis of marital condition and industrial status.

25 John Burnett, *Idle Hands: The Experience of Unemployment, 1790–1990* (London: Routledge, 1994), p. 211. A sample of working-class job advertisements in the *Birmingham Mail* in 1930 showed that half excluded the middle aged. John Benson, *Prime Time: A History of the Middle Aged in Twentieth Century Britain* (London: Longman, 1997), figure 4.4.

26 Bourke, *Dismembering the Male*, p. 74.

27 In 1939, 641,000 pensions were still being paid to amputees. *Ibid.*, p. 33.

28 Burnett, *Idle Hands*, pp. 212 and 218.

29 'Certificate of Character', 16 February 1916, Bristol Education Committee, North Street Wesleyan School (held by author).

30 Glucksmann, *Women Assemble*, pp. 109–11.

31 Alice Kessler-Harris, *In Pursuit of Equity: Women, Men and the Quest for Economic Citizenship in Twentieth Century America* (Oxford: Oxford University Press, 2001).

32 Glucksmann, *Women Assemble*, p. 111.

33 *Census General Report*, 1931, p. 152; Pam Taylor, 'Daughters and Mistresses – Mothers and Maids: Domestic Service between the Wars' in J. Clarke, C. Critcher and R. Johnson (eds), *Working-class Culture: Studies in History and Theory* (London: Hutchinson, 1979).

34 Tweedy, *Consider her Palaces*, pp. 30–31.

35 *Ibid.*, pp. 28–9.

36 Davidoff, *Worlds Between*, p. 173.

37 *University Women's Review*, June 1938.

38 Dulcie Groves, 'Onward, Spinsters, Onward! The National Spinsters Pension Associa-

tion 1935–58', paper presented at the Centennial Suffrage Conference, Victoria University, Wellington, New Zealand, August 1993; H. Smith, 'Gender and the Welfare State: The Old Age and Widows' Pensions Act', *History*, 80 (1995).

39 Groves, 'Onward, Spinsters, Onward!'.

40 Smith, 'Gender and the Welfare State', *Spinster* (February 1938), p. 3, and (March 1938).

41 Groves, 'Onward, Spinsters, Onward!'.

42 *Ibid.*; Smith, 'Gender and the Welfare State'.

43 Burnett, *Idle Hands*, p. 262.

44 H. Llewellyn Smith, 'The Homeless Poor' in *NSLLL* vol 3, p. 272.

45 *Ibid.*, p. 273.

46 National Archive, London (hereafter NA), HLG/49/21 Mr Tudor Owen, 'Minute sheet', 3 November 1926; Mrs Cecil Chesterton, *In Darkest London* (London: Stanley Paul and Co, fourth edition, 1927).

47 *Ibid.*, pp. 86–7; Virginia Woolf, *A Room of One's Own*, 1929 (London: Grafton Books, 1977).

48 Marjorie Hillis, *Live Alone and Like It: A Guide for the Extra Woman* (London: Duckworth, 1936).

49 Mary Scharlieb, *The Bachelor Woman and her Problems* (London: Williams and Norgate, 1929), pp. 66–8.

50 Fiona Hackney, 'Careers for Girls and Modern Women?', in unpublished paper '"They Opened Up a Whole New World": Feminine Modernity and British Women's Magazines 1919–1939'.

51 National Council of Women, 'List of Hostels and Other Accommodation in London and the Provinces for Women in the Professions and in Industry, compiled by the National Council of Women of Great Britain and Ireland' (London, n.p., 1923).

52 Garfield, *We Are at War*, p. 49.

53 London School of Economics, Archive, NSLLL, Hampstead (middle-class), cards. 0014, 0398, 0566, 0857, 0801, 0576 0578, 0581, 0804, 0144, 0156.

54 *London Opinion*, 11 January 1930, p. 357, and June 1939, p. 36.

55 *Ibid.*, back covers of edition for 3 May, 28 June and 12 July 1930.

56 *Ibid.*, front cover, 10 May 1930

57 *1921 Census, General Report*, table 39.

58 Carol Dyhouse, *No Distinction of Sex? Women in British Universities, 1870–1939* (London: UCL Press, 1995), p. 23.

59 Penny Tinkler, *Constructing Girlhood: Popular Magazines for Girls Growing up in England, 1920–1950* (London: Taylor and Francis, 1995); Vynrwy Biscoe, *300 Careers for Women* (London: Lovat Dickson, 1932).

60 Oram, *Women Teachers and Feminist Politics*, p. 8 and tables 3 and 8.

61 *1931 Census: Occupation Tables*, tables 7 and 11; Guy Routh, *Occupations of the People of Great Britain, 1801–1981* (London: Macmillan, 1987), p. 31.

62 Margaret Cole, *Marriage, Past and Present* (London: J. M. Dent, 1939), p. 142.

63 Defined as 'those occupations that require some years of study at universities or institutions of a similar nature', Routh, *Occupations*, p. 25.

64 *Ibid.*

65 Ken Sanderson, 'A Pension to Look Forward to …?': Women Civil Servant Clerks in London, 1925–1939, in Leonore Davidoff and Belinda Westover (eds), *Our Work*,

Our Lives, Our Words: Women's History and Women's Work (Basingstoke: Macmillan, 1986).

66 Hilda Martindale, *From One Generation to Another: 1839–1944* (London: George Allen and Unwin, 1944), p. 195.

67 Oram, *Women Teachers and Feminist Politics*, p. 25.

68 *Ibid.*, p. 197.

69 June Hannam, '"Married to the Labour Party": Single Women and British Labour Politics between the Wars', paper presented at the 12th annual conference of the West of England and South Wales Women's History Network, 'Single Women in History, 1000–2000', 23 June 2006.

70 See for example *Careers for Boys: Prospects in Twenty Trades and Professions Dealt with by Experts* (Manchester: Allied Newspapers, 1925), p. 103.

71 The 1931 census shows 12 per cent of single men in managerial positions (including widowers) aged thirty-five to forty-four compared with 16 per cent unmarried (excluding widowers) out of all professional men of this age.

72 *1931 Census: Occupation Tables*, table 6.

73 Jeremy A. Crang, *The British Army and the People's War, 1939–1945* (Manchester: Manchester University Press, 2000), pp. 21 and 46.

74 Penelope Lively, *Oleander Jacaranda: A Childhood Perceived* (Harmondsworth: Penguin, 1995), pp. 33–4.

75 R. M. Braithwaite, 'The Evacuation Scheme in World War Two from the Point of View of a London Probation Officer', unpublished paper held by author (also in the Imperial War Museum).

76 Benson, *A History of the Middle Aged*, pp. 63–4.

77 Crang, *The British Army*, p. 2.

78 Penny Summerfield, *Women Workers in the Second World War: Production and Patriarchy in Conflict* (London: Croom Helm, 1984), pp. 59–60.

79 Katherine Holden, 'Family, Caring and Unpaid Work', in Ina Zweiniger Bargielowska (ed.), *Women in Twentieth Century Britain* (London: Pearson, 2001), p. 145.

80 Norah Lea-Wilson, unpublished autobiography (1972).

81 Letter from Norah Lea-Wilson to Lilly Dodds written on a train between Ceylon and Madrass, 3rd January 1940.

82 Summerfield, *Reconstructing Women's Wartime Lives*, ch. 7, pp. 261 and 278.

83 Sue Bruley, 'A New Perspective on Women Workers in the Second World War: The Industrial Diary of Kathleen Church-Bliss and Elsie Whiteman', *Labour History Review* 68:2 (2003).

84 Diana Brinton Lee, File Report No. 2059, 'Will the Factory Girl Want to Stay Put or Go Home? Angus Calder and Dorothy Sheridan', *Speak for Yourself: A Mass Observation Anthology* (Oxford: Oxford University Press, 1984), p. 179.

85 Diary entry, 12 May 1946, in Simon Garfield (ed.), *Our Hidden Lives: The Remarkable Diaries of Post-war Britain*, 2004 (London: Ebury Press, 2005), p. 216.

86 'Cadwallader' and 'Nudnick' [pseudonyms of Paul Clemens and Patrick Nerney], *The Little Black Book: A Manual for Bachelors* (London: Hutchinson, 1958); Froy, *How to Avoid Matrimony*, p. 19.

87 Froy, *How to Avoid Matrimony*, p. 19. The Marriage Guidance Council opened its first office in London in 1943. See J. Lewis, D. Clark and D. J. H. Morgan, *Whom God Hath Joined Together: The Work of Marriage Guidance* (London: Routledge, 1992).

88 ESDS Qualidata, University of Essex, National Social Policy and Social Change Archive, SN4723, FLOP, 1865–1955, interview with WAD.

89 Harriet Jones, 'The State and Social Policy', in Bargielowska, *Women in Twentieth Century Britain*.

90 Pauline Gregg, *The Welfare State: An Economic and Social History of Great Britain from 1945 to the Present* (London: Harrap, 1967), p. 267.

91 FLOP, Miss M. G. interviewed 19 August 1955. See *FLOP*, pp. 192–3.

92 Gregg, *The Welfare State*, p. 232.

93 Peter Townsend, *The Last Refuge: A Survey of Residential Institutions and Homes for the Aged in England and Wales* (London: Routledge, abridged edition, 1964), p. 239.

94 *FLOP*, p. 192.

95 1951, *Census, General Report*, p. 87 and table 35.

96 National Social Policy and Social Change Archive, Mabel E. Mitchell, 'The Problem of the Aged, the Infirm and the Aged Sick: A Social Study of 550 Institutional Cases', Unpublished MD thesis (2 vols), 1952, p. 157.

97 By 1953, 699 small Homes in England and Wales had been opened with accommodation for 20,000 persons. *Report of Ministry of Health for Year Ended 31st December 1953*, Cmd. 9321, Part 1, Section 2.

98 Mitchell, 'The Problem of the Aged, the Infirm and the Aged Sick', p. 157.

99 *Ibid.*, p. 183.

100 *1961 Census, Summary Tables*, table 24, 'Institutions: Age and Marital Condition of inmates'.

101 Townsend, *The Last Refuge*, pp. 66 and 92.

102 *Ibid.*, p. 222.

103 *Ibid.*, p. 39.

3

Family standbys:
brothers, sisters, daughters, sons

Well I had lots of commitments myself. Because my sister-in-law had two sons, and my father's last words were … he said 'my maid' he said, 'I would like you to have married but…' cos he said, he thought I was rather good, I won't say what he said. But he said, 'I couldn't give you an education, but you see the little boys get an education'. So I was paying for one of the boys to go to school, one of my nephews … my brother and his wife couldn't pay for the other one, they couldn't afford it, so that's why I couldn't marry really. Well you can't if you've got that, can you, because you've got – and then I had mother and I couldn't leave mother could I, mother had to be looked after. (Interview with Ellen)

Introduction

THE STATEMENTS ABOVE MADE by an eighty-five-year-old retired health visitor, born in 1908, show how attachment to family shaped the life story of an unmarried woman in mid-twentieth-century England, providing her with a rationale for her life and work, justifications for not having married, and multiple identities of daughter, sister and aunt, endlessly available to give care. Ellen's work and indeed her entire life-history were circumscribed by the injunction to care for her family. Her education was cut short when her father was thrown out of work by an injury, and this early experience of coping with illness and her training as a nurse made it appear natural that she rather than her unmarried brother should become the family carer even though he lived in the parental home and she did not. Her decision to train as a health visitor shortly before the Second World War was made on the grounds of family need for care, as was her move back to her home town, which meant she had to forgo promotion.

Ellen's position as a family standby did not leave her without any power. When she returned to live with her parents during the war, she brought with her a close friend with whom she had shared her life and work since their training days and who subsequently married her brother. Her friend's presence as a sister-in-law probably helped Ellen adjust to living at home again, particularly as it enabled her to become an aunt. Yet although she regarded him as 'a very selfish man', she saw her brother rather than her sister-in-law as having given her 'two delightful boys'. As we shall see in chapter 8, for single childless people relations with children (however important) were always provisional. It was the blood relationship with her nephews that took precedence, and even then, she could not take the relationship for granted in the way that most parents could. Although she knew the work she did and the relationships she formed were of value, Ellen had internalised the nuclear norm which equates family with marriage and motherhood. She was trapped by expectations that she should have married, and her devotion to her work and her relatives was presented primarily as compensation for not marrying and not having a family of her own.

The identities of uncle, brother, son and nephew were also important for single men. 'Gay' bachelor stereotypes might situate single men as free-floating individuals, but evidence from mid-twentieth-century social surveys suggests that most bachelors either lived with other people's families in lodgings, or remained in the parental home. Still, the links between masculinity and individualism hide men's dependence on (and contribution to) family and domestic labour,[1] and accounts comparable to that of Ellen, or indeed any other biographical sources which illuminate single men's familial roles, are therefore much scarcer.[2]

With these concerns in mind, this chapter examines single people's identity within their families and shows how this was influenced by issues such as family size and structure, class, the allocation of material resources, health and employment. How were single people living within 'families' categorised by themselves and by others? Did the identity of family standby cut across class and gender relationship or did its meaning vary between men and women and between different social groups? And what tensions existed within the identities of brother, sister, daughter and son?

One important arena for discussion is the role of government welfare and unemployment policies: how far working-class single people were treated as an economically useful group and regarded as independent from, dependent on or indistinguishable within the families and households to which they were attached. A second area of debate is at the level of representation. Single people appeared in many different guises, variously as selfish, pampered, selfless, heroic, dutiful, submissive or downtrodden; tied to parents, missing or happily escaping family life. But in what ways did these images influence the construction of personal narratives? All these concerns will be investigated by drawing upon a wide variety of sources including social surveys, government reports and correspondence, newspapers, magazines and novels, and finally, most importantly, through the voices of single women and men themselves.

The New Survey of London Life and Labour

Household surveys are important sources for revealing the lifestyles of families. From the late nineteenth century, a succession of researchers investigated the consequences of unemployment, industrial depression, and wartime dislocation and reconstruction on working-class populations, with the aim of improving the health and welfare of the nation.[3] These surveys yield useful information about household composition, employment and sources of financial and practical support. But although they might be expected to reveal data about the position of single people within the family, the documentation has often since been destroyed,[4] and the marginal status of the single as a category means that this group was largely ignored in the published material. Even in cases where records remain, locating unmarried men and women within them is not straightforward, mainly because researchers based their estimates of poverty on a household model, which assumed a static hierarchical family structure with husband/father as head, and in which financial and domestic resources between related (but not unrelated) household members were presumed to be shared. This model disguises the actual power relations within families and makes it hard to tell how far single related and unrelated household members were included in or excluded from the core family group.

These problems are manifest in *NSLLL*, for which records have been preserved and contain useful data on the jobs, income and lifestyles of single people.[5] However, having access to data only in statistical form, tidied up in order to become machine readable, may obscure as much as it reveals. This became apparent when I examined the record cards for three inner London boroughs with diverse populations, Hampstead, Chelsea and Deptford,[6] and attempted an assessment both of the numbers of spinsters and bachelors aged over thirty living in these areas and the of variety of living situations in which they were found (see appendices 1 and 2).

Of the three and a half thousand working-class people whose details were recorded in these three boroughs, 152 were single and over thirty.[7] The significance of family, particularly for older single men, is suggested by the fact that two thirds were living with family members, compared with just under half the single women in the same age group. Yet these statistics of themselves do not tell much about how these people conducted their lives. The familial model suggested by the categories given on the record cards, together with Llewellyn Smith's instructions and definitions, proved inadequate when interviewers were faced with differing family and household structures.[8] Categories worked to obscure the number and significance of single people within the family, while the policy of designating the eldest married man (or in his absence his widow) as head of household,[9] regardless of their income, made it difficult to tell who was actually supporting whom within the family. The majority of unmarried people appeared simply as sisters, daughters, brothers or sons, but while their marital status is suggested by their lack of an obvious in-law, other categories of singleness, such as separated wives and widows living with parents and siblings, are often indistinguishable from the never-married with this method of record keeping.

The categories of spinster and bachelor were only used when men and women were living independently, either alone or with other, unrelated single people. However, although never-married women could not achieve head-of-household status if they were living with married people, the same was not always the case for men. A widow lost her position as head of the family in cases where married sons or daughters were in the family, when 'the married man of the younger generation was counted as head',[10] but some interviewers also extended this policy to single male relatives, believing that gender should override marital status. Disregarding instructions, they sometimes placed unmarried sons as heads of households on the grounds that they were taking full responsibility for the home even though their single sisters were also in full-time work. The same was not true of unmarried daughters, who remained in a subordinate position no matter how large their contribution was to the family budget, rather than being viewed as independent adults. Because poverty was regarded as a family rather than an individual affair, their earnings were included in the family budget on the principle that all income was being pooled. Thus, it is not immediately apparent whether single adult children generally paid their own board and keep to their parents and retained the rest of their earnings, or contributed to the support of parents and/or other family members. The difficulty of separating the single from their families is particularly noticeable for out-of work daughters, whose dependent position within the family was variously categorised as 'at home', 'domesticated', 'domestic' or 'home duties', with no source of income given, whereas sons were more often recorded as 'unemployed' and claiming unemployment benefit in their own right.

The *New Survey* records need to be read in the context of an economic climate where women's earnings were increasing in importance as a source of family finance. As we have seen, during the 1920s and 1930s, the steady decline of Britain's old heavy industries undermined male employment opportunities, whilst expanding occupations were mainly in the new light-industry, clerical and service sectors that thrived on lower-paid, mainly female employment. Despite the ideal of a family wage, it was difficult for families to survive solely on the earnings or unemployment allowance of the male head,[11] and since married women were increasingly being discouraged from taking up regular paid employment, the contribution of an unmarried daughter or son was particularly valuable. Records from the London Borough of Deptford show that out of 529 working-class families under half were in traditional families with husband, wife and dependent children or husband and wife alone, and more than 40 per cent contained earning single adult members.

The position for single men and women was not, however, the same. The assumption that all men had families to support was built into the concept of the family wage, and the earnings of single sons were therefore usually considerably higher than the earnings of daughters. The difference can be seen by looking at the relative positions of two widows in Deptford, both drawing 10s a week pension and living in similar rented accommodation. The household with two sons aged fifty and thirty-six working as dock labourers had an income of six pounds a week. This was 50 per cent more than the one containing daughters of similar ages who were both shop assistants, with a weekly household income of only just over four pounds. Yet having sons rather than daughters did not always advantage women. Another widow in Chelsea lived in a poorly furnished two-room flat with an unmarried son (designated head of the household) who earned only two pounds a week, and since he was described as 'never home before ten o'clock at night', he may well have been spending his earnings in the pub.[12]

Marital status and dependency: the equal pay debate

The anomalies revealed by *NSLLL* records must be viewed in relation to debates surrounding this subject during the interwar years over equal pay and access to welfare and unemployment benefits. The former issue came to a head in 1921 in a post-war climate of rising unemployment, when Seebohm Rowntree and Frank Stuart published their report *The Responsibility of Women Workers for Dependants*. This had been commissioned to answer a report by the Fabian Women's Group which claimed that, since over half of working women were responsible for the maintenance of dependants, they should have equal pay with men. Rowntree and Stuart's aim was to discover on a 'scientific basis' whether in fixing women's wages any allowance should be made for dependants. Their estimate, that only 12 per cent really had any degree of family responsibility, challenged the reliability of the Fabian Women's research, which it was argued was biased towards professional women.[13]

However, despite their claims to objectivity, Rowntree and Stuart's own research criteria were structured by a priori assumptions about gender and marital status. They 'regarded a person as dependent, or partially dependent, on a worker, if the latter's wage, whether large or small, had to be shared between two, but no equivalent service was demanded from the former'. Thus they maintained that a widowed mother whose daughters jointly contributed to her upkeep should not be regarded as dependent on them because they 'would really be employing her as their housekeeper', ignoring the fact that a married man who demanded housekeeping services of his wife was fully justified in claiming *her* as his dependant. Equally, a woman who paid her family more than the market price for board and lodging would not be regarded as having dependants 'if the income of the chief wage earner is sufficiently high to render such action on her part unnecessary'.[14] This assumed that a chief wage earner would necessarily share his whole wage earnings with his wife and dependent family, while a daughter would be expected to support only herself. Yet as we have seen, economic relationships within working-class families are not so clear-cut. Families might depend on a daughter or other female relative's earnings in the not-infrequent cases where the father or chief (male) wage earner kept a substantial portion of his earnings for his own use, or was unemployed, ill or absent.[15] These situations were ignored and obscured by Rowntree and Stuart's criteria.

One reason for the large discrepancy between the figures of Rowntree and Stuart and those of the Fabian Women's Committee was the much higher average age (thirty-four) of the latter's women inform-ants. Rowntree and Stuart admitted that their own survey also showed a dramatic rise in the number of women with dependants in the thirty to forty age cohort (26 six per cent compared with an average of only 13 per cent in all age groups). Since 87 per cent of their respondents were single, and more than two thirds of those who were designated as having dependants gained them through the death or illness of a father, it is likely that a substantial number of these cases were of single women supporting their mothers. Since it was in this age group that men might be expected to have the largest number of non-earning children, a case for a greater degree of equivalency of wages between married men and older single women could have been made. However, Rowntree and Stuart believed such cases could be adequately dealt with by improving widow's pensions and increasing grants paid under the national health insurance scheme to chronic invalids.

This debate illustrates the way in which expectations relating to gender and marital status shaped men's and women's relationship to work. The division of the category 'woman' into *either* childless worker without dependants *or* dependent non-working mother was achieved in the interwar years by using the institution of marriage as gate-keeper. And this division was never successfully challenged by a feminist movement fragmented after the war over issues of equality and difference.[16] Eleanor Rathbone, leader of the National Union of Societies for Equal Citizenship,[17] saw equality for men and women in the labour market as contingent upon enabling married women to gain independence from their husbands through a system of allowances which would pay them directly for their family responsibilities. In *The Disinherited Family* (1924), she was critical particularly of bachelors who occupied 'a vantage point for bargaining which is not open to women' and were indistinguishably lumped together with men with dependent families, enabling them to 'fight the battle of high wages from behind the petticoats of their comrades' wives and children'.[18] Yet her own position as a woman of independent means suggests that she too may not have sufficiently recognised the difficulties which the equation of marriage and family responsibilities posed for the working-class single woman living with her family. Like Rowntree and Stuart, she assumed that insurance benefits for the old and infirm should be sufficient to remove any familial burdens taken on by them, and had little sympathy for the Fabians' cause. In her analysis, women were polarised into single 'workers' and married 'mothers'. The latter as 'mothers' had needs and social responsibilities which entitled them to *different* treatment as women. The former should, she believed, be given *equal* treatment with men and, like them, be regarded as having no family responsibilities.

Single sons and daughters and the state in the interwar years

The question of family responsibility also arose in relation to the payment of welfare and unemployment benefits during the interwar years. Against a background of strikes, industrial disputes and rising unemployment, which hit many families hard and undermined the position of the male as breadwinner, interwar governments made use of the earning power of the single. Although often denied full access to welfare benefits, they were still required in times of hardship to support their families or else be supported by them. Both men and women could be in this position and many single people did help finance families, often receiving in return domestic services from mothers, sisters or aunts. Yet as we have seen, the higher wages a man could command, regarded as necessary for the support of his future family, also enabled men to pay, or if unemployed receive an allowance, for these services. In the early 1930s, an unemployed bachelor could obtain seven shillings benefit for a dependent house-keeper, who could be a female relative, while single women had no such entitlement.[19]

The anomalous position of the single woman worker proved to be of considerable value to the state in 1919 when the Ministry of Labour attempted to prevent women who they believed had no real intention of working from claiming unemployment benefit on the basis that they had paid insurance contributions as munitions or other workers during the war. Belief that any woman seeking work should accept a job in domestic service led to accusations in *The Times* that if women refused employ-ment 'because it was not exactly to their taste, they ought not to be paid out of the public purse and so enabled to live a life of idleness'.[20] Histo-rians have used this as an example of injustice to married women which prevented them claiming dole, pointing out that such accusations had no basis in fact.[21] Yet its effect was equally if not more damaging to single women, many of whom were ejected from relatively well-paid war work and denied the possibility of claiming benefit.[22]

Further restrictions came in 1922 when the rising tide of unemploy-ment led the government to introduce a means test. Single people living with relatives were excluded from claiming unless they could prove that they were entirely self-supporting when in work and could not reason-ably look to their relatives for support when unemployed. This involved proof of a regular payment equivalent to board and lodging and the appli-cation of a crude, all-or-nothing means test to the household.[23] Given the connection means tests had with the stigma of the Poor Law, many women would have been unwilling to put their relatives through such a test, even if they had been able to satisfy the first requirement. They were thus left with the option of taking any job, however poor the conditions, or relying on relatives for support, which put them in a dependent position similar to but without the status of a wife.[24] Of those who did make claims between August 1925 and April 1928, over half of the 465,265 disallowed because household income was sufficient for their needs were from single persons living with relatives, and many more women's than men's claims failed.[25] However, when in 1931 a Royal Commission on Unemployment Insurance followed up the cases of 2,354 disallowed persons in eight areas, they found that 43.8 per cent of single women found work in the six- to thirteen-week period following their appeals, compared with 33.1 per cent of single men.[26] At a time of high male unemployment, this suggests the continuing availability of low-paid service work for women and a greater perceived necessity for them not to rely on relatives for support.

However, the notion of family responsibility could cut both ways, requiring single people also to support their families. Family responsibility was a principle widely invoked and applied by relieving authorities in the 1920s and 1930s, an area fraught with confusion and contradictions dating back to the Elizabethan Poor Law Act of 1601, which had imposed obligations on parents to support children, husbands to support wives, adults to support aged parents, and grandparents to support grandchildren.[27] As Crowther points out, 'By the 1930s there was an inconsistency between the legal definition of the family and the practice of official bodies responsible for the relief of the poor and unemployed. The State tolerated and even exploited this inconsistency for economic reasons.' Thus not only could working single sons and daughters be required to support parents, but single people could be compelled to support brothers, sisters, nieces and nephews or even more distant relatives if they lived in the same house. Yet inconsistencies in scales of poor relief and assessment of claims introduced some striking anomalies. For example, a father might or might not be paid an allowance for his unemployed unmarried daughter, according to how usual it was for unmarried daughters to work in that particular area.[28] Equally, unemployed men or women who could prove they had been supporting an aunt towards whom they had no legal liability on some occasions were paid an allowance for her as a dependant.[29]

In 1937, sociologist Professor Ford pointed out the inconsistency of the state's position and the unfairness of burdening earning children with long-term responsibility for their parents. This situation had been depicted by Walter Greenwood in his novel *Love on the Dole* (1933), which showed the desperation during the Depression of a family whose male members are unemployed, forced by the means test to survive on the wages of their only daughter.[30] It is unclear how far adult children left home in order to avoid maintaining parents, though evidence from a Poor Law Commissioner suggests that daughters were 'ready to do their share' while grownup sons often disregarded their parents' needs.[31] However, to avoid such cases the Unemployment Assistance Board during the 1930s created a fictitious definition of the household known as the 'constructive family', whereby children who left home to evade regulations could still be assessed as part of the family unless they could prove they had been evicted.[32]

Sons and daughters in wartime and post-war England

It could be argued that the Second World War was the ultimate social force to weaken family ties, creating a major disjuncture in the lives of many single adults still living in the parental home. Not only were all men aged between eighteen and forty not in reserved occupations called up to do national service,[33] but from 1941, single women between the ages of twenty and thirty (extended in 1942 to forty and later to fifty) were required to register at labour exchanges. Those with no dependants were regarded as mobile and could be posted wherever work was needed, often away from home.[34] Summerfield argues that wartime propaganda offered representations of 'the patriotically disintegrating family' with loyal parents shown as abrogating their authority to the state, while those that resisted were depicted as selfish and unreasonable. But the nuclear family was still maintained as the cornerstone of British society, and new constructions of familial dynamics which placed daughters outside the home in the service of the state did not entirely replace older ones of dutiful domesticity.[35]

The nuclear norm was reinforced even more strongly in post-war Britain, but although the welfare state was established around a model of the male breadwinner, not all its provisions disadvantaged the single. For example, the new national insurance system based on the recommendations of William Beveridge's report, *Social Insurance and Allied Services* (1942), no longer applied a means test to wage-earning families, which removed the obligation on single sons and daughters living at home to support parents if they were out of work. Still, the post-war housing shortage meant that there were few opportunities excepting the despised bed-sitting room for those on low or even middling incomes to live alone, with new housing in the outer suburbs being reserved primarily for families with dependent children. An article in *The Times* offered sympathy to the inhabitants of bedsits and particularly to bachelor civil servants whose opportunities for courtship, it was argued, were severely restricted. [36] And, although the new system of family allowances reduced the disparity between the living standards of bachelors and married men with children, the equal pay debate remained unresolved, with arguments about the relative familial and housekeeping responsibilities of married men and single men and women continuing to be voiced in the press.[37]

It was in this context that a new set of social surveys was undertaken in

London in the mid-1950s by researchers from the Institute of Community Studies in Bethnal Green. These had much more interest in how familial relationships actually worked than did pre-war projects. Described as 'a marriage between anthropology and sociology',[38] their aims and methods were also different from those of Llewellyn Smith. Peter Willmott and Michael Young were interested in the effects of post-war housing policies which were moving working-class communities from inner London out to housing estates in the suburbs, but here it was kinship rather than household relationships that were the key concern, with a strong focus on 'the wider family'.[39] Yet, while single people could have been a significant element in their study, the researchers made it clear that their main interest was in nuclear families, with husbands and wives as 'the principal actors' through whose eyes they looked at kinship.[40]

Peter Townsend's study had a broader focus and criticised traditional definitions of family, by pointing out 'that for much social analysis a working definition of "household" [defined by the census as a number of people sleeping together under the same roof and eating together at the same table] that was applied too rigidly may cause part of the truth about people's home relationships to be missed or misrepresented'. The difficulties of separating a household from a dwelling (which might contain more than one household within it) are shown up by the complexity of family relations in cases where some meals but not others were shared, or where meals were eaten separately but relatives were on call and offered other kinds of help. Equally, Townsend questioned whether a single man living in the same house as his widowed mother, eating all his meals out and spending all his weekends away from home, should be regarded as living in the same household.[41] These examples illustrate the inherent problems within the doctrine of family responsibility, warn us against making assumptions about the meaning of single people's patterns of co-residence, and show the importance of bringing gender into the analysis.

The 203 pensioners who were Townsend's principal subjects had a total of eighty-three unmarried children, most of whom were over twenty-five and more than half over thirty-five. All but seven of these children lived in the parental home, showing that despite wartime disruptions, it was still rare in this locality for working-class single adults with surviving parents to live independently. Analysis of his interview data, which includes both the child and the parent's perspective, suggested that many of these children were under some pressure, particularly from mothers, to remain unmarried: 'There were various references by old people and children alike, to unmarried children or siblings who were "too comfortable at home" or "didn't want to leave Mum".' This led Townsend to speculate that a father's authority in the home was more likely than a mother's to be challenged by grownup sons and daughters. He was especially struck by the closeness of relationships where mothers were widowed and had become particularly anxious not to be parted from their children (a position that was often related to weakness and femininity, as in the character of Private Pike in the 1960s TV series *Dad's Army*). It is noticeable, however, that mothers were accused of pampering sons, while daughters were said to have refused marriage proposals to care for infirm mothers. In the absence of a marriage partner, single children who remained living at home would often be identified with the position occupied by the missing parent and become substitute spouses for their fathers or mothers. One single son was described as 'being like a husband to his mother', while a widow of eighty whose husband had died young described her misery when she lost her sixty-year-old unmarried son:

> When he was at hospital, they said he never talked about anyone else. They said they'd never heard a son talking about his mother like that. He never got worried about women. I miss him, oh how I miss him. We used to keep the home going. We were never apart.[42]

While responses from hospital staff show that such close relationships were perceived not to be entirely normal, Townsend observed that 'it seemed wholly natural for the remaining unmarried child at home to take on the care of a parent'. Such a child might be singled out to take on more than a fair share of the burden of care 'simply because the old person found a need to replace a spouse with someone in almost the same intimate standing' and sometimes undertook 'tasks of a personal nature … previously borne by the husband or wife'.[43]

Oral history evidence

My 1990s interviews with unmarried men and women born in the first three decades of the twentieth century offer some interesting comparative evidence here which both supports and complicates Townsend's analysis. From a similar age cohort to that of the children of his principal subjects, my group was much more diverse in background, current location, and geographical origin; they included domestic servants, manual labourers, and white-collar and professional workers, and were located in towns and villages in north east England and in southern English counties, cities and towns. A further difference is that my subjects, interviewed at the end of their lives, were recreating a picture of their earlier lives from memories and spoke with hindsight, whereas Townsend's were describing their current situation. The similarities which appear between the two groups suggest that mid-twentieth-century discourses about the importance of single sons and daughters as carers fitted the late twentieth-century agenda I imposed upon them, which was to offer me explanations for why they had not married, thus making it easier for some of my subjects to identify themselves as closely attached to their families.

Gender divisions in family roles also emerged in my interviews. For example Sid (born 1925), after returning in 1946 from four traumatic years in a German POW camp, continued to live with the grandmother and grandfather who had brought him up. Sid's relatively high wages as a miner were more than sufficient to pay his board and keep, leaving him plenty of disposable income to spend in the pub, and he had no interest in married life, preferring the company of men to women. Sid's account also suggested that like Townsend's subjects he might have been too comfortable at home to want to change his situation.

Dorset farm labourer Bert also received domestic services from his mother, who did all the cooking and washing. But because his father had given up the family farm when Bert was only nineteen and his mother had been in poor health, he became the principal wage earner, working a sixty-hour week during the 1950s to support both his parents. He had also been needed at home (in a rural area with limited public transport) because they couldn't drive. Yet despite his breadwinning and later caring role when his mother was ill, and the positive affirmation of this position given by me as interviewer, Bert still believed his mother had made life too easy for him and that he had exploited her:

B: That's the trouble warn'it, stayed at home (laughed) easy life, really.
KH: *There's something to be said for that.*
B: Yes, that's what it's for when you think about it. Cruelty in'it.
KH: *Why is it cruelty?*
B: Making her work.
KH: *What, your mother?*
B: Yeah (long pause) – too late now.

Bert's narrative suggests that he felt trapped by his parents as well as by his own need of them and that he had internalised critical beliefs about bachelorhood. The first words that came into his mind associated with being single were 'down and out'. He appeared to believe that by not marrying he must have been selfish, and also that I would be in agreement with this image. Thus, when I asked him how he would respond if people asked him why he hadn't married, he replied:

B: Like I say I don't know, never got round to it. Like I say, I'm a loner. Whether it was meanness, greed or what I don't know (laughed) – you'd probably say both.

KH: *I don't know. Meanness, now that's an interesting one isn't it. Why mean?*

B: Keep what you got, that sort of stuff …

KH: *I'm wondering if that's what other people would think or if that's from you.*

B: I don't know. I never thought about it in that way … I don't know, perhaps I didn't believe in share and share alike.

The idea that single men were bad at sharing was also voiced by Peter (born 1928), the son of an optician, who had lost his father in 1946: 'I realise myself, I could never get married because I'd got far too many ideas of my own which I could never expect to share with anybody at all.' Peter also saw himself as a 'loner' and had lived apart from his mother during his early working years, never supporting her financially. Nevertheless, she had been an important figure throughout his adult life. She had supported his career choice against the advice of his critical, disciplinarian father. He had remained living near her, visiting her very regularly during the early part of his career and later sharing a home with her. Her practical value is suggested by her role as his laundress, who provided a regular supply of ironed shirts. Unwilling to make any personal revelations or cite his mother as any direct influence on his marriage prospects (though hinting that she had made social life more difficult), he stressed the strength of the attachment between them. Thus this loner who believed he had led a selfish life was also a family standby, seeing the full-time commitment he had given to his mother's care in old age as his major life contribution as a single middle-class man.

Townsend's belief that single sons and daughters often became replacement husbands for widowed mothers seems to be borne out by this and a number of other interviews across the class spectrum, and it was by no means only daughters who gave physical care. Many of the single men I interviewed left alone to care for parents in old age found themselves faced with 'tasks of a personal nature', which were part of the burden of becoming a substitute spouse.

This was the case with Bob, son of a boilermaker (born 1933), the only child in a family of eight not to marry, who after his return from four years national service in the mid-1950s had remained living at home after all his siblings had left. Bob's image of bachelorhood did not emphasise loneliness or selfishness but rather fun and sociability. He had loved to dance with women, longed to travel the world, but also regretted not having married. Yet because as a child, he felt excluded from his mother's love by her need to care for his father (who had been gassed in the First World War) and also by a favoured younger brother, Bob was eager to jump in and replace his father and actively embraced the identity of family standby. Despite the fact that he had placed other men in the position of 'second daddies' when he was younger, after his father's death he guarded his mother jealously, determined that she should not marry again.

As she grew older Bob had also given his mother the kind of intimate bodily care which would normally been done by women or by a husband, arousing strong feelings that had had no other outlet, and he described his mother's ageing body as 'a precious jewel'. Yet he knew that to feel that way towards his mother breached the incest taboo and was crossing a socially unacceptable boundary:

> When you're talking about [a] man would like to see a woman naked, and that never happened to me, and yet I had to see Mum in her naked-ness, and that hurt me, because Mum was beyond a wife you under-stand.

Parental need as well as attachment to parents and the parental home were powerful motivations for men and women interviewees alike. A number of women regarded themselves as having been destined to be carers, because of parental illness or infirmity that began quite early in their lives. For example, Dora (born 1903), the daughter of a railway signalman, had given up office work in her early twenties after her mother's health had deteriorated, and looked after her brother's child after his wife died. For her, home was the place where she was needed most, and she hadn't minded giving up work.

The 'good' daughter image was, however, no more stable than that of the 'selfish' son. For Dora, remaining in a subservient position when she was doing all the housework was not easy, and this part of her story was at odds with the image of a happily unmarried carer:

> Well 'cos Mum still wanted to be … it was her home and, you know, we didn't quarrel, but I'd do different things … Once I was home, a lot of times she stayed in bed. If she felt like it she'd get up and then perhaps she'd do the potatoes, peel apples or anything like that, but she just did it when she felt like it and she got up when she liked and that sort of thing but she didn't have the responsibility of anything.

Other 'dutiful daughters' described parental death as 'gaining my freedom', expressed resentment about the very different expectations that were held of their brothers, and regretted that they had been forced to give up or modify career ambitions in order to give care.[44]

Doreen (born 1911), whose mother owned the family farm, used the identity of a caring daughter both as a justification for not having pursued a more adventurous life-path and as a way of working out difficulties in her relationship with her father. While her mother offered a model of female authority, the frustration her father felt at having to take orders from his wife may have been taken out on Doreen, and he later made it difficult for her to have boyfriends. In an attempt to escape, she tried unsuccessfully to persuade her parents to allow her to become a missionary, until one day she received a message from God:

> I knew 100% from God that he didn't want me to be a missionary … you do just know, and that at some stage I'd have my parents to look after. And that to me was the worst possible thing … I wasn't in any doubt about it. He didn't want me to be a missionary. But he didn't leave me without a job, and that ultimately I would be responsible for my parents. And that I didn't want to accept at all because I just knew it was going to be very, very hard.

Despite the burden God had placed upon her, Doreen was able to gain power following her mother's death. When she and her brother and sister inherited the farm, her father was allowed no say in what happened to it. And although Doreen's missionary ambitions were compromised by having to look after her father, she used her belief in God to represent her caring responsibilities as divinely ordained and also a justification for not marrying. Thus, any anger or sadness about frustrated ambitions was denied or submerged into her religious faith.

Dutiful daughters and wayward sons: representations of single men and women and the family

The life stories discussed above carry elements of different fictional discourses and exhibit tensions between duty, sacrifice and personal fulfilment. Images of dutiful daughters were particularly common in women's magazines and fiction during the interwar years, at a time when concern about plight of women who supposedly could not marry because of the war was at its height. For example, in 1929, Mrs Marryat's column in *Women's Weekly* denied that there could be any conflict of interests between parents and daughters and claimed (like my interviewee Dora) that the girl who was 'the mainstay of the home' should not be pitied or looked upon as 'a martyr to duty'. She held rather that:

> Love is the driving force … Her affection for her parents makes what she does for them a delight, not a fulfilment of a dry duty … A home

of her own – isn't she in one? What home could be more her own than this she shares with those she loves? Would it be a happier one if she were married to a rich man who doled out a little help perforce – to her people whom he despised for being poor?[45]

But although daughters in this position had apparently made no sacrifice, the column's subtitle 'in praise of unknown heroines' appears rather to contradict this claim, and parents could as easily be cast in the role of villains demanding too much from their daughters. A letter in an earlier edition of the same magazine took this line, arguing that: 'The most pathetic sight in the world to my mind is the spinster woman of uncertain years who has all her chance of happiness spoilt by her too selfish parents.'[46]

The power which parents could exert over daughters and parents' dependence upon daughters for support were also common themes in women's novels during the interwar years. Radclyffe Hall's *The Unlit Lamp* (1924) and May Sinclair's *The Life and Death of Harriet Frean* (1922) depicted daughters being held at home in bonds of service, compelling them to internalise their parents' needs so that, like my interviewees' Ellen and Doreen, they felt they could not leave their parents.[47] Yet not all parents in this position were pictured as preventing their daughters from marrying. In E. M. Delafield's *Thank Heaven Fasting* (1932), the demands of a mother that her daughter should marry left the daughter carrying a terrible burden of disgrace, forcing her to see marriage primarily as an escape from parental disapproval.[48] And more radically, the heroine of Winifred Holtby's *The Crowded Street* (1924) was pushed into discarding the dependent daughter role by the realisation that her mother didn't really need her at home but only wanted her to marry, and found a new independence both from her family and from men.[49]

Each of these authors portrayed the family as locking daughters into cycles of self-denial, where parents' wishes took on an overweening importance and independent action became increasingly difficult. However, their radical potential lay in their acknowledgement that the major difficulty for these unfortunate women was not simply that they could not marry, but rather that marriage was their only viable means of escape.

It has been argued that such images heralded a new sense of freedom for women after the First World War and a rejection of the Victorian image of the self-sacrificing daughter who missed out on marriage, confirming Virginia Woolf's belief that 'the modern woman was born in or about 1910, because she began to develop a sense of what it was to act freely and for herself'.[50] Yet while it is true that Delafield, Holtby, Hall and Sinclair were all critical of the ways families trap daughters and prevent them from growing into independent women, the story of the dutiful daughter, which was repeatedly retold by my interviewees in the 1990s, cannot be so easily dismissed as an anachronism in this period. Popular support for the spinsters' pension campaign suggests this was an image which still drew public sympathy in the late 1930s and 1940s.[51] Furthermore, it was just such a daughter, Mary Jocelyn, heroine of Flora Mayor's *The Rector's Daughter*, who was one of the best-loved spinster heroines of the 1920s.

This book, regarded as Mayor's crowning achievement, sold well and received very favourable reviews.[52] What inspired readers to love Mary was her ability to transform the despised spinster role to a vehicle for sainthood. As one reviewer put it, 'Mary Jocelyn is one of those sad figures of whom it is said that nothing ever happens. Mrs Mayor reveals the meaningless of that phrase. Mary Jocelyn's "nothing" is a full rich state of being.'[53] Thus, although Mary remained tied to and dominated by her father, she was admired for accepting her lot without bitterness and recognising that her task was to help alleviate suffering. Oldfield believed that Mayor, who was herself a Victorian spinster, wanted to champion the older spinster model, 'those sexual and social failures who she saw as despised and discounted by the young and thriving'.[54] It could be argued that by valuing the role of the spinster daughter who stayed at home, Mayor was also challenging the inevitability of marriage as women's destiny. Still, although she may have offered comfort to real 'dutiful daughters', the emphasis on the saintly and heroic nature of Mary's life's work makes readers all the more aware of what she has given up, and we are haunted (as my interviewee Ellen was) by the shadow of a marriage that might have been.

Images of heroic sons refusing marriage in order to stay with their parents in books read by men are much rarer. Rather, the maternal figure often appears in the guise of other characters. In this period the archetypal fictional bachelor was Bertie Wooster, an upper-class playboy looked after by his butler Jeeves, who was also a single man. The enduring appeal of the eternally popular Jeeves and Wooster, chronicled in fourteen comic books and repeatedly adapted for television and stage, lies partly in its author P. G. Wodehouse's ability to play with gender stereotypes. Calm, clever and inscrutable, Jeeves is a father figure for his wayward and irresponsible master Wooster, protecting him from dangerous feminine influences and in particular from predatory women. But while this could suggest a rejection of the feminine, Jeeves also acts like a mother, aunt or wife by offering his master domestic services. His endless ability to come to the rescue when Wooster is in trouble is also suggestive of a mother protecting her son. Jeeves's maternal role becomes particularly obvious in

Thank You, Jeeves (1934) when he gives notice. Bertie 'did not care to think what existence would be like without him' and, like a child who thought his mother had deserted him for ever and then finds her again, can hardly contain his joy when his manservant agrees to return: 'You get a moment like this – supreme as you might say – with all the clouds cleared away and the good old sun buzzing on all six cylinders – and you feel … well dash it!'[55] Maternal relationships between male servants and their masters were not confined to the comic novel. For example, Dorothy Sayers' bachelor detective Lord Peter Wimsey had a manservant who looked after him, as did the forty-year-old hero of one many reruns of the Jane Eyre story, *Bachelors have Such Fun!* (1938), by the prolific romantic novelist Barbara Stanton. This latter story made a direct connection between mothers and manservants, with Charles 'having been at hand when his master cut his first tooth, [understanding] him as a mother understands her favourite child' and running his flat like clockwork.[56]

While Wodehouse's books remained popular throughout the period, by the 1950s the demise of indoor domestic service made accounts of the upper-class Englishman nurtured by his butler seem somewhat old fashioned. In *How to Avoid Matrimony* (1957) Froy depicted the 'true bachelor' as being without the support of either servant or mother, endlessly chasing and seducing but never marrying women. He believed a bachelor should live alone, and dissociated the term from 'insipid milky types of men' who are 'just Unmarried', insisting that the man who lives with his mother is not a 'true bachelor'.[57] Imagery of this kind, which circulated in all-male environments in the 1950s, 1960s and 1970s (my copy of this book previously belonged to the Officers' Mess library at RAF Linton on Ouse),[58] may have had some influence on my male interviewees, many of whom went into National Service during the 1950s, perhaps making it easier to relate to an image of the selfish 'loner' and harder to present themselves unambiguously as dutiful sons.

Brothers and sisters in fiction

Froy's chart of marriage risk by age groups places the older bachelor aged fifty to seventy as in a marriage danger zone, 'beginning to fret for someone to darn his socks',[59] while Stanton concludes her book with the view that while bachelorhood might be normal for younger men, older bachelors are 'only half alive'. Single men of this age group could, however, be resuscitated (though not always entirely successfully) by being portrayed in the role of a brother. Foregrounding the sibling relationship, which, Davidoff has argued, remains the source of 'some of the most powerful emotional bonds and practical human interactions',[60] has been particularly necessary for unmarried people because, after parental death, it offered them their strongest connection to family. But the presence of siblings could also be 'potentially divisive, fragmenting material, cultural and emotional resources' because (unlike marriage) it offers no possibility for 'either the formation of family or its continuance'.[61]

This paradox was encapsulated in a comic novella, *The Day of the Tortoise* (1961), by the popular pastoral novelist H. E. Bates, which told a story about four unmarried siblings in late middle age. Described by a reviewer as portraying 'a typically English ménage', the book showed through an inversion of gender roles the power of the sibling relationship but also its tyranny and ultimate sterility. The central character, fifty-seven-year-old Fred, was an unlikely hero. He did indeed seem half alive at the start of the book, 'wearing carpet slippers of a faded red plum colour', with 'tired looking hair and moustache' and 'the absent air of an unhurried dog trying to remember, though not very successfully, where it had hidden a favourite bone the day before yesterday'.[62] Fred was held in thrall by his eccentric, spinster sisters, who used him as their servant, making him play the Cinderella part by doing all the cooking and housework. However, the nameless 'princess' who transformed his life and awakened his latent sexuality turned out to be an equally emblematic figure in post-war Britain. Mirroring contemporary concerns about juvenile delinquency and 'problem' families, she was a homeless, young, pregnant woman who had been abandoned by her family.

While Bates' earlier and more famous book *The Darling Buds of May* absorbed a young bachelor into the Larkin family as partner for the eldest daughter,[63] in *Day of the Tortoise* the middle-aged bachelor brother ended up rejecting a family identity by rebelling against his tyrannical sisters. The outcast girl's pregnancy could be seen as a symbol of fertility, but the escape she offered Fred from the sterility of single siblinghood was not into marriage but rather was closer to Froy's vision of the 'true bachelor'. She got him to dance and get drunk, and kindled his desire with a kiss. Thus, while the union was never fully consummated and she left to be reunited with her baby's father, Fred's discovery of the pleasures of an independent single life meant that his relations with his sisters would never be the same again.[64]

Weakness and overdependence on siblings (which had prevented Fred from developing into a real man) were also depicted in relationships between sisters in interwar women's novels. For example, in Delafield's *Thank Heaven Fasting* the bond between the Marlowe sisters Frederica and Cecily is seen as destructive, ruining their marriage prospects, and in *The*

Misses Mallett (1922) by E. H. Young, two spinster sisters are shown as a negative influence on a younger sister and niece, attempting to put them off marriage: 'The Mallets don't care for marrying. Look at us, free as the air and with plenty of amusing memories. In this world nobody gets more than that, and we have been saved much trouble. Don't marry, my dear Rose.'[65] Yet, although Delafield and Young both appear to have considered sisterly ties to take second place to marriage, these portrayals were far from being wholesale rejections of the sibling relationship. Rather the emotional sustenance single women were shown to draw from their sisterhood suggests that, at a time when so many sisters did in reality live together, it was viewed as a relationship of considerable significance.

Brothers and sisters in social surveys and oral history

The importance of the sibling relationship for unmarried people is borne out by evidence from social surveys and oral history showing that fictional sibling households had many real-life equivalents. The *New Survey* shows single siblings living together without any married relations present, with the domestic role sometimes taken by a sister who kept house for working siblings of both sexes. But when there was only a single brother and sister, they were presented as operating more like quasi-married couples.[66] A railwayman's written account depicts his sister in terms similar to a wife with little or no independent life apart from her sibling. The couple regularly went on outings and holidays together, with the sister following the routines imposed by her brother's work:

> The nature of my employment does not allow for regular hours of meals or sleep. When on day duty, usually rise about 5.15 a.m. and retire 10.30 pm to 11 pm. Night duty, the order is reversed, the hour of rising being between 5.30 pm and 6 pm and bedtime 10.30 a.m. It therefore necessarily follows that mealtimes are also irregular for myself, and, incidentally my sister too.[67]

This was a position also adopted by my interviewee Dora, when describing her relationship with her twin bachelor brother.

Yet in a case where two single sisters lived together without a brother, neither was designated as housekeeper.[68] Like the majority of unrelated working-class single women in the survey, both had paid employment and were self-supporting. Their lower wages would not have allowed one to remain in the home. Thus although a brother could enlist a sister as a substitute wife, for older working women domestic support of this kind would have been regarded as a privilege, not an expectation.

Oral interviews suggest the complexities of these relationships which household surveys can do little to illuminate. One particularly interesting example was recounted by Daisy, who worked as a live-in domestic servant and who had experienced a conflict of loyalties between her elder sister May and unmarried employer Freda, both of whom she adored. After Freda's elder sister had died, Daisy was able to demonstrate the power she held over her employer's affections by persuading her to let May move in with them in a most unusual arrangement. May had gone out to work each day and paid Freda for her keep but had also shared Daisy's bedroom. Daisy explained: 'It was a difficult situation in some ways. The three of us. I loved my sister. I loved Miss Freda. Miss Freda liked me very much, she quite liked May but, she liked me and you see it was three. I had to be canny.'

The categories adopted by household surveys of 'head', 'servant' and 'lodger' would have done little to explain the economic and emotional complexities of these relationships, in which class, employment status, kinship, money, affection and passionate feelings were all implicated. However, it seems likely that Freda knew she would only be able to hold onto Daisy as a servant if she accepted her sister as part of the bargain.

Townsend's interviews with unmarried brothers and sisters show a web of familial interconnections within and between sibling households,[69] and he stressed the particular significance of this relationship for unmarried people, both in Bethnal Green and more widely.[70] He was struck by the extent to which married siblings saw themselves as protecting and watching over unmarried siblings, and gave an example of a married woman with an infirm unmarried brother living nearby who cleaned and cooked for him. But he also found unmarried sisters who did not live together sharing shopping and meals and offering physical care during periods of ill-health, as well as unmarried brothers and sisters living in close-knit partnerships whose dynamics often imitated those of husand/wife, father/daughter or mother/son.[71] One example which made a particular impression on him was a family of three orthodox Jewish siblings in their seventies and eighties whose parents had died when the brother was only nineteen. The brother had become a substitute father, discouraging his two much younger sisters from marriage and using them as his housekeepers.

The life-story of two single sisters illustrates the fluidity of sibling exchanges over time:

A big family sort of got on my mother's nerves and there were three single sisters left. To be quite frank with you she nagged a little bit and we all left to find lodgings near by. I wouldn't advise anybody to leave their mother like that. The other two were together for some time and then when one of them married I left the sister, who had a family, who I was living with, and me and my sister have lived together ever since.

The sisters had worked making handstitched buttonholes and when interviewed were in their seventies, retired and supplementing their pensions by taking in lodgers. They were described as moving between lodgings, married and unmarried sibling households, including weekend shifts looking after nephews and nieces. Townsend was also told in confidence that one of the sisters could have married her brother-in-law after his wife died. The strength of the sibling relationship is shown by the fact that she turned him down. While this was partly on the grounds that he still had his youngest daughter at home to look after him, the main declared reason was to ensure that her sister would not be left alone.[72]

The idea that single people were 'family standbys', suggested at the start of this chapter, was actively embraced by Townsend and he tried (often successfully) to attach this identity to his unmarried interviewees. Many other sources discussed here could lead to similar conclusions. Unmarried men and women often felt their lives had been validated by the care or support they had given to parents and other relatives and, while strongly promoting marriage, the government was still happy to make use of both their earning and domestic labour power. But there have also been alternative discourses at play. Being a family standby could be frustrating and humiliating for unmarried people who felt restricted by parents or elder siblings and unable either to marry or to fulfil other personal ambitions. Yet, although it was a struggle for many to achieve autonomy and independence in their relationships, some found ways of achieving it. The imagery attached to unmarried people is also ambivalent. For men the cult of the bachelor playboy was created in opposition to hen-pecked husbands, but also to pampered sons tied to their mothers' apron strings, while daughters were often pitied or criticised for failing to escape from mothers and become liberated, modern women. These kinds of paradoxes will be explored further later in the book where I examine another important aspect of single people's relationship to family: their relationships with children.

Notes

1 Davidoff, *Worlds Between*, p. 233.
2 The absence of men in family history is discussed in Davidoff *et al.*, *The Family Story*, and Loftus, 'The Self in Society'.
3 See for example Booth's *London Life and Labour of the People* (1889), Rowntree's

surveys of York (1901, 1936 and 1950), and Bowley's surveys of Bolton, Northhampton, Reading, Stanley and Warrington (1913–14 and 1923–4).

4 For example Herbert Tout, *The Standard of Living in Bristol* (Bristol: University of Bristol, 1937). See Peter Wardley and Mathew Woollard, 'Retrieving the Past: A Reclamation and Reconstruction of the Social Survey of Bristol 1937', *History and Computing*, 6:2 (1994). See also M. Bulmer, K. Bales and K. Kish Sklar, 'The Social Survey in Historical Perspective' in M. Bulmer (ed.), *Essays on the History of British Sociological Research* (Cambridge: Cambridge University Press, 1985). Social surveys up to 1934 are listed in A. F. Wells, *The Local Social Survey in Great Britain* (London: George Allen and Unwin, 1935).

5 See Colin A. Linsley and Christine L. Linsley, 'Booth, Rowntree, and Llewelyn Smith: A Reassessment of Interwar Poverty', *Economic History Review*, 46:1 (1993). The *NSLLL* records can now be accessed electronically through the UK Data Archive.

6 Hampstead was a predominantly middle-class borough with the lowest proportion of people living below the poverty line and high population mobility (less than half were born in London). Deptford was a mainly working-class borough with 14.5 per cent over the poverty line and a much more stable population (71 per cent were London born). Chelsea was the smallest borough, relatively wealthy but with pockets of poverty. *NSLLL* vol. 3, p. 373, and vol. 6, pp. 419–25.

7 This compares with a national average including all classes of eight per cent in these age groups. Source: *Census 1931, General Report*, table XLVI. It was not always possible to tell unmarried people apart from other categories of singleness.

8 See *NSLLL* vol. 3, pp. 413–23.

9 *Ibid.*, p. 414.

10 *Ibid.*

11 See Selina Todd, *Young Women, Work and Family in England 1918–1950* (Oxford: Oxford University Press, 2005), for a discussion of this issue.

12 *NSLLL*, Deptford (working-class) files 470 and 418; Chelsea (working-class) file 153.

13 B. Seebohm Rowntree and Frank Stuart, *The Responsibility of Women Workers for Dependants* (Oxford: Clarendon Press, 1921).

14 *Ibid.*, pp. 7–9.

15 Miriam Glucksmannn, 'Some Do, Some Don't (But in Fact They All Do Really). Some Will, Some Won't; Some Have, Some Haven't: Women, Men, Work, And Washing Machines', *Gender and History*, 7:2 (1995); J. Pahl, *Money and Marriage* (London: Macmillan, 1989).

16 Harold L. Smith, 'British Feminism in the Nineteen Twenties' in Harold L. Smith (ed.), *British Feminism in the Twentieth Century* (Aldershot: Elgar, 1990); Susan Kingsley Kent, *Making Peace: The Reconstruction of Gender in Interwar Britain* (Princeton, NJ: Princeton University Press, 1993), ch. 6.

17 On Rathbone see Mary Stocks, *Eleanor Rathbone* (London: Gollancz, 1949); Joanna Alberti, *Eleanor Rathbone* (London: Sage, 1996); Susan Pederson, *Eleanor Rathbone and the Politics of Conscience* (London: Yale University Press, 2004).

18 Eleanor Rathbone, *The Disinherited Family*, 1924 (Bristol: Falling Wall Press, 1986), p. 136.

19 *NSLLL* vol. 3, p. 423.

20 Jane Lewis, 'Dealing with Dependency: State Practices and Social Realities, 1870–1945' in Jane Lewis (ed.), *Women's Welfare, Women's Rights* (London: Croom Helm, 1983).

See also Braybon, *Women Workers in World War One*, who argues that the view of single women as dependants of their parents was widespread (p. 175).

21 Alan Deacon, *In Search of the Scrounger: The Administration of Unemployment Insurance in Britain, 1920–1931*, Occasional Papers in Social Administration, No. 60 (London: G. Bell and Sons, 1976), p. 25; Pat Thane, *The Foundations of the Welfare State* (London: Longman, 1982); Lewis, 'Dealing with Dependency', p. 25.

22 Braybon, *Women Workers in World War One*.

23 Deacon, *In Search of the Scrounger*, p. 26.

24 Several women from middle-class families in my interview sample were forced by the Depression to take whatever work they could find or had for some periods of time to rely on impoverished families for support.

25 Deacon, *In Search of the Scrounger*, p. 55.

26 Thane, *Foundations of the Welfare State*, pp. 175–6.

27 These liabilities, which applied even if the persons concerned were not co-resident, were retained unaltered by the consolidating Poor Law Acts of 1930 and 1934. M. A Crowther, 'Family Responsibility and State Responsibility in Britain before the Welfare State', *Historical Journal*, 25 (1982), p. 132.

28 *Ibid.*, pp. 132 and 141.

29 *Ibid.*, p. 140. P. Ford, *Incomes, Means Tests and Personal Responsibility* (London: P. S. King and Son, 1939), shows the great variations between households in different areas.

30 P. Ford, 'Means Tests and Responsibility for Needy Relatives', *Sociological Review*, 24 (1937), p. 188.

31 Ford, *Incomes*, p. 13; Walter Greenwood, *Love on the Dole*, 1933 (London: Vintage, 1993).

32 Crowther, 'Family Responsibility', p. 142. See also Michael Anderson, 'The Impact on the Family of the Elderly of Changes since Victorian Times in Governmental Income-Maintenance Provision' in Ethel Shanas and Marvin B. Sussman (eds), *Family, Bureaucracy and the Elderly* (Durham, NC: Duke University Press, 1977).

33 The top age limit was later extended to fifty-one.

34 Gerry Holloway, *Women and Work in Britain since 1840* (London: Routledge, 2005), p.164.

35 Summerfield, *Reconstructing Women's Wartime Lives*, p. 48.

36 *The Times*, 12, November 1949, p. 5; Davidoff *et al.*, *The Family Story*, p. 202.

37 See for example the correspondence 'Equal Pay for Women', *The Times*, 12 February 1955, p. 7, and Kathleen Lewis 'Subsidizing the Married', *The Times*, 10 May, 1954, p. 7.

38 Janet Fink and Julie Charlesworth, 'Historians and Social-Science Research Data: The Peter Townsend Collection', *History Workshop Journal*, 51 (2001), p. 210.

39 Michael Young and Peter Willmott, *The Family and Kinship in East London*, 1957 (Harmondsworth: Penguin, 1962), p. 12.

40 *Ibid.*, p. 17. For a critique of Young and Willmott's focus on companionate marriage see Janet Finch and Penny Summerfield, 'Social Reconstruction and the Emergence of Companionate Marriage, 1945–59' in David Clarke (ed.), *Marriage, Domestic Life and Social Change: Writings for Jacqueline Burgoyne, 1944–88* (London: Routledge, 1991).

41 *FLOP*, p. 35.

42 *Ibid.*, pp. 95–6, 42, 123–4.

43 *Ibid.*, p. 72.

44 See also Janet Finch, *Family Obligations and Social Change* (Cambridge: Polity, 1989); Jane Lewis and Barbara Meredith, *Daughters who Care: Daughters Caring for Mothers at Home* (London: Routledge, 1988).

45 *Woman's Weekly*, 21 September 1929.

46 *Woman's Weekly*, 27 January 1923. Dutiful daughters looking after selfish parents also appear in magazine fiction, sometimes achieving the status of heroine, for example in *Modern Home* (June 1930) and *Good Housekeeping* (July 1933).

47 May Sinclair's own early life was dominated by the demands of her role as her mother's companion, and her involvement with psychoanalytic ideas led her to identify the stifling environment of the family as a negative influence on women's lives. Sandra Ellesley, 'May Sinclair and the Medico-Psychological Clinic: A Case study in the Cultural Reception of Psycho-analysis', unpublished MA dissertation, University of Essex, 1990, p. 21.

48 E. M. Delafield, *Thank Heaven Fasting*, 1932 (London: Virago, 1988).

49 Winifred Holtby, *The Crowded Street*, 1924 (London: Virago, 1981).

50 Nicola Beauman, *A Very Great Profession: The Woman's Novel 1914–1939* (London: Virago, 1983).

51 In the *Spinster* (March, 1938), a story of this kind was used as propaganda for their campaign to receive pensions at fifty-five.

52 Sybil Oldfield, *Spinsters of this Parish: The Life and Times of F. M. Mayor and Mary Sheepshanks* (London: Virago, 1984), pp. 240 and 315, n. 1.

53 Review by Sylvia Lynd, *Time and Tide*, 18 July, 1924, quoted in Oldfield, *Spinsters of this Parish*, p. 242.

54 Oldfield, *Spinsters of this Parish*, p. 236.

55 P. G. Wodehouse, *Thank You, Jeeves*, 1934 (Harmondsworth: Penguin, 1999), pp. 11 and 229.

56 Barbara Stanton, *Bachelors Have Such Fun!* (London: Hurts and Blackett, 1938, second impression), p. 19. Her popularity is suggested by the fact that she published fifty novels between 1932 and 1963.

57 Froy, *How to Avoid Matrimony*, pp. 211–12.

58 See also William Davis (ed.), *The Punch Book of Women* (London: Hodder, 1974). Some of Froy's advice is now on the internet.

59 Froy, *How to Avoid Matrimony* (inside front and back cover).

60 Davidoff, *Worlds Between*, p. 206.

61 *Ibid.*, p. 207.

62 H. E. Bates, *The Day of the Tortoise* (London: Michael Joseph, 1961), pp 5–6. This book was described as 'joyously readable' in the *Times Literary Supplement*, 8 December 1961, p. 877.

63 H. E. Bates, *The Darling Buds of May* (London: Michael Joseph, 1958).

64 Written in the same period, Barbara Golden's *The Linnet in the Cage* (London: Heinemann, 1958) portrays a bachelor uncle as a fairy godfather who encourages a pregnant niece to return to her baby's father.

65 E. H. Young, *The Misses Mallett* (London: Virago, 1984), p. 25.

66 See NSLLL, boxes 9, 10 and 18, Deptford (working-class) file 436a, Deptford (middle-class) card 0082, Chelsea (working-class) file 4, Hampstead (middle-class) card 0019, Hampstead (working-class) file 221.

67 *NSLLL* vol. 9, pp. 403–6.

68   NSLLL boxes 10 and 18, Deptford (working-class) file 465, Hampstead (working-class), file 252.

69   *FLOP*; Townsend's informants consisted of eighteen unmarried pensioners (six men and twelve women).

70   The high number of single siblings living together in Bethnal Green was in line with a national sample from the 1951 census, which showed 39 per cent of single women living with siblings compared with only 1 per cent of married women.

71   For example FLOP, interview with Miss A. W., 26 January 1954.

72   *Ibid.*, interview with H. H., 30 August 1955.

4

Relations without a name:
sex and intimacy

[In] establishing a number of celibate professions for women, marriage bars made the sacrifice of normal human relationships the intolerable condition of professional success and economic security ...[and] provided many women who had no natural taste for life-long virginity with a direct and powerful incentive to the very irregular unions which were held in such abhorrence by contemporary society.[1]

Then she cried more than ever and all the repressed misery of her past life burst out in a flood – how grey, how negative it had been, how women hadn't loved her nor men married her ...

Feel Phyllis's society would be more tolerable than anyone's at the moment, simply because she has absolutely no claim on me except what I care to admit.[2]

Introduction

IN 1932, VERA BRITTAIN and Phyllis Bentley developed a close but short-lived friendship. Brittain was attempting to combine marriage, motherhood, a career in journalism and a glittering social life amongst the literary elite, whilst working out her grief at the loss of her fiancé, brother and men friends during the war in her autobiography *Testament of Youth*. Bentley, unconfident and provincial, still single at the age of thirty-seven, had recently achieved success with her latest novel and was enjoying her new-found fame in London.

Like many of her contemporaries, Brittain dwelled frequently in both her diary and published writings on the frustrations and dangers of spinsterhood and the adverse effects of 'sex starvation', of which Bentley provided a good example.[3] Bentley's confession that she had neither been loved by women nor married by men suggests a broader definition of intimacy than could easily be admitted in public, but it was one which would have resonated with Brittain's own experience. Her marriage after the war had brought her security, status and children, but no passionate romance, and her husband was often away from home. Despite her belief that more single women should be able to marry, the attraction of Bentley as a friend lay in that fact that she could be placed outside her network of familial responsibility and obligation. Furthermore, Brittain's closest and arguably her most important relationship was with another unmarried woman, the journalist and novelist Winifred Holtby, who shared her home and whose life was celebrated by Brittain after Holtby's death at the age of thirty-seven in a biography *Testament of Friendship.* Yet, because this relationship carried no social recognition, it could not compete publicly with her marriage.[4]

The problems the institution of marriage posed for unmarried women such as Bentley and Holtby, for their relationships with other women but also with men, were not insignificant. Not only did they have to grapple with their society's confused and contradictory expectations of unmarried women in relation to sex, but also it was not always easy to know how to name or attach meaning to relationships whose claims were not recognised in either law or custom. What space could they occupy if the alternative to being a wife was to be dubbed a predatory 'mistress', a 'sexual invert' or a 'frustrated spinster'?[5] What meanings were available for them to attach to friendships in a society where intimate (sexual) relationships outside marriage were condemned, where strong expressions of emotion between women were discouraged, where celibate women were in danger of 'inferiority complexes', and where marriage was regarded as the most important happening in a women's life? This chapter will examine these paradoxes by considering how unmarried people's needs for friendship, intimacy and sex were discussed and categorised and by uncovering public and private channels through which their close physical and emotional relationships could be expressed.

As the case above illustrates, the power of marriage in this period lay primarily in the authority it conferred on an exclusive sexual partnership between one man and one woman, making all other forms of adult intimacy appear deviant or second best. This belief was strengthened by the loss of so many marriageable young men in the First and Second World Wars and by the idea that women of this generation had been deprived of the opportunity ever to marry. Those who accepted that 'second best' might have been in an illicit or adulterous heterosexual relationship or in a same-sex partnership, whether platonic or erotic. But in each case, single people often felt unable to speak honestly or openly about what such a relationship meant to them, and were constrained by the knowledge that it would never be perceived as being as significant as a marriage.

A further and equally important consequence of the married/single sexual dichotomy has been the production of mutual envy, stemming from both sides of the divide. The frequent idealisation of intimate relations within marriage and the envy felt by the single ignored the brutal reality of many marriages in which power was unequally distributed. A rapidly rising divorce rate and widening of grounds for divorce suggest that, despite the growing belief that marriage should be an equal physical partnership in which sexual enjoyment should be shared, some marriage partners longed to escape. Single people's freedom appeared enviable to some and so also did their different (often less restricted) kinds of intimate relationships and friendships, which did not carry any claims or obligations, in public at least. However, in order to survive marriage, these feelings usually had to be buried and were sometimes displaced, with married people projecting their own discontents onto single people.

The power of marriage to define intimacy was also different for men and women. The counterpart of the stereotype of the embittered, sex-starved spinster was the carefree, irresponsible bachelor, a ubiquitous figure in films, novels and magazines, whose ease of access to women meant that he could do very well without marriage. Such representations suggest that intimacy created few problems for single men and disguised the power relations inherent within them. Beliefs that men's sex drive was more active than women's, that the male sex function was unproblematic and that men's needs for emotional intimacy were less significant than women's had important consequences for single people. The view that it was normal and natural for unmarried men but not for unmarried women to 'sow their wild oats' made sexually active women either seem to be victims of male lust or be labelled promiscuous and likened to prostitutes, as 'hard-boiled' or 'amateurs'.[6] Anxieties about single male's sexual functions and behaviour had to be hidden,[7] while single women's sexual and emotional problems were more openly discussed by doctors and psychologists. There were also differences in homosexual relationships, which, though perceived by many people as undesirable for both sexes, were illegal only for men.

Between 1885 and 1967, sex between men in both public and private locations was liable to prosecution and custodial sentences. The need to hide evidence of such activity meant that it commonly took place outside the home in all-male environments, often within institutions such as the armed services, boarding schools and colleges, religious communities and men's clubs and societies. To preserve their privacy and respectability, men frequenting these institutions generally closed ranks, and their homosocial networks and homosexual relationships have only relatively recently been revealed in autobiography and life-history interviews.[8] My own gender, class and sexual orientation as a middle-class, heterosexual woman also meant that that these kinds of relationships were not always revealed to me in interviews, particularly where my interviewee's class position was different from my own.

Lesbianism, although perceived as undesirable and unhealthy, was never made illegal. Yet similar levels of secrecy and silence surrounded intimate relationships between women, which also often flourished in all-female environments. Concern about revealing too much and fear of criticism and social ostracism, which lasted even beyond the grave, have resulted in the frequent destruction of personal papers which might have revealed socially unacceptable feelings or illicit liaisons. Thus, feminist and lesbian historians writing institutional, professional and personal histories have had to work hard to find sources which uncover the intimate relationships of single women.[9]

These gaps in sources have contributed to a long-running debate amongst historians about the extent to which the First World War was a significant watershed in sexual and social change. The commonly held belief that women gained new sexual freedom needs to be supported by hard evidence of increased sexual activity outside marriage, rather than by anecdotal opinion. But while questions have been raised about why people thought sexual activity outside marriage increased during and after the war, it is still not altogether clear what lies behind these beliefs.[10]

Despite a lack of hard evidence demonstrating that most single women during the 1920s and 1930s really were bereaved partners of soldiers, the idea of a lost generation of women consigned to 'imaginary widowhood' and compelled to seek solace either in the company of other women or in adulterous extramarital liaisons should not be dismissed. Rather, images of 'doomed youth', and 'superfluous' women have themselves cast shadows over the lives of this generation of unmarried women and men and affected their sexual and intimate relationships in multiple and long-lasting ways.[11] The first step to bringing these invisible relationships out of the shadows must therefore be to understand the beliefs and myths that surrounded them.

Gendered sexualities

One important belief generated by the 'lost generation' myth was that because the war had deprived so many women of heterosexual experience within marriage, they must be a problematic group. Thus while single men's sexual difficulties were rarely discussed in public, those of single women became a focus of medical and media attention. Educated women in particular who delayed or avoided marriage and motherhood were heavily criticised and regarded as deviant.[12] Yet such concerns about the physical and emotional health of the unmarried woman were hardly new and were not simply fuelled by the demographic imbalance, which had itself been an issue of ongoing concern for more than half a century. Similar medical and psychoanalytical views from both within and outside Britain about normative sexuality, sexual deviance and same-sex relationships can be discovered considerably earlier than the war. These views can be linked to changes in women's position within marriage and the dissemination of the ideas of sexologists and psychoanalysts, principally Havelock Ellis and Sigmund Freud, that sexual energy was the principal motivating force in adult life[13] and that it was as normal for women as for men to experience sexual desire and pleasure.[14] This meant that by the First World War the desirability of the heterosexual norm for women within marriage was commonly established through reference to the sexual deprivation, frustration or perversion suffered by the unmarried woman.[15]

These changes in understanding the nature of female sexuality took place without an accompanying shift in the sexual double standard, which helps to explain why, in public at least, single women were regarded as more problematic than single men. This is evident even in literature aimed at married people. For example, the opening passage of *Ideal Marriage*, an influential marriage manual which became the standard text during the 1940s and 1950s,[16] saw marriage as offering 'the only – even though relative – security to the women's love of love and of *giving* in love' (emphasis in original) while 'men too, on the whole, find in the permanent recognition and responsibility of marriage, the best background for useful and efficient work'.[17] While singleness is not mentioned, it is clear that not to be married was worse for women, because they were deprived of the opportunity to give and receive love in a secure sexual relationship, even though such security within marriage could not be guaranteed. By contrast, single men's ease of access to impermanent sexual relations outside marriage meant that although marriage might be perceived as a better option, it was not their only one.

Birth control pioneer Marie Stopes, arguably the most influential woman in sexual matters during the 1920s,[18] showed a similar understanding of the deprivations of unmarried women. In her best-selling book *Married Love* (1918), she noted particular problems after the age of thirty and referred to the prevalence of nerves and sleeplessness among women who had 'never had any normal sex-life or allowed any relief to their desires'.[19] She was by no means alone in being concerned about the effects of celibacy. In the previous century, socialist August Bebel stressed the importance of satisfying the sex impulse and the much higher rates of lunacy and suicide among the unmarried,[20] but these ideas were much more widely disseminated after the war in relation to women. Similar views were voiced in the interwar years by progressive intellectuals who stressed the importance of heterosexual relations for women's health and happiness.

For example, Bertrand Russell in *Marriage and Morals* (1929) used images of perpetual virgins, intellectually timid, jealous and disapproving because they were denied the satisfaction of loving partnerships with men, to promote new forms of marriage. [21] In *Motherhood and its Enemies* (1927) Charlotte Haldane, a former suffragette and wife of geneticist J. B. Haldane, saw the interests of the unmarried as being in direct opposition to married women arguing that 'undersexed' celibate women had lost interest in sex as a result of poor diet stemming from their inexperience in housekeeping.[22] And in *Psychology of Sex* (1933) Havelock Ellis, now a household name, stated that sexual abstinence caused mental worry and erotic obsessions that could produce 'an unwholesome sexual hyperanaesthesia which especially in women often takes the form of prudery'. This was a particular problem for women, who could not easily form sexual relationships outside marriage and were less likely to relieve themselves through spontaneous orgasms in their sleep.[23] Images of prudish, frigid spinsters were also common in interwar fiction with spinsterhood often now viewed as a sexual rather than an economic problem, particularly for middle-class women. George Orwell typifies this trend in *The Clergyman's Daughter* (1935), offering a quasi-Freudian explanation (unconvincing even to some of his contemporaries[24]) for his heroine Dorothy's failure to marry. Her resistance to marriage was presented as the result of early sexual trauma 'which left a deep-seated wound in her mind', rather than a result of her lifestyle of poverty-stricken respectability caring for an elderly father, and Orwell stressed the ubiquity of this kind of 'abnormality' amongst the educated women of his day.[25]

While these authors said little or nothing about celibacy for men, it would be a mistake to see abstinence as being viewed only as a female problem. Stopes' private correspondence shows that she was also consulted by unmarried men and that the views of sex and marriage voiced by experts in the public domain masked much more confused and contradictory ideas about male chastity. Although men had always had more sexual licence than women, Victorian beliefs about true manliness had demanded that men should also lead chaste and blameless lives.[26] In the new sexual climate of the 1920s and 1930s, these ideas were being undermined by an alternative view that long-term chastity for men was even more harmful and debilitating than it was for women. With this in mind, a thirty-year-old unmarried clerk who believed celibacy had made him unfit for marriage saw his only hope in seeking sexual union beforehand, and asked Stopes if she knew of any facilities for sexual intercourse in his city without fear of catching venereal disease, while another physically fit bachelor aged twenty-nine, who 'hadn't sown [his] wild oats', worried that 'continued abstinence and forced self-control is going to prove harmful to all my best powers'. A third man, who believed he was oversexed, felt that perhaps his pent-up sexual energies would harm his future wife, if ever he did get married, and turn her into a wreck. The fear touching all these correspondents was expressed by one as 'because a man is not married he is often suspected of being not too good', and he and others begged Stopes to find a solution for the unmarried.[27]

Yet Stopes could do little to relieve their anxieties, beyond recommending early marriage, the standard advice given by most commentators at this time. Her difficulties in this respect must be viewed in the context of a society in which virginity was still highly valued but where levels of sexual surveillance and parental control were decreasing. Some loosening of social restrictions on young people, which led to fears that levels of extramarital sexual activity might rise, is suggested by the decline of chaperonage amongst the middle and upper classes, new job opportunities enabling greater economic independence particularly for middle-class women, and the growth of cinema and dance-hall cultures offering a much wider range of meeting places for men and women outside the home than before the war.[28]

In such a sexual climate, it was imperative that Stopes should not jeopardise the dissemination of contraceptive information to married women through claims by the church and other moralists that it would offer a licence for fornication amongst the unmarried.[29] Indeed *Married Love* would have been banned as obscene had there been any hint that single people might benefit from its contents.[30] Thus, although sexual satisfaction for both partners within marriage was promoted as essential for health and happiness, Stopes could not promote the benefits of sex to the single, and when male correspondents asked whether under the circumstances they might legitimately have recourse to prostitutes or indeed any sexual relationship outside marriage, they received stern warnings that there was 'absolutely no guarantee of safety' and such liaisons were 'morally deplorable'.[31]

The contradictions inherent within her position were pointed out by an Oxford academic who wrote to her privately to protest:

> Why is it [sex] not a just and harmless pleasure between other than married people? For you say elsewhere that for a man to restrain himself for longer than 14 days ([*Married Love*] pp 80–2) or a month takes out of him energy, which properly belongs to other forms of activity, and that unlike woman's, man's desire is almost ever present. If this is true, I can't understand what is to become of men such as myself, unmarried and unlikely to be able to marry for some years. Here we are with a constant desire, losing energy if we restrain ourselves longer than a fortnight or a month, forbidden to practise fornication (as well as knowing it to be unsafe) and unable to marry. Clearly a most impossible position and the strongest argument for masturbation.[32]

However, here as elsewhere Stopes was unable to resolve the conflict between nature, economics and morality he posed. Until 1884, Oxford dons had been barred from marriage,[33] and although the ban was no longer imposed, male-centred college lifestyles, low salaries and the high ratio of men to women in universities made marriage difficult for men in his profession. Yet the idea that thousands of women were desperate to marry made the Oxford don's position appear less tenable than it had in the nineteenth century, when sexuality was less in the public domain. Long-term singleness for men was not simply undesirable, but also called into question their masculinity, and was indicative of their inadequacy as men. Thus in her reply, while pointing out the dangers of masturbation, Stopes gave her usual advice that he should marry as soon as possible and use birth control.

The question of sex outside marriage for unmarried women is more complex and must be understood in terms of class as much as gender. Although the number of women having sex with men they did not intend to marry was increasing, they were still a small minority, with the only sizeable, visible group working as prostitutes.[34] Fears that allowing young unmarried women the same pleasures as married women would lead to an increase in prostitution, pregnancy and venereal disease were voiced by some older middle-class (often also unmarried) philanthropists, who worried that the birth control advice in *Married Love* might undermine their efforts to maintain high moral standards among working-class girls. One such correspondent, who worked in a YWCA girls' club, wrote to Stopes in 1922 that she had been 'told that you have a clinic in Bethnal Green where you treat girls and teach them to treat each other for this purpose and that prostitutes have been heard to rejoice that they can now carry on with no results – in the way of children'.[35] Although Stopes insisted that her fears were groundless and that her clinics were only for married women, such concerns may be viewed in part as a defensive response to attacks on their own celibacy and lack of heterosexual experience, which before the war had seemed less problematic.

A number of instruments of social control instigated or supported by middle-class women were deployed in an attempt to counter any increase in sexual activity among young girls and working women. For example, the new women's auxiliary police force took on the task of patrolling parks and open spaces to protect young women from sexual encounters, while the British Social Hygiene Council spread information about venereal disease through meetings, lectures and conferences. Their message was reinforced by commercial propaganda films such as *Damaged Goods* (1919),[36] in which the unmarried hero catches syphilis and, despite warnings by doctors, goes on to marry and infect his wife and child. Running as a sub-plot is the story of the source of his infection, an unmarried woman who 'fell' into a life of disease and prostitution after being raped by her employer and bearing an illegitimate child.

Films of this kind, in line with much of the cinema of the period, constructed clear boundaries between male and female sexuality in relationship to marriage. Women were shown as essentially innocent but vulnerable to corruption and once corrupted become dangerous to themselves and others, while men were neither pure nor automatically disgraced by sexual initiation.[37] Thus, while such films carried warnings for both unmarried women and men about the dangers of extramarital sex, the message to women was that sexual experience would disqualify them permanently from marrying, while for a man who had already 'fallen', marriage to a virtuous wife offered redemption and a safe haven against the dangers of the prostitute.

These films were shown at the cinema in some areas but more frequently screened in town halls by social reform groups. The films thus reached a variety of different audience, offering salutary warnings to young men and women with limited knowledge of sex and reproductive practices. Such was the case for Molly (born 1899), who worked during the 1920s as a still-room maid in a Bath hotel and never subsequently married. She saw *Damaged Goods* at the town's Assembly Rooms and never forgot it. More than seventy years later, her memory of the film's content was not of a man contracting VD and giving it to his wife but rather that it was 'about a girl who got into trouble', a taboo subject in her family and community that she had never felt safe to discuss even with her friends. Thus, it appears that the film (the only one she remembered seeing) may have achieved its objective by giving a shape to her unspoken fears.[38]

It is clear, however, that not all women accepted such warnings (aimed mainly at a working-class audience) about the dangers of sex outside marriage. Stopes' claim that sexual desire was normal for women led to a number of requests for solutions to sexual frustration. For example, in October 1921, soon after the publication of census statistics had highlighted 'the surplus women problem' in the press,[39] a nurse wrote to Stopes about the dilemmas facing her clients:

> We all know that since the war there is a shortage of men, therefore many, many girls must go unmarried. These girls are only human, they feel the longing for a mate. They have all the (unexpressed) restless stirring after something they can not have. Must their longing simply be squashed! Will this not account for many unmarried mothers? Can we blame them if they see no future in getting legally what they want?[40]

While Stopes seemed unable to help this woman and often failed to reply to letters of this kind, other interwar feminists took a rather different line. For example, socialist feminist Stella Brown stressed the variety and variability of the sexual impulse among women, including the possibility of 'natural nuns' and homosexual relationships as well as heterosexual relationships both within and outside marriage. She herself had a number of male lovers and argued that all women should have access to contraception in order for women to be truly emancipated and economically secure.[41] Winifred Holtby, who had formed strong emotional relationships and friendships with both sexes, also denied that celibacy should be regarded as a problem. In *Women* (1934) she challenged the prevailing view of spinsters as frustrated, asking why 'even when all their appetites for intimacy, power, passion and devotion are satisfied' single women must ask themselves what they were missing, while 'neither sexual experience nor social activity for a man was presumed to depend upon his marriage'. Thus, although women were advised not to dread 'the shadow of the manless thirties', she pointed out that no similar advice was ever given to bachelors of the same age.[42]

Solutions to celibacy

Although Stopes had difficulty in helping unmarried people, other advice books appearing between the late 1920s and the early 1950s and aimed at the general reader sought solutions for the problems of singleness and celibacy. Discussions were wide-ranging and included masturbation; heterosexual relationships; sublimation of the sex drive through close platonic friendships, socially useful work or creative endeavours and same-sex relationships. Each of these solutions will be considered alongside evidence of single women's and men's personal experiences of and engagement with them.

Masturbation

Expert opinion was split about the dangers of masturbation. Stopes advised her male correspondents that to indulge in the practice regularly might disable them for normal sexual intercourse. However, for women over thirty with no other sexual outlet, if they understood it was dangerous and controlled the use to not more than twice a month, it 'was *sometimes* beneficial' (emphasis in the original).[43] By the 1930s, most medical experts concluded it was physically harmless for either sex if practised in moderation, and rarely condemned it outright as immoral, but still looked for ways to reduce levels of activity. Havelock Ellis believed it was more common in adult women, since they did not have the same access as men to 'sexual gratification with the opposite sex', and for older celibate women it might have a sedative effect on the nervous system.[44]

It was in the psychic realm that most doubts were expressed, particularly about masturbators' frequent feelings of exhaustion and shame. Ellis saw self-righteousness and religiosity often appearing as a protection against remorse and stressed the shy, solitary and suspicious nature of many male masturbators.[45] Advice to women after the Second World War was even more critical. For example, M. B. Smith, in *The Single Woman of Today: Her Problems and Adjustment*, maintained that being self-centred and without the give and take of normal love relationships, masturbation tended to 'disorganise the personality'.[46] In *Unmarried but Happy* (1947), journalist Leonora Eyles (who had previously been an agony aunt for the magazine *Modern Woman*) thought that even if it brought physical relief for women, very rarely did it bring mental or spiritual peace. She offered practical advice such as exercise before bedtime, warm baths, hot drinks with an aspirin and uplifting books, in order to take the mind off the problem, or if this failed a system of rationing to twice and then, after a month, once a week.[47]

The least censorious advice was given by Laura Hutton, a clinical psychologist at the Tavistock Clinic. In *The Single Woman and her Emotional Problems* she adopted the Freudian view that transition to sexual maturity involved the centre of greatest sexual response passing from the clitoris to the vagina and that masturbation might cause women trouble in getting full physical pleasure from a man.[48] However, for some single women it offered 'the best possible occasional solution for the problem of the relief of psychosexual tension', provided there were no accompanying feelings of guilt or failure. It was the mental conflict rather than the physical act that produced deleterious effects, and she described a girl's discovery that a practice she had considered harmless was considered by one doctor as a vice which might lead to insanity. Although she ceased masturbating, this woman was haunted throughout her life by shame and guilt 'rooted in the memory of a "vicious" life – a life in reality spent in unselfish service to others'.[49]

It is more difficult to know how widely single men and women were affected by these views. Certainly Stopes' single male correspondents during the 1920s struggled not to give way to the practice, with one man physically relieved but mentally debased because he had lost power over his actions, while another described the practice as 'the very cream of one's blood being thrown away'.[50] However, by 1949 the responses of the mainly middle-class single men who replied to MO's 'Little Kinsey' survey seemed more sanguine, with many regarding it as normal, although one thirty-four-year old did express some unease, seeing it as 'adolescent and no substitute for sex life'. While fewer women wrote to Stopes about masturbation,[51] the silence and fear which still surrounded this subject during the 1920s was suggested by a forty-year-old woman who thought she could never marry because she was deaf and who suffered agonies in an effort to curb what she thought was 'wrong'.[52]

This woman had been relieved from the shame of this experience by meeting Jessie Murray, one of the first British psychoanalysts, who had written the preface to *Married Love* and who had encouraged this woman to read the book. She was lucky to have received such enlightened advice. Smith in *The Single Woman of Today* cited a 1929 American survey of single women from well-educated or professional backgrounds which found that nearly all reported masturbation and that 80 per cent had begun the practice after the age of thirty. Yet few admitted this openly because of social taboos.[53] And while by 1949, Dr Chesser's survey of 300 men examined in the army found 100 per cent admitted to the practice, less than a third of his 600 general women patients did so. The responses of single women from lower middle or middle-class backgrounds between the ages of thirty-two and sixty-six in MOs 'Little Kinsey' survey also show embarrassment was common. We do not know how far this was the case for working-class women, but oral history evidence indicates that amongst respectable working-class families there was very little discussion of sex and that the practice would probably have been taboo and viewed as shameful.

One MO respondent, who had extensive knowledge of masturbation through reading, linked her own experience to the views of psychologists and sexologists, seeing herself as sexually normal physically but psychologically abnormal, because she was interested in the attentions of men but loathed the 'final act'. Like Orwell's Dorothy, she had used this as a reason not to marry:

> Occasionally I am forced to become aware of an accumulation of sexual energy in myself. Always at night and I try to go to sleep so that the energy may be discharged by way of a sexual dream. If I cannot sleep, I do something about it, always knowing that, in spite of any process of intellectual feeling, I shall suffer for some days from a guilt feeling. This does not happen very often thank goodness, maybe three or four times a year. Anyway, you can see why I was embarrassed at answering your questions 33a and b.[54]

Heterosexual relationships

While masturbation remained a shameful secret for most women, the containment of sex within marriage was more openly discussed. Stella Brown's enlightened views on the rights to contraception of the single woman can be associated with the new, more flexible forms of heterosexual union that were being suggested during the interwar years by progressive thinkers such as Bertrand Russell and Harley Street specialist Dr Norman Haire, chairman of the World League for Sex Reform.[55] Both men drew upon the ideas of American judge Ben Lindsay, who spoke out for a new form of companionate marriage, with legalised birth control, and with the right to divorce by mutual consent for childless couples, but they went further in suggesting the possibility of sexual relations outside marriage and the gradual replacement of the professional prostitute with the voluntary mistress.[56] But while by the 1930s a recognisably modern sexual culture was beginning to emerge in which discussions of sex were becoming more acceptable in newspapers and magazines,[57] these ideas were far from mainstream.

The prominent eugenicist Sybil Neville-Rolfe, a long-time supporter of social purity campaigns, illustrates some of the contradictory beliefs about extramarital sex in the interwar years in her report for the *New Survey of London Life and Labour*, published in 1935. The numbers of prostitutes had been reduced and though in the new, more open sexual climate, girls might still contract venereal disease and have unwanted pregnancies, they were less likely to pursue promiscuity as an occupation. Thus, she was unsure whether promiscuity might not actually have increased as result of the growth of the non-commercial extramarital 'sex-adventure', but was still convinced that the vast majority of these relationships had 'some emotional content, and any suggestion that it is in any way allied to prostitution would be rebutted with indignation by those concerned'.[58] However, in her advice book *Why Marry?* (1935) she argued that no case could be made for such arrangements, and that trial or companionate marriages must not be encouraged, since a few people's 'brief happiness' could not compensate for the 'acute suffering, disappointment or maladjustment to life' suffered by many others.[59]

Advice books in the 1930s aimed at the single woman and written by psychologists were concerned to uncover the root causes of such maladjustments and were therefore less condemnatory. Laura Hutton admitted that in rare circumstances psychosexually mature women could receive great physical and emotional benefit from 'love consummated in full sexual union'. Yet she stressed the rarity of such a mature response and warned of the difficulties, such as pregnancy and 'deviations from normal sexual intercourse in order to avoid it', inevitable in most 'irregular relationships'. If the relationship was transitory, the normal woman's difficulty in separating her mental and emotional life from that of her body led to injuries in self-esteem, which usually resulted in deterioration into promiscuity and often drink or drug addiction.[60] The Jungian psychologist Esther Harding agreed about the dangers of casual, pleasure-seeking sex, but approved serious extramarital relationships undertaken by mature, self-supporting (by which she meant middle-class) women. She saw the repression of love which accompanied complete chastity as resulting in feelings of inferiority and unfulfilment, and while acknowledging the inevitable moral and emotional conflicts, noted the advantages of a relationship without social obligations, which could be more alive and reach a freedom often absent in marriage.[61]

These relatively enlightened views were not repeated in advice literature to unmarried women during the 1940s and 1950s. During the Second World War, social dislocation diminished levels of community surveillance and offered young single women and men greater opportunities for sexual adventure,[62] particularly if they were posted away from home.[63] But the reinforcement of marriage and the nuclear family during the immediate post-war years coincided with heightened fears of prostitution, resulting in a campaign to clean up the streets and culminating in the Wolfenden Report (1957), which recommended increased penalties for street offences, the remand of convicted prostitutes in custody for social and medical reports, and referrals to moral welfare workers.[64] Such a climate of 'moral panic' made extramarital sex appear particularly threatening. Yet Hera Cook points to the paradox that a more socially conservative and rigid post-war gender culture, in which heterosexual male dominance was reinforced, coexisted with a loosening of sexual restrictions on women outside the public domain. The publication in 1948 and 1953 of Alfred Kinsey's studies of American male and female sexual behaviour, widely publicised in Britain, was less centred upon married couples and questioned the abnormality of deviant sexual behaviour.[65] More middle-class men now expected to have mistresses of their own class and, with contraception more easily available, there was a concurrent willingness on the part of some middle-class women to have premarital and extramarital affairs even though they bore the costs in terms of back-street abortions and illegitimate babies.[66] The hugely popular film *Brief Encounter* (1945), which featured a secret, unconsummated affair, offered a vicarious experience of such forbidden desires, although some viewers found it hard to understand why it stopped short of a full sexual relationship.[67]

Smith in *The Single Woman of Today* saw the enigma of the single women in love with the married man as 'touching the roots of our social structure ... undermining the rule of family and moral code by which we live', and offered the Freudian explanation that some women in this position were acting out 'a subconscious desire to play safe and avoid marriage, whilst consciously desiring it'. Still, for her such women were more pitiable than culpable, and she described the hundreds of letters she had received and discussions with 'countless spinsters' who believed their lives were 'outside the law of Nature' or described the desperation of being the 'other woman'.[68]

Contemporary accounts by women, unmediated by psychologists or journalists, are harder to come by. However, life-history evidence suggests that it was not uncommon for single working women to be faced with conflicts between love and morality. Margot (born 1905) described her attachments to a number of bosses as 'a bit of fondness and that was that', but she had also found the experience of being repeatedly wooed by married men both 'trying' and 'sad'. Amelia (born 1905) had suffered harassment from a married boss whose attentions she had avoided, but had also fallen in love with a married man, a memory she still cherished: 'There was a chap who was married and we both knew better, and he didn't lead me on at all, so there is really nothing to tell, only I learned what it was to be madly in love. If you haven't ever been you wouldn't know, would you.'

A single woman, born in 1920, writing for MO described the conflict of values in a wartime romance with a married man. While it seemed to be 'genuine, live and was certainly exciting', she repeatedly told her lover he must go back to his wife. Yet when after four months he was posted away, still 'it was shattering to realise [she] would never see him again.'[69]

These kinds of affairs between single women and married men were endlessly replayed in women's film, novels and magazines throughout our period, with liaisons often positioned abroad, symbolising danger and excitement but also set apart from and therefore less threatening to the safety of the home and marital bed. The ambivalence which many single and married people felt about such 'live' but illicit relationships was suggested by contrasting the lovers' passion with the sterility of the man's loveless marriage. One of the best known of this genre was one of the most acclaimed Hollywood productions, *Now Voyager* (1941), starring Bette Davis, in which a frustrated spinster who had been held in thrall by a dominating mother enters into a shipboard romance with a married man who had been neglected by his wife.[70] In a society where love, sex and ideally also motherhood were regarded as a woman's birthright, yet were still denied to most single working women, the appeal of *Now Voyager*'s ending is obvious. However, many other stories which highlighted the sex appeal of the older spinster either ended in marriage, or showed repression of the sex drive in a more negative light as resulting in frustration or perversion.

The sex life of the unmarried man was described in very different terms, with avoidance of marriage and extramarital affairs presented as both normal and forgivable. Indeed, popular literature and journalism for men often suggested that bachelorhood was a more desirable state for men than marriage. The message throughout our period in the men's magazine *London Opinion* was of bachelors' ready availability for sex. But by the beginning of the Second World War, this had become more overt, with cartoons of men seducing sexy women (including a nanny whose 'knowledge' of soldiers was such that 'she could call the roll of the Brigade of guards if they lost it any morning').[71] Such imagery excluded and debased women readers and when, in 1954, *London Opinion* merged with another similarly misogynistic men's lifestyle magazine, *Men Only*, it became, like its American counterpart *Playboy*, primarily a vehicle for soft pornography. This shift can be linked to a more aggressive and tough masculine culture characteristic of the 1950s. Two years' compulsory National Service in the armed forces encouraged men to identify being a male with an eternal state of bachelorhood, in which effeminacy was despised and swearing, drinking and seducing women celebrated, whether or not they acted upon their desires.[72] Froy's *How to Avoid Matrimony* (1957) was dedicated to a long list of women's first names (which ended with 'and to all members of the Women's Royal Airforce wherever they might be'). But although the bachelor might be 'a lone wolf' or a 'stag at bay', he was still not immune from marrying. We are therefore presented with a chart in which men's risk of marriage in different age groups is assessed using the language of nuclear war, with warnings of matrimonial landmines, restricted areas, and danger zones where men must wear protective clothing.[73]

Yet this kind of literature also displayed evidence of anxiety that not all bachelors were single by choice and that men needed to be tall and physically and mentally fit to be desired by women. Thus during the 1930s, when the beneficial effects of fresh air and recreational exercise were being widely promoted for both men and women,[74]we find in *London Opinion* a cartoon of an undersized, 'rabbity'-looking single man being rejected by a robust and furious tennis girl as a suitable partner. Advertisements for bodybuilding promised small men who were losing out in both the job and marriage markets that if they followed the right exercise regime, they too could 'increase height and be a Man'. By the 1950s, psychological reasons for long-term bachelorhood had come to the fore and it was suggested that 'where a person had not been able to find a marriage partner in the normal way, they might be emotionally unstable – or neurotic?'[75]

Single men's own accounts suggest that the idea of pursuit by women could be used as a narrative which helped them to make sense of their own sexual histories and, particularly, their ability to overcome any underlying reticence about approaching the opposite sex. A bachelor (born 1932) writing for the MO Close Relationships survey adopted this perspective:

> My experience with girls started around 1952/3 with typists in the office (I flirted and fooled around so much it's a wonder I didn't get the sack) … I was late in having sexual experiences (about 21) mainly through shyness and reluctance to make the first move, for fear of rejection. Yet whenever I DID make advances, my fears were unfounded. Girls simply accepted me into their arms, gracefully. It was as though I hankered after fruit; it was there hanging.[76]

Adultery could also be explained in rather different terms from the unmarried women's accounts above, with no great emotional or physical conflicts suggested and women cast as the active agents in consummating relationships. Thus, Ian's affair with the wife of a fellow service man in the RAF in the mid-1950s was justified on the grounds that 'she was sexually highly motivated and her husband had been posted to Germany and she was quite happy to get into bed with someone'.

However, for other men this kind of narrative was at odds with their own memories of sexual difficulties they had encountered. Another bachelor writing for MO born 1910, who had suffered from psoriasis, described the difficulties of enforced celibacy and the belief that when he finally at the age of thirty found a woman who wanted to have sex with him, it had caused his impotence. He was also anxious to dispel the myth that men and women were incapable of close platonic relationships, describing his long-term friendships with two women as the one constant factor in his life, without which he might well have been lost in despair.[77]

Sublimation

The relationship with a friend described by the man above would have been regarded by psychologists as offering a way of sublimating the sex drive, an idea commonly recommended to unmarried people. Here sex energy was regarded as a 'source of power to carry on lines of activity that are not all related to the force from which they draw part of their motive and strength', examples being friendships, religion, work or other kinds of creative activity. US sociologist Ernest R. Groves saw sublimation as necessary for a 'multitude of young women and a sizeable group of men' but stressed that it was more likely to be a 'continuous programme' for women, since for men marriage was a virtual certainty, even though for economic reasons they might be forced to delay it. For such women devotion to business, painting, art or literature might drive out the consciousness of sex and provide psychic relief. But a more successful method was often to substitute another relationship for a sexual one, for example with friends, other people's children (an idea explored in later chapters) or parents. However, he noted the danger of repressed sexual feelings in such relationships leading to fixation.[78]

Hutton argued that because sublimation was in the main an unconscious process rooted in early childhood, it could have negative aspects, particularly if sexual and emotional energy became concentrated into one obsession or compulsive form of behaviour, such as excessive religious observance and zeal or doting on a pet. In such cases, the only practical remedy was to '*distribute* this emotional energy into more and more varied interests', and though she recognised that this was difficult for many, there was 'scope for definite efforts of *will*' (emphasis in the original). [79] Others took a more negative stance. Harding believed that a preoccupation with professional life often involved the repression of love and hid 'a deeply buried sense of inferiority and unfulfilment',[80] while Smith quoted the social psychologist Kimball Young (in Young's *Personality and the Problems of Adjustment* (1940)), who believed there was 'always a physiological and psychological price to be paid for her [the single woman's] sublimation'.[81] It was also a class-based concept, as the US doctor and lecturer Ira Wile pointed out by asking 'What is the sublimating content of domestic and personal service in which two-thirds of the 3,166,603 female workers were not married? Are the lives of laundresses, practical nurses, cooks and waitresses happily chaste in thought and deed?'[82]

It is difficult to know how far single people themselves understood the concept of sublimation or saw their work, relationships and other activities in that light, but it is clear that for some men and women who never married 'fixation' on an alternative love object such as a pet brought solace and respite from loneliness. My interviewee Doreen (born 1911) described her love for the pigs on the family farm, which had given her the affection her father had denied her, while an MO single male correspondent (born 1932) felt the strongest, most long-lasting love he was capable of feeling was for a dog that died in 1959.[83] Another MO contributor, who kept a daily diary during the 1940s, and who was familiar with the work of the psychologist Esther Harding, described her feelings for her cats in terms of transferred affection:

> Each one becomes a friend with a distinct individuality, and the loss each time is a deeply personal one. No one else ever replaces that person exactly but new personalities help you to forget your grief at the loss of others. Living would be quite unbearable if you could not transfer your affections in this way.[84]

Same-sex Relationships

Close emotional and/or physical relationships with member of the same sex were more problematic and sometimes regarded as a danger to marriage. Since the politics of homosexuality in this period have been extensively analysed by historians elsewhere,[85] my discussion of this subject relates to friendships and partnerships between unmarried people rather than on homoerotic identities and practices more broadly.

The problems for men were a legacy of the Criminal Law Amendment Act in 1885 (often known as the blackmailer's charter), which resulted in suspicion being cast on close male friendships.[86] The competing models and explanations offered by sexologists and psychoanalysts seeking to understand the nature of homosexuality did little to alleviate fears and anxieties about public opinion and the possibility of press exposure. However, interviews carried out during the 1970s with homosexual men who reached adulthood between 1910 and 1940 suggest that in practice such anxieties coexisted with a range of different sexual strategies, ranging from abstinence to integration into (usually secret) gay subcultures to the use of male prostitutes.[87]

Bachelors of all social classes living in same-sex living partnerships, whether platonic or homosexual, were particularly at risk of exposure, and discretion had to be exercised if they were to avoid becoming objects of public scrutiny. For economic reasons, however, such partnerships were probably rarer amongst working-class bachelors, most of whom remained living with relatives or in lodgings. Yet here too partnerships were not unknown. For example, records of the New Survey show bachelors aged fifty-two and forty living together in a one-bedroom flat in Deptford, one employed as a labourer and the other with no other source of income in what appears to be the role of a housewife.[88] The suspicion that these kinds of domestic arrangements might have aroused is suggested by another record of a single male café proprietor and his manager, both in their forties, living at the same address. In this latter case, situated in a much wealthier area of town, the enumerator made a special note establishing the economic nature of their relationship. 'Mr D resides at this address with Mr W and acts as manager at salary set out on other side of the card. Both men are bachelors'.[89]

Views of these kinds of relationships from the inside offer rather different viewpoints. One of Porter and Week's informants, who had been a sergeant in the army (born 1892), spoke about his seven-year partnership with a plasterer during the 1920s as being 'just like a wife to come home to'. Yet because both men were working, they maintained an egalitarian regime, atypical of most marriages at that time, sharing household chores and cooking. It is also clear that few people who knew them well would have been in much doubt about the nature of their partnership, with the couple believing that friends and family didn't know 'but had a very good suspicion'. And they felt confident enough to declare 'as long as we love each other what's it got to do with other people'.[90] Another man from a middle-class background (born 1897), who worked as a consulting engineer and was described as a 'pillar of his community', described a mixture of private tolerance and intolerance of his long-term living partnership. The parents of this man's friend had suggested that he move in with their son and had treated him like a son-in-law, yet his own father was horrified and had advised him not to tell his mother.

Women's partnerships did not escape criticism, but because lesbianism was not illegal, suspicions were focused less directly on sexual activity and more on physical difference and emotional abnormality. Nineteenth-century writers had largely denied the possibility or avoided the subject of erotic love between women, enabling a concealment of women's passion from the public gaze with 'equivocations and silences',[91] but by the early twentieth century, the focus of concern centred increasingly on the erotic element of these friendships. This shift can be linked to the creation of a new framework for understanding the nature of same-sex erotic relationships by Havelock Ellis, which included both men and women. Ellis' ideas, set out in his multi-volume *Studies in the Psychology of Sex*, were taken up and recycled during the interwar years by a range of social commentators, and were made available to a wider audience in his handbook for students and medical practitioners, *Psychology of Sex* (1933). His theory, first laid out in *Sexual Inversion* (1897), was that homosexuality was not a disease but rather a congenital condition common to all societies, which, although classified as 'a highly abnormal aberration' and related to minor neurotic conditions, must nevertheless be accepted and tolerated rather than cured or punished. [92] But while Ellis' views were relatively enlightened, his image of the congenital invert as well as his descriptions of acquired inversion in same-sex institutions, drawn from studies of boarding-school friendships and from stories told by his wife and her friends, gave rise to much more negative and perverse views of same-sex relationships, particularly between older and younger women in institutional contexts, which served to underscore the desirability of married rather than single life. His work thus offered a model for representations of dominating, power-hungry lesbians who ruined young girls' lives and put them off marriage, representations which became ubiquitous in advice literature and fiction from the 1920s to the 1950s.[93] As Laura Doan has shown, the trial and subsequent banning of Radclyffe Hall's novel *The Well of Loneliness*, which pleaded for showing tolerance to the invert, brought this knowledge much more into the public domain, creating a new language and visibility for lesbians, shattering the silence that had previously surrounded female homosexuality.[94]

Marguerite Steen's novel *The Wise and Foolish Virgins* (1932) typifies this post-1928 literature, warning of the dangers of an older spinster's influence over a younger woman. Praised by a contemporary reviewer for 'so much realism',[95] it was published in the midst of the Depression at a time when feminism was at a low ebb, and concern about the declining birth rate coupled with high male unemployment made the sight of working women appear particularly threatening. The book featured a spinster teacher, Miss Gatty, who exerted an undesirable influence over Catherine, an ex-pupil attracted to her ordered but narrow, sterile home because of its contrast with her own background of dirt, prostitution and immorality.[96] Although Catherine's attraction to Miss Gatty was desirable in so far as it was a means to separate her from her depraved family, if she was to grow up into a normal young woman, it could not be allowed to continue. The prudishness, sexual frustration and selfish hypocrisy of the teacher were exposed when, on discovering that her servant's sister was a prostitute, Miss Gatty physically and verbally attacked Catherine 'using words – phrases – that she had never known she knew the meaning of'.[97] The solace Catherine eventually found in the arms of a man who would take her away from her past life was presented as a necessary way of enabling her to escape from the unhealthy influence of the spinster, establishing her difference from both the celibate and the prostitute, by showing her as a woman whose sexuality would be contained within a heterosexual union.

Relationships between women were often treated with suspicion by doctors and psychologists, particularly if there was any disparity in age between the two women concerned. Mary Scharlieb, a feminist doctor from the pre-war generation less influenced by the new psychology, suggested in *The Bachelor Woman and her Problems* (1929) that the dangers of obsessive friendships could be overcome if the love of the elder was sufficiently 'motherly'. Hutton disagreed. The seeking of a 'mother substitute' on the one side and 'thwarted maternal instincts' on the other, which produced such 'unequal friendships', could never be 'regarded as a really sane and satisfactory compensation for the normal fulfilment for either of the friends'.[98] Psychologists writing about the care or development of adolescent girls were more likely to see the influence of older women like Miss Gatty as positively harmful. Child psychologist Mary Chadwick in *Adolescent Girlhood* (1932) suggests that friendships of this nature are the products of 'repressed and perverted sexual desire on the part of the older woman'. Such women, who are only capable of gratifying love impulses with other women, 'frequently cherish a good deal of hostility towards men, either consciously or unconsciously. Their attitude will generally become transferred to the girls who come under their influence, by example or precept which will not be advantageous for their future happy or healthy development'.[99]

Similar fears that girls and young women coming under the influence of 'abnormals' might be irretrievably damaged and turned away from marriage and domesticity can be read in psychological, medical and educational literature of the period and intensified still further during the 1940s and 1950s when homosexuality came more strongly under attack by the police.[100]

The virulence of these attacks undermined the female culture which originally enabled middle-class single women to create spaces in which they could operate away from their families without overt criticism. In forming communities modelled upon the bourgeois family,[101] they had offered girls and younger women in their care a place of safety and familiarity. However, by maintaining certain occupations as women-only spheres of influence, limited through marriage bars to unmarried women, a space had also been created in which relationships between women had flourished and could be valued more highly than the marital bond. These relationships had more difficulty in surviving the 'aggressively married and heterosexual' climate of the interwar and post-war years, when women were increasingly being defined in terms of their sexuality rather than their moral authority. That many commentators considered all-female environments, such as women's colleges and boarding schools, a threat to the institution of marriage is all too clear from the literature of the period.[102]

Yet not all psychologists were critical of same-sex relationships. If they were set up on an equal basis, Hutton and Harding saw them as generally positive, regarding a home made by two women friends as a much more satisfactory alternative than hostels, lodgings or the child-like position adopted in the parental residence. Hutton maintained that although a single woman could sublimate one part of her normal instincts, that of motherhood, through work such as teaching and nursing, this could not meet all her needs: 'both her mating as well as her maternal instincts have to be taken into account, understood, made use of and controlled, if her personal contacts with her own sex are to do anything to alleviate her loneliness, and offer her some substitute for wifehood and mother-hood'.[103]

These women were even more atypical in endorsing sexual relation-ships under certain circumstances between mature women, even though in Harding's view such homosexual friendships should be regarded as 'a transitional phase of civilisation'. She regarded unmarried women as often 'the most vital and enterprising, the ones with the greatest intelligence and initiative', and stressed the unprecedented importance of friendship amongst this class of women.[104] Yet such friendships could only ever be regarded as 'substitutes' for marriage. Hutton, perhaps because she had found a new confidence in her own lesbian identity in the years after the *Well of Loneliness* trial,[105] astutely recognised that two women setting up house together lacked all social support and got 'nothing comparable to the hopeful start of every normal marriage'.[106]

The lack of social support for women's partnerships meant that although they were common throughout our period and aroused little surprise or overt comment, neither their emotional nor practical value was usually discussed in public by the women themselves. Personal papers were often destroyed and caution was exercised about saying too much lest their friendships be ridiculed or stigmatised. Susan Pedersen, in her insightful and moving biography of Eleanor Rathbone, explores the tragic paradox which can be found in the work and partnerships of many other single women at this time. In order for Rathbone to pursue her lifetime goal of honouring and giving adequate financial compensation for the work of wives and mothers, she both had to 'avoid her own mother's fate and escape her own family's grasp'. Yet her friend Elizabeth Macadam, who embodied the ideal of female autonomy and played a crucial part in enabling Rathbone to achieve these goals, was determined that her own role should be erased from the public record. Macadam shared

Rathbone's life for more than forty years, pursuing her own career in social work and taking care of her friend both practically and emotionally in a relationship which brought both women 'real emotional fulfilment'. Yet she insisted that their relationship was left out of the story in Mary Stock's biography of her friend and ensured that her own correspondence with Rathbone would be burned after her death. Stocks, however, did not entirely concur with Macadam's demands. She describes the beginning of Rathbone's relationship with Macadam as 'a momentous development which bears no date' and invokes the marriage ceremony by calling her 'the friend and companion of Eleanor's existence until death did them part, and at no subsequent period was Eleanor lonely'.[107]

A similar caution pervades an edited collection of letters from a teacher, E. E. Lawrence, to her friend M. F. S., which was published by the latter under the title You Will Remember (1933). The two women lived and worked together as co-principals of a private girls' boarding school from 1900 until 1929, when Lawrence died, writing to each other on every day that they were not in each other's company. While a few clues as to the strength of their partnership can be gleaned from entries which mention the frustrations of the postal service delaying letters during the coal strike, and frequent references to 'sharing', which are often in capitals or inverted commas, the editor herself remains silent, nameless and largely invisible within the narrative.[108]

Evidence of the nature of working-class women's partnerships is even scarcer, though the New Survey records reveal a number of single women living together in households in which income was pooled and in some cases bedrooms shared. Some of these were working women, some were unemployed, while others were living on income from tenancies, and in many cases, neither woman was clearly designated as household head, making them appear to be egalitarian partnerships not dissimilar to a companionate marriage. A waitress and a book-keeper in their forties living together in Chelsea (both unemployed) described themselves as 'just dragging along and did not know how they were existing', and the interviewer noted disapprovingly that 'both women smelled strongly of drink'.[109] By contrast, the economic relationship is made clear between two women living together in Hampstead who ran a small shop and tea-house, making six pounds between them, described as 'an excellent business for such small premises... patronised by middle-class people in the neighbourhood'.[110] However, in the absence of any personal written testimony, it is impossible to know what such domestic arrangements really meant or what their emotional or physical basis was.

The Second World War offered increased opportunities for gay and lesbian relationships to flourish, in the forces or in other war work. Although acts of indecency between males carried the penalty of court martial, in practice this was used only for the most blatant indiscretions.[111] A loosening of social and sexual restrictions may also be reflected in positive representations of spinster partnerships in some British films, particularly those focusing on the role of women in the war. For example, in Powell and Pressburger's film, *A Canterbury Tale* (1944), a woman taking the male role in running a farm with her sister raises doubts about marriage by telling a land girl that she hadn't married because she didn't want to live in 'a long street with every house a different sort of sadness in it'. And in Frank Launder's melodrama *2000 Women* (1944), two middle-aged spinsters in a French internment camp are shown having an intimate relationship which included at one point sharing a bed, while their removal to a punishment camp is accompanied by a chorus of 'For they are jolly good fellows' from the other inmates.[112]

But while both lesbian and gay oral histories often represent the war as a golden age, 'when all one's gay friends appeared in the most gorgeous uniforms' and periods in the forces facilitated the development of short- and long-term same-sex partnerships, it became harder for men openly to express love for other men or women for other women during the uncom- promisingly heterosexual climate of the 1950s. For men living in London there were still recognised gay venues, such as the gallery in the Sadlers Wells theatre, and partners could also be found through carefully coded advertisements in the *New Statesman* for bachelors to share houses.[113] And for women, *The Well of Loneliness*, read illicitly during the 1930s and 1940s and finally released for publication in 1949, offered a way of recognising themselves and others as lesbian, reducing feelings of isolation, although some women found it hard to identify with the 'short back and sided male suited' lesbian identity it promoted.[114]

Yet oral history interviews also indicate that where single men and women were isolated from gay subcultures it was difficult for them to make sense of feelings and desires which were never discussed in public. Meg (born 1902) described her shock when a woman approached her and gave her *The Well of Loneliness* to read, because she had not known what lesbianism was, while Rona (born 1930) spoke of her difficulty as a young adult in acknowledging her feelings towards other women whom she feared might not reciprocate or understand them, and also her need to escape from men because she could not explain why she was not attracted to them.[115]

Homosexuality was often still associated with mental abnormality and believed to be contagious during the post-war years, with the number of prosecutions spiralling rapidly upwards. Fears of abnormality or longings not to be described as abnormal were expressed by a number of single people in the 1949 'Little Kinsey' survey.[116] But by the end of the 1950s, some moves had been made towards greater acceptance of 'an unfortunate condition', whatever the causes, with increasing pressure from gay men to reform the law.[117] Thus, when in 1956–7 (around the time that the Wolfenden Report recommended that homosexual acts between consenting adults in private should be decriminalised) Lionel was treated for clinical depression, he was asked by the psychiatrist if he was homosexual, because at that time 'the usual suggestion [was] that the orientation may be a cause of nervous trouble'. Yet Lionel himself was far from convinced this was the case and was 'baffled' by advice that he should sublimate his sexual urges into some kind of activity, even though he did not become fully sexually active until the mid-1960s. Rona also sought help from psychiatrists during the late 1950s but her experience had a happier outcome, enabling her to feel more comfortable with her sexuality. In the late 1950s, she joined a Neurotics Anonymous group and was subsequently introduced by another member to the Gateways Club, a well-known lesbian venue that had been in existence since the 1930s, where she could at last feel at home.

Each of these 'solutions' to celibacy was opposed to and regarded as inferior to sex within marriage. Masturbation and sublimation were poor substitutes for marital sex; heterosexual and homosexual relationships outside marriage were undesirable and at times dangerous substitutes. Yet the paradox that both Harding and Holtby recognised was that relation-ships outside marriage were often more satisfying and 'alive' than many marriages, and offered a relief from the stifling exclusivity of conjugality. Lionel understood his function was to provide that relief in the multiple (and in most cases long-term) sexual liaisons he had with married men, which they hid from their wives. B. Charles, writing in 1945, may have had similar experiences: in his MO diary he stated repeatedly that he thought most men had homosexual desires or experiences, and that the reason for the frequent savage sentences for sex offences was that 'the judge who tries the case … is a bit jealous that HE hadn't done the same'.[118]

It was not only sex or intimacy that could not be contained within marriage but also the production of children. In the next chapter, I look at the consequences of the exclusion of unmarried men and women rom legitimate parenthood.

Notes

1   Vera Brittain, *Halcyon or the Future of Monogamy* (London: Kegan Paul, Trench and Trubner, 1929).

2   Vera Brittain, *Chronicle of Friendship: Vera Brittain's Diary of the Thirties* ed. Alan Bishop A (ed.), (London: Gollancz, 1986), entries for 29 May and 25 August 1932, pp. 45 and 79.

3   *Ibid.*, 16 and 17 June 1932, pp. 52–4.

4   This relationship and its possible lesbian nature have been much discussed. See Pam Johnson, "'The Best Friend that Life Has Given Me": Does Winifred Holtby have a Place in Lesbian History?' in Lesbian History Group (eds), *Not a Passing Phase: Recovering Lesbians in History 1840–1985* (London: Women's Press, 1985), pp. 141–57; Jean E. Kennard, *Vera Brittain and Winifred Holtby: A Working Partnership* (London: University Press of New England, 1989); Clay, *British Women Writers*; Marion Shaw, *The Clear Stream: A Life of Winifred Holtby* (London: Virago, 1999); Deborah Gorham: *Vera Brittain: A Feminist Life* (Oxford: Blackwell, 1996).

5   Brittain attributed this latter identity to Bentley but Holtby vehemently rejected it. See Winifred Holtby, *Women* (London: John Lane, Bodley Head, 1934), pp. 131–2.

6   Esther Harding, *The Way of All Women* (London: Longman, 1934), p. 218, describes promiscuous women in these terms. For reflections on 'sowing wild oats' in the context of 1920s' England see 'A Teacher's Life' in Kevin Porter and Jeffrey Weeks, *Between the Acts: Lives of Homosexual Men 1885–1967* (London: Routledge, 1991), p. 42.

7   See Lesley Hall, *Hidden Anxieties: Male Sexuality 1900–1950* (Cambridge: Polity, 1991).

8   Weeks and Porter carried out life-history interviews with gay men in the late 1970s but published their accounts only more than ten years later, when many of the men had died. See also Matt Houlbrook, *Queer London: Space, Identities and Male Practices, 1918–1957* (Chicago: University of Chicago Press, 2005). On the creation of the homosexual 'closet' in nineteenth century Britain, see Harry Cocks, *Nameless Offences: Homosexual Desire in the Nineteenth Century* (London: I. B. Tauris, 2003). For the twentieth century see also Hugh David, *On Queer Street: A Social History of Homosexuality, 1895–1995* (London: HarperCollins, 1997).

9   For important recent work in this area, see Laura Doan, *Fashioning Sapphism: The Origins of a Modern English Lesbian Culture* (New York: Columbia University Press, 2000, and Clay, *British Women Writers*.

10 This debate is discussed in Gail Braybon, 'Winners or Losers: Women's Role in the War Story' in Gail Braybon (ed.), *Evidence, History and the Great War* (Oxford: Berghahn Books, 2003).

11 See Holden, 'Imaginary Widows'.

12 Anti-spinster rhetoric was voiced by commentators from many different backgrounds, including the birth control pioneer Marie Stopes in *Enduring Passion* (1928) and *Sex and the Young* (1926), eugenicist Arabella Keneally in *Feminism and Sex Extinction* (1920), philosopher Bertrand Russell in *Marriage and Morals* (1929), writer and ex-teacher Clemence Dane in *Regiment of Women* (1917) and *The Women's Side* (1926), and child psychologist Mary Chadwick in *Adolescent Girlhood* (1932). For discussions of this subject see Jeffreys, *The Spinster and her Enemies*; Oram, *Women Teachers*. A collection of useful primary sources on lesbian history

can be found in Alison Oram and Annmarie Turnbull, *The Lesbian History Source-book: Love and Sex between Women in Britain from 1780 to 1970* (London: Routledge, 2001).

13 By the 1920s, Freudian ideas were already well known amongst the middle classes. Alison Oram, 'Repressed and Thwarted, or Bearer of the New World? The Spinster in Interwar Discourses, *Women's History Review*, 1:3 (1992), p. 419; Dean Rapp, 'The Early Discovery of Freud by the British General Educated Public, 1912–19', *Social History of Medicine*, 3:2 (1990). For a discussion of the influence of Freud's ideas and the difficulties of connecting them to a history of physical experience, see Hera Cook, *The Long Sexual Revolution: English Women, Sex and Contraception 1800–1973* (Oxford: Oxford University Press, 2004), pp. 167–8.

14 Most famously in Marie Stopes, *Married Love*, which sold 2,000 copies within two weeks of publication in 1918, and went through seven editions in the first year. Richard Soloway, *Birth Control and the Population Question in England, 1877–1930* (Chapel Hill, NC: North Carolina University Press, 1982), p. 211.

15 See for example the 'Spinster by One' in the *Freewoman*, 23 November 1911.

16 Cook, *The Long Sexual Revolution*, p. 196.

17 T. H. Van de Velde, *Ideal Marriage: Its Physiology and Technique*, 1926, trans. Stella Browne (New York: Random House, 1930), p. 2.

18 Lesley Hall, 'Feminist Reconfigurations of Heterosexuality in the 1920s', in Lucy Bland and Laura Doan (eds), *Sexology in Culture: Labelling Bodies and Desires* (Chicago: University of Chicago Press/Cambridge: Polity, 1998), p. 146.

19 Marie Stopes, *Married Love*, 1918 (London: G. P. Putnam's Sons, 1930), p. 78.

20 August Bebel, *Woman in the Past, Present and Future*, 1883 (London: Reeves, undated edition), p. 47. On celibacy see Andreas Hall, '"May the Doctor Advise Extramarital Intercourse?": Medical Debates on Sexual Abstinence in Germany, c. 1900' in Roy Porter and Mikuláš Teich (eds), *Sexual Knowledge, Sexual Science: The History of Attitudes to Sexuality* (Cambridge: Cambridge University Press, 1994).

21 Bertrand Russell, *Marriage and Morals* (London: George Allen and Unwin, 1929), pp. 212 and 221–2.

22 Charlotte Haldane, *Motherhood and its Enemies* (London: Chatto and Windus, 1927), pp. 125–57.

23 Havelock Ellis, *Psychology of Sex*, 1933 (London: William Heineman, fifth edition, 1939). This was a distillation of his seven-volume *Studies in the Psychology of Sex* into a more popular introductory book.

24 Jeffrey Meyers (ed.), *George Orwell: The Critical Heritage* (London: Routledge and Kegan Paul, 1975), p. 10.

25 George Orwell, *The Clergyman's Daughter*, 1935 (Harmondsworth: Penguin, 1975), pp. 76–7.

26 Hall, *Hidden Anxieties*, pp. 27–8.

27 Welcome Library for the History and Understanding of Medicine, London, Archives and Manuscripts, Marie Stopes Papers (hereafter MSP), PP/MCS/A166, MCD to MCS, 1920; A70, JD to MCS, 1919; A71,GHD to MCS, 1929; A216, RHS to MCS, 1922.

28 Sybil Neville-Rolfe, 'Sex Delinquency', in *NSLLL* vol. 4, p. 295. See also Jeffrey Weeks, *Sex, Politics and Society: The Regulation of Sexuality since 1800* (London: Longman, second edition, 1989), p. 207; Cate Haste, *Rules of Desire: Sex in Britain: World War I to the Present* (London: Chatto and Windus, 1992), ch. 4.

29 *Daily Herald*, 23 February 1925. See also *Manchester Guardian*, 21 May, 1926 and 30 January, 1935.

30 June Rose, *Marie Stopes and the Sexual Revolution* (London: Faber and Faber, 1992), p. 118.

31 MSP, PP/MCS/A166.

32 *Ibid.*, A218, AHS to MCS, 1920.

33 Joseph Bristow, 'Symonds' History, Ellis's Heredity', in Bland and Doan, *Sexology in Culture*, p. 85.

34 Cook, *The Long Sexual Revolution*, p. 178.

35 MSP, PP/MCS/A48, EAB to MCS, 14 March 1922.

36 A British production by G. B. Samuelson.

37 Annette Kuhn, *Cinema, Censorship and Sexuality, 1909–1925* (London: Routledge, 1989), pp. 55 and 63–4.

38 Interview with Molly, 23 September 1993.

39 *The Times*, 25 August 25, p. 9d, 26 August, 1921, p. 13c, 31 August 1921, p. 6g, and 5 September 1921, pp. 4c and 10a.

40 MSP, PP/MCS/A43, DMB to MC, 18 October 1921.

41 Hall, 'Feminist Reconfigurations', pp. 136–7.

42 Holtby, *Women*, pp. 130–2.

43 MCS to MM, 1922, in Ruth Hall (ed.), *Dear Dr Stopes: Sex in the 1920s* (London: André Deutsch, 1975), p. 175; MSP, PP/MCS/A218, AHS, 1920.

44 Ellis, *Psychology of Sex*, pp. 102–14.

45 *Ibid.*, pp. 111–12. See also Laura Hutton, *The Single Woman and her Emotional Problems* (London: Bailliere, Tindall and Cox, 1935), p. 70; Leonora Eyles, *Unmarried but Happy* (London: Gollancz, 1947), p. 104.

46 M. B. Smith, *The Single Woman of Today: Her Problems and Adjustment* (London: Watts, 1951), pp. 120–1.

47 Eyles, *Unmarried but Happy*, p. 104.

48 Hutton, *The Single Woman and her Emotional Problems*, pp. 67–70. Laqueur sees this advice as evidence of female masturbation being viewed as a regression to an immature sexual phase, while for men the penis 'remains invariant as the source of genital pleasure': Thomas Laqueur, *Solitary Sex: A Cultural History of Masturbation* (New York: Zone Books, 2003), pp. 393–4.

49 Hutton, *The Single Woman and her Emotional Problems*, p. 77.

50 MSP, PP/MCS/A71, GHD, 1929; A70, FED, 26/6/29; A107, JHG, 24/7/27.

51 Laqueur, *Solitary Sex*, p. 375.

52 MSP, PP/MCS/A218, DS, undated but probably 1923.

53 Smith, *The Single Woman of Today*, p. 120.

54 MO Archive, Sussex University, Sexual Behaviour 1939–50, Box 12, Form A9/2 Questionnaire (Panel D94/3) 1949, 12/12/B, index 458, ref. 361.

55 Haire was a prominent member of the British Sexology Society, whose views on the subject of birth control were often quoted by journalists, for example *Manchester Guardian*, 21 May 1926. See Weeks, *Sex, Politics and Society*, pp. 184–5; Jeffreys, *The Spinster and Her Enemies*, p. 159; Roy Porter and Lesley Hall, *The Facts of Life: The Creation of Sexual Knowledge in Britain, 1650–1950* (London: Yale University Press, 1995), p. 210.

56 Russell, *Marriage and Morals*; Norman Haire, *Hymen or the Future of Marriage*

(London: Kegan, Paul, Trench, Trubner, 1927); Judge Ben B. Lindsay and Wainwright Evans, *The Companionate Marriage* (London: Brentano's, 1928).

57 Cook, *The Long Sexual Revolution*, p. 183.

58 Rolfe, 'Sex Delinquency', p. 296.

59 Sybil Neville-Rolfe, *Why Marry?* (London: Faber and Faber, 1935), p. 42.

60 Hutton, *The Single Woman and her Emotional Problems*, pp. 82–4.

61 Esther Harding, *The Way of All Women* (London: Longmans, 1934), pp. 252–69.

62 Cook, *The Long Sexual Revolution*, p. 184.

63 Penny Summerfield and Nicole Crockett, '"You Weren't Taught that with the Welding': Lessons in Sexuality in the Second World War', *Women's History Review*, 1:3 (1992). See also Gail Braybon and Penny Summerfield, *Out of the Cage: Women's Experiences in Two World Wars* (London: Routledge and Kegan Paul, 1987).

64 *Report of the Committee on Homosexual Offences and Prostitution*, Cmd. 247 (London: HMSO, 1957), p. 116.

65 Stanley, *Sex Surveyed*, p. 36.

66 Cook, *The Long Sexual Revolution*, pp. 184–5.

67 Stephen Bourne, *Brief Encounters: Lesbians and Gays in British Cinema, 1930–1971* (London: Cassell, 1996), p. 78.

68 Smith, *The Single Woman of Today*, pp. 38–40.

69 MO, Close Relationships File (1990), H670.

70 For a discussion of this film see Janet Fink and Katherine Holden, 'Pictures from the Margins of Marriage: Representations of Spinsters and Single Mothers in the Mid-Victorian Novel, Interwar Hollywood Melodrama and British Film of the 1950s and 1960s', *Gender and History*, 11:2 (1999). See also chapter 6.

71 *London Opinion*, May 1939.

72 Lynne Segal, *Slow Motion: Changing Masculinities, Changing Men* (London: Virago, second edition, 1997), pp. 18–20.

73 Froy, *How to Avoid Matrimony*, inside cover and p. 7.

74 On exercise for women, see Jill Julius Matthews, '"They Had Such a Lot of Fun": The Women's League of Health and Beauty', *History Workshop Journal*, 30 (1990).

75 *London Opinion*, 31 May, 1930, p. 211 and 20 September 1930, p. 27, Peter Williams, 'A Marriage Has Been Arranged', *London Opinion*, January 1953, pp. 21–4.

76 MO, Close Relationships File, H828.

77 MO, Close Relationships File, G2192.

78 Ernest R. Groves, 'Sex Psychology of the Unmarried Adult', in Ira Wile (ed.), *The Sex Life of the Unmarried Adult* (London: George Allen and Unwin, 1934), p. 110–11. Groves was a pioneer educator on sex, marriage and the family.

79 Hutton, *The Single Woman and her Emotional Problems*, pp. 144 and 146–7.

80 Harding, *The Way of All Women*, p. 254.

81 Smith, *The Single Woman of Today*, p. 127.

82 Wile, *The Sex Life*, p. 40.

83 MO, Close Relationships File, H828.

84 Garfield, *Hidden Lives*, p. 368.

85 For example Jeffrey Weeks, *Coming Out: Homosexual Politics from the Nineteenth Century to the Present* (London: Quartet Books, 1977); David, *On Queer Street*; Houlbrook, *Queer London*; Doan, *Fashioning Sapphism*.

86 A gay man writing an MO diary referred to the unfairness created by this anomaly in

the law. Garfield, *Hidden Lives*, pp. 142 and 320–1.

87 Weeks, *Sex, Politics and Society*, p. 220; Porter and Weeks, *Between the Acts*. See also David, *On Queer Street*.

88 NSLLL, Deptford (working-class) file 433.

89 NSLLL, Hampstead (middle-class) record 0002.

90 Weeks and Porter, *Between the Acts*, pp. 7–8

91 Vicinus, *Intimate Friends*, p. 202.

92 Ellis, *Psychology of Sex*, p. 188 and ch. 5.

93 Vicinus, *Intimate Friends*, p. 202.

94 Doan, *Fashioning Sapphism*, p. 194.

95 Eric Linklater, 'Review of Marguerite Steen, *The Wise and Foolish Virgins*', *Listener*, 18 May 1932.

96 Marguerite Steen, *The Wise and Foolish Virgins* (London: Gollancz, 1932), p. 180.

97 *Ibid.*, p. 272.

98 Scharlieb, *The Bachelor Woman*, p. 51; Hutton, *The Single Woman and her Emotional Problems*, p. 17.

99 Chadwick, *Adolescent Girlhood*, pp. 256–7. See also p. 237.

100 Neville-Rolfe, *Why Marry?*; Phyllis Blanchard, *The Care of the Adolescent Girl* (London: Kegan Paul, Trench and Trubner, 1921); Anthony Ludovici, *Woman: A Vindication* (London: Constable, 1923); Keneally, *Feminism and Sex Extinction*; Haldane, *Motherhood and its Enemies*. See also Oram, *Women Teachers*; Jeffreys, *The Spinster and her Enemies*; Sheila Jeffreys, 'Sex Reform and Anti-Feminism in the 1920s' in Sheila Jeffreys, *The Sexual Dynamics of History* (London: Pluto, 1983).

101 Elizabeth Edwards, *Women in Teacher Training Colleges, 1900–1960: A Culture of Femininity* (London: Routledge, 2001); Vicinus, *Independent Women*.

102 Vicinus, *Independent Women*, pp. 12 and 41; Oram, 'Repressed and Thwarted', p. 421.

103 Hutton, *The Single Woman and her Emotional Problems*, p. 8.

104 Harding, *The Way of all Women*, pp. 132 and 104.

105 Clay, *British Women Writers*, ch. 5.

106 Hutton, *The Single Woman and her Emotional Problems*, pp. 103–4 and pp. 40–1. See also Oram, 'Repressed and Thwarted', pp. 421–2.

107 Stocks, *Eleanor Rathbone*, pp. 8 and 58; Pederson, 'Eleanor Rathbone and the Politics of Conscience, pp. 4–5 and 167.

108 *You Will Remember* (London: Oxford University Press, 1933), pp. 264–9.

109 NSLLL, Chelsea (working-class) file 178.

110 NSLLL, Hampstead (middle-class), Card 0842. See also Cards 0482, 0062, and 0120; Deptford (middle-class) cards 1230 and 1224; Deptford (working-class) files 460, and 466.

111 Haste, *Rules of Desire*, p. 118.

112 Bourne, *Brief Encounters*, pp. 68–9.

113 Porter and Weeks, *Between the Acts*, p. 112.

114 Rachel O'Rourke, *Reflecting on The Well of Loneliness* (London: Routledge, 1989), pp. 17–41; Hall Carpenter Archives Group, *Inventing Ourselves: Lesbian Life Stories* (London: Routledge, 1989), p. 47. See also Doan, *Fashioning Sapphism*, on the creation of this identity.

115 Meg told me this during a second, unrecorded interview, not having felt confident enough to speak on the record.

116 MO, Sexual Behaviour 1939–50: Box 12, Form A9/2 Questionnaire (Panel D94/3)

12/12/B, ref. 440, index no. 4215 (male aged 23) and 12/12/A, ref. 162, index no. 0161 (female aged 38); Box 9, 12/9/G 9, Public Habit sample, Form A9/4 (male aged 40).

117 Weeks, *Coming Out*, p. 166.

118 Garfield, *Hidden Lives*, pp. 141–2.

5

Mad or bad?
Parenthood outside marriage

As one woman, not herself a trained [social] worker, put it 'In my young days these women were thought of as "bad women". You were sorry for them, you tried to help, but they had to be made to realise they'd gone wrong before you could help them go right. Now it seems that they're all mad, not bad. They can't help themselves. There's no free will any more, no point in moral effort. If you're born to have an illegitimate baby, have it you will.'[1]

I had no desire to marry but I had a fairly rampant sexual urge … I have wondered from time to time what happened to her and the child, it hasn't been a major worry in my life. In any case, I'm sure I would be bad news if I suddenly turned up.[2]

Introduction

THIS CHAPTER EXAMINES UNMARRIED parenthood from the 1910s to the 1960s viewed through the lenses of social policy, popular culture and personal testimony. It explores the practical and emotional impact of the increasing involvement of the state and voluntary organisations in rescuing and reforming the 'unmarried mother', and the complex and often contradictory relationships that arose between women and men who had children outside marriage, the children who were named as illegitimate, the families who sheltered or rejected them, and the professional and voluntary workers who attempted to regulate their lives.

The extent to which parenthood was uncontained by marriage in this period is suggested by the frequency with which people today claim illegitimacy as a family secret, often discovered in the process of researching their own personal histories.[3] Illegitimate births emerged unexpectedly during the research for this book, particularly in oral history interviews.

Women I had assumed to be childless were found to have children; one man (quoted above) confessed to not knowing the fate of a child he had fathered out of wedlock; and several lifelong single men and women had concealed their own illegitimacy. These personal narratives are set against accounts of legislative change and shifts in social and public policy in order to bring out diversity in individual experience and to show the significance of family, community, voluntary or state support systems. Both personal and public stories are also set in the context of a range of images, beliefs and ideas about single motherhood and fatherhood voiced in advice literature, novels and films of the period.

The perceived necessity of regulating unmarried parenthood suggests the fragility of the institution of marriage in the first half of the twentieth century. Yet there has been relatively little research into public policy in this area, with no in-depth study for the first half of the century.[4] We know even less about experiences of parenthood outside marriage, other than anecdotal accounts which indicate unexplored depths of pain, shame and concealment. For an unmarried woman to bear a child brought her in touch with a central aspect of being female, but like the childless spinster she remained on the margins of society, positioned outside the normative boundaries of womanhood.[5] Fear of being shamed led some women to give up their children or hide their illegitimate status by posing as an aunt, older sister or adoptive mother,[6] and although it was easier for unmarried men to evade the responsibilities of fatherhood, they too were constrained by the necessity of concealing evidence of their child's paternity. While most unmarried parents eventually married,[7] it has been more problematic in this chapter to separate those who never married from those who did. For both groups, bearing or fathering a child at a time when they were not married was a source of shame and often secrecy which meant that (whatever their subsequent history) they were less likely to have openly named themselves as that child's mother or father or to have played an active part in its upbringing.

Statistical surveys give limited help in discovering the number of lifelong single men and women who fathered or bore children. While the Registrar-General breaks down illegitimate births to women by age, it is impossible to discover how many of those women remained single. Equally, although we can chart illegitimate births in relation to the number of unmarried women and also discover the per centage of all registered live births that were outside marriage, some of these births were to married women whose husbands had refused to accept paternity. In addition, many mothers unmarried at the time of their child's birth were actually cohabiting (often with the father) and may have married after the event. It was only when illegitimacy began to be investigated in the late 1940s and 1950s that women in these different situations were counted, albeit only in small-scale studies. But, as Janet Fink has argued, such studies are problematic, since they drew mainly on the relatively small number of cases who were known to voluntary organisations, and could not follow up women with illegitimate children who evaded discovery or 'who simply melted into their surrounding social or familial network'.[8] The census was of limited help in this respect since, until the end of the 1960s, it seriously underestimated the numbers of unmarried mothers living with their families. In three-generation families both the mother and her child often appeared as children of the head of household.[9]

The difficulty of tracing unmarried fathers is even greater. The law tied paternity closely to marriage, and an unmarried man could evade all responsibility if the mother did not name him or if he could prove the mother might have had intercourse with another man at the time of the child's conception.[10] Even if he did acknowledge paternity, he gained paternal rights and a full legal relationship to the child only by marrying the mother.[11] In law, he was described only as a 'putative father'; and if the mother of the child was already married, her husband rather than its natural father had paternal rights. It was not until 1959 that a Legitimacy Act was passed which allowed putative fathers to apply to the courts for access and custody rights.[12] Thus, the law worked in favour of those who avoided being named as father. The lack of a legal relationship, compounded by the stigma of illegitimacy, actively discouraged unmarried men from acknowledging their children and made it difficult to persuade them to pay maintenance. Correspondence with the Home Office in 1927 made it clear that a putative father should not be described as a parent and had no legal liability towards his child other than one which was actually in force by a court order.[13] The 1953 *Report of the Departmental Committee on the Adoption of Children* pointed out the anomaly that only natural fathers subject to affiliation orders were required to give their consent to their child's adoption, while fathers who voluntarily maintained their child (and sometimes also its mother) without an agreement had no such rights.[14]

Linguistic differences implied by the phrases 'to mother' and 'to father' are also important in that they reflect major gender divisions in parenting roles. To become a mother assumes having given birth and to mother a child suggests care and nurturance, but to father a child assumes biological paternity without any expectation of child care. This asymmetry in meaning made men who became fathers less likely to see close relationships with children as part of a masculine identity. Thus, while unmarried mothers were expected to take responsibility for their babies, unmarried fathers could not easily play an active part in childrearing and the pressures on them either to marry the mother or to deny or ignore the existence of their child were strong.

'Fallen women': bad blood and hidden mothers

During the early and mid-twentieth century several conflicting sets of ideas, images and stories relating to single motherhood were in circulation. The oldest of these was the 'fallen woman' who had transgressed sexual boundaries and had to pay for her sin, a belief that still influenced attitudes and policies towards single mothers in the first three decades of the twentieth century and remained influential in some quarters into the 1960s and beyond. The welfare reforms of the post-1906 Liberal government were framed with this image in mind, reinforcing unmarried mothers' outcast status by denying them insured benefits such as maternity or unemployment allowances. This meant that their only eligibility was for an affiliation order to be made from the child's putative father towards its maintenance, and the only statutory provision a place in the workhouse, which usually separated them from their children.[15] By the eve of the First World War, 'fallen women' were increasingly regarded as a source of contamination, and the idea that they should be separated from their communities was given scientific and legal backing. Loose morals were linked with hereditary weakness and this connection helped to shape to the Mental Deficiency Act of 1913, which allowed unmarried mothers to be classified as mentally and morally defective if they had more than one child.[16] If they were in receipt of poor relief when pregnant or at the time of giving birth, from 1927 local authorities were empowered to detain them indefinitely in a secure institution apart from their children, who were generally accommodated in orphanages.[17] However, in practice, the term 'mental defective' was loosely defined and often included mothers who were simply homeless or destitute, on the grounds that costs to the tax payer would be reduced by the mother's institutionalisation and she would be prevented from getting pregnant again.[18]

The deterrent effect of the Mental Deficiency Act was remembered by health visitor Ellen, who explained how it had worked in practice in a Wiltshire workhouse where her father was on the Board of Guardians. In 1927, at the age of eighteen, she had taken a job in the sewing room, where she came into contact with young unmarried mothers whose children had been sent to sex-segregated Homes. This experience had left a deep impression and she stressed the disgrace an illegitimate child would have represented in her own family, but also noted the women inmates' sense of powerlessness and injustice in the face of an uncaring and incomprehensible system:

> I can tell you that they were supposed to be seen by a psychiatrist once a year. He would see forty in a morning. So one girl, I said to her, 'I'm very interested in this. What did they ask you?' She said 'They're daft in there.' They were not stupid these girls. They might be a bit loose … but they hadn't had the chance. One girl was a girl from the circus, a very nice girl. She should never have been locked up, but they were literally locked up. And he [the psychiatrist] said: 'Now you tell me the difference between a sparrow's tail and a cow's tail.' I said: 'what did you say?' She said: [to the psychiatrist]: 'Well if you don't know I'm not going to tell you' which I thought was rather nice. And then that was her there for another year. That was the rule that they had to be seen once a year … They were all there, well I think they were there twenty years … And I was so sorry because I thought, poor things, there all that time with no money, no anything. I don't know if they had any training.

Daisy (born 1908), whose mother had fostered illegitimate babies born during the First World War, suggested it was not only mothers who suffered in such a system but also the babies who had been neglected. She described unmarried mothers in a maternity hospital working in the laundry while the nurses had pushed bottles into the babies' mouths and left them to feed themselves, removing them after a set time, even if the bottles had slipped. Yet mothers could also resist such harsh regimes. One stole milk from the kitchen to feed her baby and later left the hospital to live with Daisy's family, going out to work to support her baby while Daisy's mother cared for it.

This account reminds us of the networks of informal care and support from families and communities which enabled women to escape incarceration. Not all women remained locked up. Some were released by their families, while others, believed to have been reformed, were allowed out initially on licence to go into residential domestic service.[19] However, the main thrust of Ellen's and Daisy's tales reproduces a common turn of the twentieth-century narrative about the harsh treatment of unmarried mothers over the last century. Women who had children outside marriage continued to be treated as 'fallen' until the 1970s, and some remained in institutions until the advent of community care in the 1980s. From the early 1990s, there have been a number of plays, films and TV documentary exposures[20] which have contributed to and helped to shape our collective memory of this subject. Such stories enable us to distance ourselves from our recent history and tend to play down the fact that families, communities and local authorities widely colluded with policies to incarcerate unmarried mothers[21] in the way that Ellen's father had done. He had described the workhouse mothers to Ellen as 'very bad girls' but said nothing about the nature of their crime. These stories also position us as much more enlightened than our predecessors, ignoring the continuing demonisation of young single mothers as irresponsible and delinquent.

While institutional confinement cannot be condoned, the actual number of single mothers receiving poor relief who were in danger of being institutionalised in early twentieth-century England was relatively low, with the majority remaining living within their families and communities.[22] Yet the visible and therefore potentially contaminating presence of unmarried mothers in the community was deeply problematic and productive of anxieties. The evidence of their maternity was perceived as a 'badge of unutterable shame'[23] and believed to have deleterious consequences for the British race. For example, Marie Stopes cited research undertaken by the Eugenics Education Society in her book *Sex and the Young* (1926) which concluded that feeble-mindedness, illegitimacy and pauperism tended to run in definite family strains. The illegitimate child was 'a source of weakness and racial disharmony which is to be deplored and as far as possible prevented', and she believed that 'with a few exceptions … *the illegitimate child is inherently inferior to the legitimate*' (emphasis in the original). Thus, she saw 'a racially subversive tendency' in the actions of 'some well-meaning people who desire chivalrously to protect the unmarried mother and her child'.[24]

In the face of such attitudes, many women felt compelled to hide the evidence of childbirth. Some had their children fostered or adopted by family members or friends while others pretended to be their child's aunt rather than its mother, a strategy which appears to have crossed class divisions. But while many families colluded to conceal the birth of illegitimate children to save them from being exposed and disgraced, such secrets carried costs for all parties. Unmarried women's difficulties in being called mother are matched by their families' fear of being shamed and by the pain felt by children unacknowledged by both mother and father.[25]

Such was the case with David, born in 1910 into a middle-class family. He had been told by his mother, Ida, that she was his aunt, who had adopted him after his parents had died; an ill-conceived and inconsistent story, which involved creating for him a new surname. From his early teens, he had seen through it, but did not reveal his discovery until after his mother's death. In retrospect David recognised that she had been protecting them both from exposure by this strategy, but although he remained in close touch with her throughout her life, such was the stigma attached to illegitimacy that to his lasting regret the fiction that she was his aunt was always preserved between them. Another informant born in the 1920s, who was particularly concerned to remain anonymous and unidentifiable, described the coldness of a grandmother who in old age had felt obliged to bring her up. Like David, she had known her aunt was her mother since her school days and told of her sadness that she had never been acknowledged as her daughter. The degree of secrecy, anger and resentment that such family secrets could engender is suggested by David, who reflected on the pressure his mother must have been under from her parents to get rid of him:

> I mean the credit really, if there is any credit, goes to my mother for not… hiving me off, because in those days really it wasn't a good thing to have an illegitimate child and her mother, my grandmother, disapproved very strongly of me. It's funny that she took it out on me.

The legacy of concealment was such that it was only under cover of anonymity that for the first time these two informants felt able to reveal their stories.

Despite family disapproval, the material resources available to David's mother had shielded him from wider exposure. Nellie, who had given birth to a child in the 1920s, was not so fortunate. For her the stigma of being an unmarried mother remained undiminished, and she still had not told other residents in her retirement Home that the woman who visited her was her daughter. So deep was her anxiety that she expressed concern after the interview that I might sell her story to the newspapers. Nellie's anger was directed both towards her father, who had not allowed her to have any say in what should happen to her child, and towards the working-class village community, who had shamed her. Understandably, she was not willing to reveal much about the circumstances of her daughter's birth, implying that she did not know who the father was. But she expressed deep and lasting resentment towards other women in the village who called her names, particularly as she was convinced many of their children had been fathered by Belgian refugees who had camped there during the First World War. Such narratives highlight the very different experiences of unmarried and married women who had illegitimate children and the extent to which married women could hide the evidence of marital infidelity.

Fictional portrayals of unmarried motherhood in the 1920s did little to ameliorate this bleak picture, serving rather to underscore the shame and retribution attached to unmarried motherhood, by reproducing images of fallen women as either tragic victims or moral reprobates. Mary Webb's novel *Precious Bane* (1924) contains both of these images. Awarded the 'Femina Vie Hereuse' prize for the best work of imagination in prose or verse descriptive of English life, this book was promoted by the prime minister, Stanley Baldwin,[26] and sold three quarters of a million copies during the 1930s, founding the fortunes of its publisher, Jonathan Cape.[27] Set in Napoleonic England, it tells us more about early twentieth-century ideas about marriage, morality and illegitimacy.

The book contrasts sensible, virtuous Prue, who has a hare lip but still ends up marrying the hero, with pretty, coquettish Jancis, who bears a child out of wedlock. After being rejected by the child's father as 'the devil's daughter', Jancis drowns herself and the baby, whose bad blood is suggested by the fact that it had none of the strength and vitality of a normal child.[28] However, the innocent but wronged Jancis is also juxtaposed with Tivvy, who is both morally defective and mentally deficient, 'a poor foolish creature who could hardly mind her own name', but also spiteful and sexually provocative. Tivvy represents the other face of unmarried motherhood, a woman without morals and without shame, who deliberately gets pregnant and threatens to expose her lover as a murderer if he refuses to marry her. Written at a time when Webb's own marriage was not living up to her hopes and dreams, with her husband obsessed with another woman, she assuaged her grief through a triumphant portrayal of physical and romantic love, harking back to the early days of their marriage.[29] But while we watch the heroine's progress from despised spinster to joyful wife, we are also offered stern warnings about the consequences of male greed and lust and the dangers for women of premarital sex.

Maternal love: reforming mothers and saving babies

While ideas about fallen women and bad blood were influential in public policy and family life, they were not the only way of representing single motherhood. By the mid-nineteenth century, the sinful model had already begun to be challenged. Stories stressing the sanctity of motherhood and maternal love became increasingly popular, showing mothers redeemed by sacrificing themselves for their children. These kinds of narratives became a staple of Hollywood films in the 1920s and 1930s,[30] but were also a strong force in twentieth-century social policy, influencing both the state and voluntary groups.

The belief that maternal love and sacrifice would save the child was not itself coherent or unified. As we shall see, some interested parties insisted that the mother should give up her own interest in her child and allow it to be adopted by a 'normal' family. Others argued that middle- and upper-class single women were justified in having children on the grounds of both the sanctity of maternal love and the benefits the offspring of such women would bring to the race. Yet others saw maternal love as a means of reform and argued that for a mother to remain with her child would save her from a second fall and prevent further illegitimate births. In this latter case, she was usually pictured as having been led astray and needing support to bring up her child to be a responsible citizen.

In the face of the falling birth rate, the idea that the child was a national asset and should not have to pay for its mother's sins gained ground with legislators during the interwar years, but they were reluctant to give too much support to mothers in order that costs of illegitimate births to the state should be reduced, and also to counter the perceived threat they represented to marriage and the nuclear family. The National Birth Rate Commission, which published its findings in 1920, suggested that although the numbers of illegitimate children made up for the deficiency of births in wedlock, caused by the voluntary restrictions of married couples, 'it is by no means clear that public opinion has as a whole undergone any fundamental change of attitude towards the unmarried mother, nor are there any signs of such a change coming about in the near future'.[31]

The implementation of the Maternity and Child Welfare Act of 1918, which brought the Ministry of Health into being and made local authorities responsible for the welfare of all expectant mothers and children under five, illustrates this ambivalence. A response both to the higher mortality rate of illegitimate children, publicised during the war, and to general concerns about child health, its provisions reflected a change in focus away from the sinful behaviour of the mother to a preoccupation with the value of the child to the state. Under the Act, local authorities were empowered to give grants to voluntary organisations to increase the provision of residential accommodation for unmarried mothers and also to make the Homes subject to inspection. Yet few local authorities took this responsibility seriously by providing their own Homes, and public expenditure remained low during the interwar years.[32] The continuing marginalisation of unmarried mothers is shown by the denial to those who were employed of free maternity services and of unemployment benefit during their absence from work. Public assistance institutions (former workhouses) were still the most likely places for those without familial support to go, and the survival rate of their babies remained lower than that of legitimate children.[33]

Another way in which it was believed illegitimate children could be saved, their cost to the state reduced and their birth mothers made less visible, was through adoption. Each of these agendas can be read in the congratulations given in Parliament to the promoters of the 1926 Adoption Bill, which gave adoption a legal status for the first time. The hope was expressed that all illegitimate children would now be adopted and that not only they themselves but also their parents would have happier lives.[34] Similar sentiments were expressed by a number of MPs to Miss Florence Horsbrugh, the chair of the 1936 committee to inquire into the methods of adoption societies and agencies.[35] While her chief interest was to prevent abuse and corruption in the adoption process, she was inspired in her cause by her desire to 'give children who start life with a terrible handicap ... the greatest benefit in the world, affection, a happy home and a good upbringing'.[36] By such means, it was hoped illegitimacy could largely disappear as a category. Offering illegitimate children to married couples who could legalise their status not only saved money but also solved the problem the unmarried mother presented in a society which maintained marriage as its central organising principle.

The perceived importance of a child having two parents was hard to counter and even well-known feminists such as the Christian preacher Maud Royden, who was particularly concerned in her ministry with the problems of single women, subscribed to this belief.[37] In her book *Sex and Common-Sense* (1921), she considered the case of the middle-class, childless woman who might be considering conceiving a child outside marriage, and argued that although women had the right 'to the exercise of their vocation and fulfilment of their nature', this could not be achieved through lone motherhood. The child had the right to 'a home – two parents – all that makes complete the spiritual as well as material meaning of "home".'[38] So important was this that both Royden and Eleanor Rathbone argued that unmarried women should not be entitled to an allowance under the proposed family endowment scheme, on the grounds that it might increase the number of one-parent families and encourage promiscuity.[39]

Yet in a society which saw motherhood as the woman's ultimate vocation, the costs to women both of childlessness and of giving up their children could not be ignored. These themes were particularly popular in American maternal melodrama films widely shown in Britain during the 1930s. For example, in both *Forbidden* (1932), directed by Frank Capra, and *The Old Maid* (1939) starring Bette Davis, the heroines were saved from spinsterhood by having secret affairs and became devoted mothers, shielding their children from disgrace. However, the best interests of their children eventually compelled both mothers to sacrifice their own happiness and allow the children to be adopted by childless married women.

The conflicts exposed in these films centre mainly on the choices made by the birth mothers. While they could be applauded for their sacrifice, the personal costs in rejecting motherhood are shown to be jealousy, disappointment and embittered spinsterhood. This is particularly apparent in *The Old Maid*, based on a novella by Edith Wharton, where the child is adopted by the heroine's married sister. In order to give her child a 'normal' family life, the birth mother, Charlotte, conceals her identity, posing as an aunt. But the dramatic interest of the film lies in the exposure of Charlotte's pain at having to sacrifice motherhood and her misery as a despised maiden aunt. This leads her to threaten to reveal the truth on the eve of her daughter's wedding, climaxing in a dramatic scene where she declares that 'just tonight *I* am her mother.[40]

Using a relative to adopt or foster a child born out of wedlock was a common occurrence, but did not always result in a mother sacrificing her own interests in the way portrayed in *The Old Maid*. The detective writer Dorothy Sayers (born 1893), who gave birth to a son out of wedlock in 1924 after an unhappy love affair, had a similar experience. She also failed to acknowledge her son John and did not even allow her parents to know of his existence, but gave him into the care of her unmarried cousin Ivy. A confidential letter written just after John was born suggests that, far from being a sacrifice, for Sayers it was a deliberate strategy which enabled her to carry on working yet still have the prospect of her son's company later in life:

> I won't go into the whole story – think the best you can of me – I know it won't make you love the boy any less. He really is a fine little chap – and I can't feel too bad about myself now, because it will be so jolly to have him later on. I am thirty now, and it didn't seem at all likely I should marry – I shall have something for my later age anyway … I wouldn't like to give him to anybody but you, because I know I can trust you absolutely to give him everything I can't give him these first years.[41]

Although Sayers did in fact marry and eventually adopted her son, having Ivy to care for her child provided him with a secure base in his early years and enabled her to regain him when he grew up. The impossibility of an unmarried middle-class woman with a baby retaining her job or social standing, and the distress and material disadvantages the stigma of illegitimacy would have caused her child, were sufficient justification for secrecy. Not all professional women were as fortunate as she was. In 1926, an unmarried elementary school teacher who had become very attached to her child felt obliged to have him legally adopted for his future welfare. She had taken six months' leave from her job and had not lost her permanent position, but was concerned that the existence of her child should not be known in house where she was living in case 'any suspicion of scandal might prevent her continuing in her profession'.[42]

Nevertheless, by the 1920s and 1930s, some commentators were going so far as to see single motherhood as desirable for women like Sayers. In her condemnation of unmarried mothers, Stopes made exceptions of 'women of supreme self-respect and independence of mind' who resented the fact that marriage laws gave the legal ownership of children born within marriage to the father, but she stressed that these were in a small minority.[43] Other eugenicists went further. Charles Wicksteed Armstrong's book, *The Survival of the Unfittest* (1931), praised by reviewers for introducing eugenicist ideas to the layman, encouraged single women from suitable backgrounds to become mothers. Since God had put the instinct for maternal love into the heart of every normal woman, he argued, 'we must remove the stigma from the girl who obeys Nature and from unmarried motherhood, recognising the right of every healthy man and woman to procreate, provided the children be properly cared for'.[44] Armstrong was not alone in taking this position, which could be justified by the falling birth rate. Other writers claimed that recognition should be given to unmarried mothers for the service they had done society in producing healthy, potentially useful citizens.[45]

Concern about the falling birth rate also drew attention to middle-class childless women, who became objects of pity or criticism,[46] and their position was sometimes compared unfavourably with that of working-class unmarried women who had children. Rosamund Lehmann represents this in her novel *A Note in Music* (1930), in which the tragedy of a childless wife is set against the pregnancy of an unmarried servant, whose fecundity is depicted as enviable, fully justifying her child's unorthodox conception:

> Annie with her fund of physical wisdom, was not the one of course to let her own ripeness wither unplucked: to deny the needs of her body in the pagan amplitude of its middle years ... It seemed so simple and so right: right too, that this symbol of matronly qualities should be in truth with child. Annie was a triumph for unchastity.[47]

The triumph of unmarried motherhood over a childless marriage is also voiced by Annie herself: 'That tear-stained face, pale apathetic, worn, those sunken eyes, ah poor soul! ... she guessed, well enough, what ailed poor Mrs Fairfax; how salt, how barren were the tears of her life'.[48]

While such views of unwed pregnancy were not widespread, by the interwar years, voluntary organisations were increasingly supporting unmarried mothers to bring up their babies. This was the principal aim of the National Council for the Unmarried Mother and her Child (NCUMC), set up in 1918, which fought to keep the child with its mother and saw their separation as a 'deplorable necessity, not as the normal and natural procedure temporarily interrupted by the lack of foster mothers', whose numbers had been diminished by the demand for women's labour during the war.[49] This goal would be achieved by providing suitable accommodation in mother-and-baby Homes and removing the stigma and material disadvantage of illegitimacy through reform of the Bastardy Acts.

Unlike the legislators who framed the 1926 Adoption Act, the NCUMC were concerned that the stigma attached to illegitimacy should be lifted. They rejected the punitive model where the mother was forced to do penance for her sins, which still characterised much rescue work at this time, and drew instead upon a belief in the redemptive power of motherhood as a means to rehabilitate the fallen woman. Thus while the NCUMC took a strong interest in the Adoption Act, they regarded it as second best to keeping mother and child together. Objections that they were encouraging immorality were countered by the argument that by far the best method of helping the child was to help its mother, and that 'to re-educate her for its sake was the best way of improving her moral standard' and preventing a second illegitimate birth.[50]

A similar position was taken by most of the other voluntary organisations concerned with unmarried motherhood during the 1920s, including the Jewish Association for the Protection of Girls and Women, the Salvation Army,[51] and the Church of England Moral Welfare Advisory Board (later the Moral Welfare Council) and its affiliated Moral Welfare Associations, to whom the NCUMC referred many women in need of accommodation. Many workers and leading figures in the organisations which helped single mothers were lifelong spinsters who devoted their lives to their causes, women such as Susan Musson, general secretary of the NCUMC, and Jessie Higson, awarded a CBE for her pioneering work in moral welfare. These were women who at the beginning of the century had been influenced by women's suffrage campaigns and by social purity and feminist demands to reform the sexual double standard. Critical of the conditions which led women into prostitution and premarital pregnancy, they sought both to improve these women's physical and social environment and to reform and re-educate them. And, while not actively condoning unmarried motherhood, these reformers saw the cultivation of maternal qualities as enabling mothers to bring up their illegitimate children as active and useful citizens rather than a source of shame and trouble and a drain on the public purse.

The state steps in: devoted mothers, frustrated spinsters and problem girls

The model pioneered by the NCUMC was adopted by the state during the 1940s, a decade sometimes seen as a watershed in the treatment of unmarried mothers, with post-war welfare settlements offering unprecedented levels of state support. The main catalyst for this change was the sharp rise during the Second World War, in illegitimacy rates which more than doubled from 4.2 per cent of live births in 1938 to 6.4 per cent in 1943, peaking at 9.3 per cent in 1945 (including a 41 per cent rise in the thirty to thirty-five age group).[52] This increase was associated with the extensive movement of both men and women away from their families, through government programmes including munitions and other war work, military service and evacuation.

While many illegitimate births were to women whose husbands or fiancés were abroad, and may have been subsequently legitimised, the plight of women war workers and service women who became pregnant away from their homes prompted the government into taking direct responsibility for their welfare. This culminated in 1943 with a Ministry of Health circular to all local authorities making the care of unmarried mothers their special duty rather than the preserve of the Poor Law and voluntary associations. State policy in this area followed most voluntary organisations in arguing that women should be helped rather than punished. While admitting that they could not solve the problem of illegitimacy and reiterating the traditional wisdom that 'every child needs both a father, a mother, affection, security and the shelter of a normal home',[53] authorities were expected to work closely with voluntary moral welfare associations and other religious bodies to keep mothers and children together as far as possible.

The story told by Mary, daughter of Mr Johnson, a butcher in a northern village whose wife ran the local Conservative club, suggests that attitudes to illegitimacy could be more liberal during the war. The father of Mary's baby, born at the start of the Second World War, was lost in action, but unlike Nellie, a decade earlier, Mary's community had not shamed her, although she was subjected to considerable pressure to have her child adopted. Yet it was neither the state nor voluntary organisations which enabled her to keep her child, but rather the support she received from her family:

> Mine was all a mistake from beginning to end, and there was nothing you could do but just go on. I had three offers of adoption … me mother said no he was born here and here he'll live. Of course, that just settled

the whole lot and everything. Nobody bothered any more. He was just taken as Johnson.

Mary's experience was not atypical. Ministry of Health records show that less than a third of unmarried pregnant service women during the war went back to their families, but a wider survey in 1945 of more than 7,000 births found four out of five illegitimate babies remaining with their mothers, most of whom lived with the child's grandparents or other close relatives.[54]

Nevertheless, in the decade following the war, the Ministry of Health directive was seen as an important step towards rehabilitating the unmarried mother, whose position in society was regarded as 'changed beyond recognition'.[55] A report in 1945 showed local authorities as slow in appointing qualified social workers and highlighted the shortage of foster mothers, places in residential nurseries and long-stay hostels for working mothers, but in most areas, co-operation between local authorities and voluntary groups improved despite some initial mutual distrust. Most importantly, Ferguson and Fitzgerald, writing in 1954, stressed the significance of the final demise of the Poor Law and the new National Health Service and National Assistance Acts in 1948. Under their provisions, unmarried mothers had free maternity care, a maternity grant and up to thirteen weeks' insured maternity benefit after the birth of the child. If unemployed, they could receive an allowance from the National Assistance Board for themselves and their children and were entitled to accommodation from the local authority if they were homeless.[56]

Yet we should not be lulled by such accounts into thinking that a regime of true equality had been introduced. Some later commentators pointed out that such optimism was misplaced, that claims that all mothers were now being treated equally were false, and that the post-war welfare settlement was constructed on the assumption that mothers were married and dependent on a male breadwinner. Unmarried and married mothers still often received differential treatment by the medical profession. Unmarried mothers were ineligible for family allowances unless they had more than one child, and they had often paid insufficient contributions to receive maternity or unemployment benefit. Unlike widows, whose pension was not means tested, their allowance from the National Assistance Board was set at the level of bare subsistence and any money received from the father or their family deducted from it. And homeless women were offered low-quality local authority accommodation, usually shared with the chronically sick and destitute.[57] The value of illegitimate children also depended on their ethnic origins, with black or 'mixed race' babies (often the offspring of American GIs) less likely to be accepted for adoption.[58]

Such interpretations suggest that, far from disappearing, the 'fallen woman' had taken on a new form. By the 1950s the idea that unmarried mothers, no longer widely regarded as morally defective or sinful, had psychological problems rooted in their upbringing became increasingly popular. This view had emerged during the interwar years and caused conflicts amongst moral welfare workers. By the 1930s, voluntary workers who believed women should not be separated from their children on grounds of immorality found themselves challenged by a new generation of social workers influenced by recent trends in psychology. The rights of the child increasingly took precedence and unmarried mothers were categorised not as immoral but as 'socially inadequate'. Lilla Retallach, central organiser for the Moral Welfare Council (MWC) from 1934–1944, noted the difficulties this had caused:

> This forces us to admit a certain confusion of mind and purpose in some moral welfare work. What were we really getting at? When we talked – and how we talked! – about keeping the mother and child together, were we sub-consciously influenced by a feeling consciously denied, that the parents ought not to get off scot free? Was there sometimes a personal and possessive desire to hold onto the mother in order to help her? Were we always ready to study the changing situation with the honesty and flexibility it required?[59]

Rescue work had long drawn upon the rhetoric of social motherhood, which encouraged middle-class women to develop maternal relationships with young women of a lower social class. In the late nineteenth and early twentieth centuries unmarried women could use their own chastity as a position of strength, but in the interwar years, they were now themselves under attack as frustrated spinsters and their motivations for 'holding onto the mother' had become more difficult to justify. Unmarried mothers were like spinsters in that they too lived outside the boundaries of marriage, and through this work, childless moral welfare workers gained vicarious experience of and power over maternal relationships. But some women envied and sought to punish unmarried mothers for having had children, an experience believed to be essential for normal development but from which they themselves had been excluded. This generation of women continued to be the backbone of the workforce in voluntary organisations dealing with unmarried mothers in the two decades after the Second World War, and these conflicting views of unmarried mothers as sinful, capable of reform through maternal love or socially inadequate remained in play.

The continuing stigma attached to unmarried mothers into the 1950s and early 1960s can be linked to American psychoanalytic research into unmarried motherhood, published in Britain, which influenced social work practice and especially family case work.[60] In particular, the psychologist Leontine Young's study of 100 unmarried mothers was widely used by British commentators. Young claimed that most unmarried mothers in her study had more or less serious levels of neurosis, although in a later book she made it clear that her findings were not necessarily valid outside the USA. Young's findings were cited by the child psychologist John Bowlby in his influential book *Maternal Care and Mental Health* to support his claim that unmarried mothers in Britain were emotionally disturbed, produced socially unacceptable children and were unfit to provide them with emotional stability, which resulted in many ending up in institutional care.[61] Bowlby disagreed with the approach suggested by the 1943 Ministry of Health circular and strongly encouraged adoption.

Yet, as Wimperis argued in *The Unmarried Mother and her Child* (1960), insufficient research had been done into the long-term effects to know which conditions favoured adoption or whether children were happier with adopted or natural mothers.[62] For while Bowlby and Young's views were undoubtedly influential, persuading the NCUMC to change its policy on adoption during the 1950s,[63] they were also challenged by some social workers and the MWC, who in tandem with state welfare and social services, continued to provide mother-and-baby Homes and other support services in local communities throughout the 1950s and 1960s.[64] Most moral welfare workers by this time were over fifty, knew little about psychoanalytic case work and refused to accept that all unmarried mothers were socially inadequate or neurotic. Rather, they continued to obey the Ministry of Health circular, encouraging mothers to explore all options that would enable them to keep their babies and seeing adoption only as a last resort.

Constructions of unmarried motherhood as sinful also persisted well into the 1960s.[65] Retallach noted the conservatism and confusion hampering the work in residential Homes which aimed at re-education of unmarried mothers, but which in some cases 'found it hard to break with the idea that there ought to be some element of punishment – somewhere – a legacy of the grim penitential days'. She stressed the importance of the new viewpoint of social workers whose concerns lay principally with the welfare of the child and who were 'ardently concerned not only with individual conditions but with justice and the betterment of human life'.[66] Wimperis did not place herself unequivocally in either camp, showed the complexity of the problem and warned against generalisation, but eventually allied herself with social inadequacy theorists in her tentative conclusion that '*among* unmarried mothers, as almost everyone would agree, there are an important number who are in general terms neurotic' (emphasis in the original).[67]

Fictional images in novels and films of the 1950s and early 1960s reflect these shifting beliefs about delinquent, neurotic or natural mothers. In British social problem and new wave cinema, films such as *Women of Twilight* (1952), *The L-Shaped Room* (1961) and *A Taste of Honey* (1962) (the latter two based on 1950s novels) reworked nineteenth-century images of fallen women, highlighting the marginalisation, lack of security and squalid living conditions experienced by the unmarried mothers and the absence of stability, order and familial support.[68] Yet Fink found representations of unmarried mothers in popular women's fiction in the 1950s as putting their children's interests before their own, in ways similar to the 1930s Hollywood films discussed above. In the novels she analyses, the heroines were generally comfortably off, older, middle-class women (often teachers) who were seduced as young women and who either gave up their children and found them later in life or kept them and hid their illegitimate status. In these works, usually written by women authors, the maternal bond was seen as sacred while the transgressive figures were spinsters who were often represented as frustrated and jealous, threatening mothers with exposure.[69]

This notion that unmarried women without children were more neurotic and frustrated than those with them could also be extended to the plight of unmarried women whose children had died. This was the theme of Celia Fremlin's first crime novel, *The Hours Before Dawn*, winner of the Edgar Award for best novel of 1958. Fremlin's focus on the neurotic behaviour of an unmarried middle-aged school teacher who had lost a child can be linked to a wider interest during the 1950s in the physical and emotional wellbeing of single professional women, particularly school teachers, whose maternal instincts were being frustrated and who might therefore be at risk of pregnancy.[70] The joy Miss Barron felt when she was pregnant and could 'walk with pride among the girls at last, no longer the withered, barren schoolmarm'[71] emphasised the gulf between spinster and mother, a gap which intensified when her baby died. In her grief, Miss Barron became convinced that it had been stolen by another woman, and attempted to kidnap the child and murder the mother. This theme was also the subject of the sinister and terrifying Hammer film *The Nanny* (1965), in which an unmarried woman who lost a child became a nanny, descended into madness and attempted to murder the children of her employers.

Absent fathers and paternal responsibility

Beliefs about unmarried fathers were equally contradictory. The sexual double standard condoned sex outside marriage for men as a proof of their virility and made it easy for men to evade the consequences of fatherhood. Unmarried fathers' stereotypical characteristics therefore included absence, invisibility and a determination to avoid detection. Yet there were also conflicting messages for men in this position. As John Gillis has argued of western societies more generally, 'by the 1920s and 30s there were a raft of regulations and laws on the books that not only reinforced the middle-class norm of husband/father as provider, but underlined the linkage between manhood and fatherhood'.[72] Thus, men who got girls 'into trouble' were increasingly regarded as feckless and irresponsible.

One way of calling men who fathered children to account was an increased emphasis on the duty of paternal responsibility both by law makers and by social and voluntary workers. Yet because for unmarried men fatherhood had a very narrow definition in law and they often never met their children (particularly if no personal relationship was maintained with the child's mother), this duty was hard to enforce. Emphasis was laid both on the family breadwinner model and on the Christian view that payment to the child's mother was retribution for the wrong done to her and her innocent child, but there were also strong economic considerations. By extracting maintenance payments from a putative father, the government no longer had to pay for the child's support. Yet this policy was and still is thwarted by the continuing failure of the state to encourage male involvement in family life while still attempting to impose financial responsibility.[73]

Voluntary societies concerned with unmarried mothers throughout our period tried to counter this problem and force reluctant fathers to take responsibility for their children by strengthening the enforcement of Affiliation Acts which ordered them to make maintenance payments to the mother. Persuading both parents to take responsibility was the best chance for the child and the best way of preventing illegitimate births. In the early 1920s, their main route to achieving this was through Bastardy Bills, introduced into virtually every parliamentary session until 1926, which sought to improve conditions for illegitimate children and their mothers. These Bills were promoted by a variety of philanthropic, socialist and feminist organisations including the Labour Party, the NCUMC, the National Union of Societies for Equal Citizenship (NUSEC), the National Society for the Prevention of Cruelty to Children (NSPCC) and the Salvation Army.

But debates over the Bills also show the concerns of MPs that unmarried women must not benefit at the expense of wives. For example, a clause in the Bastardy Bill of 1923, which placed a stronger obligation on the father to support his illegitimate child by increasing the maximum amount payable to the mother,[74] differentiated between children whose fathers were not married and those who were. In the former case, unmarried mothers were portrayed as innocent victims of 'unbridled male sexuality' and were compared to deserted wives. But where the father was married, a different discourse prevailed. Opponents of the clause portrayed the unmarried mother as fallen, 'an offence against the moral law', whose demands for maintenance could deprive a 'legitimate wife' of her just deserts.[75]

Bastardy and subsequently Legitimacy Bills were consistently rejected or amended by the House of Lords, and when a Legitimacy Act was finally passed in 1926, the clause which raised the maximum amount payable by the father in affiliation orders from 10s to 20s was claimed as a victory by the chair of the NCUMC Council, Lettice Fisher, wife of the former education minister H. A. L. Fisher.[76] Yet the Act also showed the powerful influence of the established church in protecting the sanctity of marriage against adultery and irregular unions, and reflects the fear that husbands might be encouraged to divorce their wives and remarry in order to give their name to an illegitimate child. It therefore differentiated between children who were the product of adultery, who could not be legitimised by their parents' subsequent marriage, and children whose parents were both unmarried at the time of their birth, who could subsequently be legitimised. The effect of this law, which remained in force until 1959, was to encourage the regularisation of unions in which both father and mother were unmarried, while simultaneously highlighting and intensifying the stigma attached to the child of the adulterous mistress, whose existence visibly threatened the stability of marriage as an institution.[77]

Unmarried men who fathered children were less likely to be categorised as immoral or neurotic than unmarried women but, by the 1950s, more interest was being taken in their identities. Wimperis calculated that about one in twenty-five men in England fell into this category, many of whom were cohabiting with the child's mother.[78] But, although the number of known non-cohabiting bachelor fathers was small, this does not take account of mothers who did not name the child's father or of cases where neither father nor mother acknowledged a relationship with their child. It is also difficult to judge how far non-cohabiting bachelor fathers took financial responsibility for their children in a country where 'the law asks little indeed of the father of an illegitimate child and enforces less'.[79]

In 1953, as few as one in seven unmarried mothers applied for affiliation orders, and they were granted by the courts to only 12 per cent of the mothers who applied. The main reasons for this appear to have been variously the reluctance of mothers to involve former partners in what was still a criminal charge, the fear of the publicity and stigma associated with police courts, the difficulties of proving paternity, the decision of the mother to have the child adopted, and the low level of maintenance awards. In 1952, the maximum award was increased from 20s to 30s, but two city court records showed magistrates fixing benefits at an average of between 15s and 17s a week. This was substantially less than the National Assistance allowance of £2 10s a week, which offered mothers bare subsistence rates. While some fathers made voluntary agreements to pay more, we do not know how many of these existed.

City court records giving the relative levels of income of unmarried mothers and bachelor fathers show the depth of the gender divide. In a comparison of twenty-eight waged unmarried mothers with children and forty-two bachelor fathers with no special responsibilities towards parents or any other person, the men earned on average nearly twice as much. Even after maintenance payments were added to the women's and deducted from the men's income, every case for which full financial details were available showed the father substantially better off than the mother. 'After board and lodging of £2 to £3 a week', Wimperis noted, 'they were, one supposes, handsomely provided with beer and tobacco'.[80]

Personal accounts from two unmarried men who fathered children in the 1950s support but also complicate the picture outlined above. Paternal absence and invisibility were encouraged by the fact that the law gave an unmarried father no right to any involvement with his child but only financial responsibilities, which might involve humiliating exposure in court. Stories told by Dickie and Ian suggest that the number of unmarried men with children could have been much higher than any contemporary investigators realised. Both men had initially reproduced the 'family breadwinner' discourse, by stating that men had a duty to support the children they brought into the world. Yet as young men doing National Service in the homophobic 1950s, they had learned to identify masculinity and being male with heterosexual conquest,[81] and had conformed to what at that time was 'the only available model of unmarried fatherhood'.[82] Evading responsibility for pregnancies, they had allowed other men to assume paternal rights and financial responsibility for their offspring, who were hidden within legitimate families with married parents.

Their justifications for this behaviour tell us much about the connections between male sexuality and paternity. Dickie was interviewed by Dulan Barber in the 1970s for a project that was seeking greater recognition and rights for unmarried fathers. He was enormously relieved that the boyfriend of the woman he had made pregnant agreed to marry her and claim paternity providing Dickie never came near them again, and had thought this condition 'pretty reasonable'. He saw his own lack of paternal responsibility as the result of a society which gave young men no clear guidance: 'I've often been told I was very irresponsible, but funnily enough it wasn't that. It was a question of trying to find out for oneself – because nobody had bothered to tell you – what responsibility meant in this area.' Yet he believed given the right social conditions men would naturally want to be fathers and disputed the stereotype of male irresponsibility: 'Once people can function in a reasonable stable environment, normal people will automatically feel paternal feelings and want to do the best for their children and take a great interest in them and so on. External pressures cause internal ones'.[83]

Ian, whom I interviewed in 1998, had a different view of fatherhood. Although he had never liked or wanted children, he also maintained his belief in paternal responsibility, arguing that he didn't think a man should walk away from a girl who was having his child. When I pointed out that he appeared not to have felt a responsibility to the woman he had made pregnant, he put this down simply to his youth and personal circumstances. Yet this was not the whole story. Four years later, he contacted me again – and wrote a letter explaining the gaps in his account which he said had continued to weigh upon his mind:

> You asked me whether if circumstances had been different, I would have cared for my pregnant girlfriend, and the child. I told you yes, I would whereas in fact I'm quite sure I would have refused responsibility and tried to make a run for it. There were two things which bothered me about this. One was that I gave you a wrong answer which was due to the fact that you asked me an unexpected question which I found difficult to answer and I gave you, off the cuff, the answer that would put me in the best light. The other was the fact that I got the girl into this position in the first place. Certainly, at the time, I didn't think anything about this. She was married and therefore I was safe. I was trapped in an all male camp, I had no desire to marry but I had a fairly rampant sexual urge. Her husband was in Germany waiting for a married quarter to become free so that he could bring her over, she had a child and, like other married women on the same camp who had propositioned me, she seemed quite enthusiastic about sex. I was also about to leave the Air Force and face the very daunting prospect at the age of twenty nine of trying to establish myself in civilian life. I have wondered from time to time what happened to her and the child, it hasn't been a major worry in my life. In any case I'm sure I would be bad news if I suddenly turned up.[84]

In the interview, Ian's desire to be seen as a responsible citizen conflicted with his memory of himself as a young man, relieved to have to escape detection. The authorities at the time had colluded with him and reinforced the view that men's sexual peccadilloes should be condoned and unmarried paternity concealed. When another airman had a similar experience and had asked the CO for advice, he was told simply 'to keep his trousers buttoned up in future'. Similarly, the RAF had responded to Ian's confession by sending the woman to Germany to join her husband and posting Ian elsewhere to avoid scandal, a move which had terminated his air force career.

But it was not simply 'rampant' young single men whose sexuality was perceived as problematic. Married women 'enthusiastic about sex' who propositioned men disrupted the harmonious ideal of companionate marriage which was being so strongly promoted in the 1950s, and the consequences of their behaviour had to be hidden. The ultimate failure of marriage to contain sexuality would be less obvious if the men and women whose activities undermined it were discouraged from acknowledging the true parentage of their children. Thus, it is arguable that attempts to persuade unmarried fathers to become family breadwinners rather than irresponsible men with guilty secrets were doomed to failure.

How often unmarried fathers remained absent throughout their children's lives is more difficult to assess, particularly those whose paternal responsibilities were not taken on by other men. David described secret, personal and financial arrangements between his unmarried parents, hiding from him both their relationship to one another and his illegitimate status. As a teenager David discovered that his 'godfather', Uncle George, was really his father and that he was not alone but one of a number of 'godchildren'. But while David did not reveal this discovery to either parent, he was critical of George's spendthrift and ostentatious lifestyle and denigrated attempts made to buy his affection. By contrast, he showed a somewhat reluctant admiration for his mother's capacity to extract money from his father:

> My mother was very good at getting money out of people for me. She certainly got the last ounce out of him, but he had it. He could have stopped perhaps lunching out at Queen's for a week. My mother was very good at persuading people that I deserved what I didn't deserve. At that time, I had no reason to be deserving of anything.

It is hard to tell how far George's willingness to pay for his son's education and attempts to buy affection were made through fear of exposure or are evidence of a genuine desire to take on paternal responsibility and create a father–son relationship with David. But his assumption of the role of 'godfather' does show the difficulty for men in his position of openly admitting to being fathers. And, while the silence that surrounded David's true parentage avoided stigma for all parties, David was left with a burden he only revealed in extreme old age. Although he had never been called a 'bastard', the fact that neither parent ever admitted he was their son troubled him to the extent that he changed his surname to that of his mother after her death.

The silence surrounding unmarried fatherhood is also reflected in the little space devoted to it in contemporary writing on unmarried motherhood. Ferguson and Fitzgerald's *Studies in the Social Services* (1954) devoted two chapters to social policy on illegitimacy in the Second World War, but barely mentioned putative fathers and had no category for them in the index. There were no serious advice books for single men, while advice books for the unmarried woman which discuss motherhood made little or no mention of the fathers of their children.

Revisiting the novels and films discussed earlier also reveals their absence. The fathers of illegitimate children were generally married or dead. Only in Mary Webb's novel *Precious Bane* do we find any detailed portrait of an unmarried father, and it is a bleak picture indeed. Tivvy's and Jancis's lover, the embittered bachelor Gideon, rejects marriage and fatherhood in pursuit of money, 'the precious bane that feeds on life's blood',[85] and as a result loses all. Haunted by the ghosts of Jancis and their child, Gideon follows them to his death by drowning himself.

The gender divide in unmarried parenthood becomes clearer if we compare the categories 'spinster' with 'unmarried mother' and 'bachelor' with 'putative father'. 'Spinster' and 'unmarried mother' were oppositional categories with unmarried women who were not mothers, or who had been mothers but had lost their children, viewed as frustrated, jealous and vengeful, and those who had children and kept them viewed as fallen women, morally suspect, delinquent and a source of contamination. Yet they could also be allies. Spinsters often supported women who had children outside marriage, aiding them to keep their babies. 'Bachelor' and 'putative father' were also oppositional categories, but there was little attempt to bring them together, with bachelorhood seen rather as an escape from paternal responsibility. As we shall see in the next chapter, single men were also largely excluded from two other means of parenting children often recommended to unmarried women: fostering and adoption.

Notes

1 Virginia Wimperis, *The Unmarried Mother and her Child* (London: George Allen and Unwin, 1960), p. 96.

2 Letter from lifelong bachelor Ian to author, 13 February 2003.

3 See Davidoff *et al.*, *The Family Story*, ch. 9, for a discussion of this issue. Ginger Frost, '"The Black Lamb of the Black Sheep": Illegitimacy in the English Working-class, 1850–1939', *Journal of Social History*, 37:2 (2003), looks at illegitimacy from the child's perspective.

4 There is no British equivalent of the US study by Regina Kunzel, *Fallen Women, Problem Girls: Unmarried Mothers and the Professionalization of Social Work, 1890–1945* (New Haven, CT: Yale University Press, 1993). Kiernan *et al.*, *Lone Motherhood*, is focused mainly on the latter part of the century.

5 Fink and Holden, 'Pictures from the Margins', p. 234.

6 Kiernan *et al.*, *Lone Motherhood*, p. 153.

7 But not necessarily to their child's father or mother.

8 Janet Fink, 'Condemned or Condoned: Investigating the Problem of Unmarried Motherhood in England, 1945–60', PhD thesis, University of Essex, 1997, pp. 228–9.

9 This was publicised by the Finer Committee in 1971, which found that 12,000 more unmarried mothers were claiming supplementary benefit than the number enumerated by the census. Kiernan *et al.*, *Lone Motherhood*, pp. 153–4.

10 In the late 1950s Virginia Wimperis estimated that approximately one in twenty-five men was a natural father, but did not suggest how many of these men were unmarried; Wimperis, *The Unmarried Mother*, pp. 122 and 126.

11 This was made legal by the Bastardy Act of 1926. Until then children born outside marriage could not be legitimised by their parent's subsequent marriage.

12 Janet Fink, 'Natural Mothers, Putative Fathers and Innocent Children: The Definition and Regulation of Parental Relationships outside Marriage, in England, 1945–195', *Journal of Family History*, 25:2 (2000), p. 178–95.

13 National Archive, London (hereafter NA), HO45/12695/496773/33 Request from the Magistrates Clerk's Office, Town Hall, Croyden, 25/2/27 and reply by S. D. Crapper 4/3/27.

14 *Report of the Departmental Committee on the Adoption of Children*, Cmd. 9248 (London: HMSO, 1953), p. 27.

15 Fink, 'Condemned or Condoned', pp. 49–50.

16 National Birthrate Commission, *Problems of Population and Parenthood: Second Report of the Chief Evidence taken by the National Birthrate Commission 1918–1920* (London: Chapman and Hall, 1920), p. 22. Russell, *Marriage and Morals*, p. 203.

17 Kiernan *et al.*, *Lone Motherhood*, p. 98.

18 Fink, 'Condemned or Condoned', pp. 50–1.

19 Pamela Dale, 'Training for Work: Domestic Service as a Route Out of Long-Stay Institutions Before 1959', *Women's History Review*, 13:3 (2004).

20 The best-known of these is the film *The Magdalene Sisters* (2002), based upon three oral histories of women who were institutionalised in Ireland.

21 Maria Luddy, 'The Welfare of Unmarried Mothers in Ireland in the early Twentieth Century', paper presented at the 10th annual conference of the West of England and South Wales Women's History Network, 'Women, Health and Welfare', June 2004.

22 Jane Lewis, 'The Problem of Lone Motherhood in Twentieth Century Britian', Welfare State Discussion paper, WSP/115, August 1995.

23 Albert Leffingwell, *Illegitimacy: A Study in Morals*, quoted in Kunzel, *Fallen Women*, p. 1.

24 Marie Stopes, *Sex and the Young* (London: Gill, 1926), p. 135.

25 See Frost, 'The Black Lamb', and Deborah Derrick (ed.), *Illegitimate: The Experience of People Born Outside Marriage* (London: One Parent Families, 1986), for evidence from children.

26 Baldwin wrote a preface to the 1927 edition of *Precious Bane*.

27 Gladys Mary Coles, *Mary Webb* (Bridgend: Seren Books, 1990), pp. 126 and 142.

28 Mary Webb, *Precious Bane*, 1924 (London: Jonathan Cape, 1933), pp. 247 and 258.

29 Coles, *Mary Webb*, ch. 7.

30 Fink and Holden, 'Pictures from the Margins'; Deborah Chambers, *Representing the Family* (London: Sage, 2001), pp. 67–9.

31 National Birthrate Commission, *Problems of Parenthood*, p. lx. The *New Survey of London Life and Labour* noted a rise in the illegitimacy rate in London from 3.59 per cent of total births in 1900 to 5.24 per cent in 1930.

32 Jane Lewis, *The Politics of Motherhood* (London: Croom Helm, 1980).

33 Sheila Ferguson and Hilde Fitzgerald, *Studies in the Social Services* (London: HMSO and Longmans, Green, 1954), pp. 86–7.

34 Hansard, 196, col. 2681.

35 Hansard, 346, cols 1474–81.

36 Hansard, 342, cols 2356–7.

37 See Oram, 'Repressed and Thwarted', pp. 424–5.

38 Maud Royden, *Sex and Common-Sense* (London: Hurst and Hackley, fifth edition, 1921), p. 61.

39 National Birthrate Commission, *Problems of Parenthood*, p. 22; Eleanor Rathbone, *The Disinherited Family*, 1924 (Bristol: Falling Wall Press, 1986), p. 369.

40 Fink and Holden, 'Pictures from the Margins', p. 242.

41 Barbara Reynolds, *Dorothy Sayers: Her Life and Soul* (London: Hodder and Stoughton, 1993), p. 127.

42 NA, HO45/12695, Notes on the present difficulties in connection with the adoption of Children Act, 1926.

43 Stopes, *Sex and the Young*, p. 135.

44 Charles Wicksteed Armstrong, *The Survival of the Unfittest* (London: C. W. Daniel, revised edition, 1931), pp. 125 and 142.

45 Haire, *Hymen*, p. 55. See also Victor Francis Calverton, *The Bankruptcy of Marriage* (London: John Hamilton, 1929), pp. 193–5.

46 See for example Charlotte Cowdroy, *Wasted Womanhood* (London: Allen and Unwin, 1933); Jean Ayling, *The Retreat from Parenthood* (London: Kegan Paul, Trench and Trubner, 1930), p. 111; Enid Charles, *The Twilight of Parenthood* (London: Watts, 1934).

47 Rosamond Lehmann, *A Note in Music* (London: Virago, 1982), p. 262.

48 *Ibid.*, pp. 263–4.

49 Lettice Fisher, *Twenty One Years* (London: NCUMC, 1939), p. 5.

50 *Ibid.*, p. 6. Fisher also took this position in her evidence to the Hopkinson Committee on Adoption in 1920.

51 *Ibid.*, p. 4.

52 Ferguson and Fitzgerald, *Studies in the Social Services*, ch. 4.

53 Circular 2866, 'The Care of Illegitimate Children', paragraph 3, cited in Wimperis, *The Unmarried Mother*, p. 178.

54 Ferguson and Fitzgerald, *Studies in the Social Services*, p. 126; *Homes and Hostels of the Future: A Report of a Conference Arranged by the NCUMC* (London: n.p., 1945). My thanks to Tanya Evans for this latter reference.

55 Ferguson and Fitzgerald, *Studies in the Social Services*, p. 140.

56 *Ibid.*, pp. 128–30 and 138–41.

57 Wimperis, *The Unmarried Mother*, pp. 158–75; Fink, 'Condemned or Condoned', ch. 3.

58 See Rickie Solinger, 'Race and "Value": Black and White Illegitimate Babies in the USA, 1945–1965', *Gender and History*, 4:3 (1992), for a discussion of this issue in the USA.

59 Lilla Retallach, quoted in Jessie E. Higson, *The Story of a Beginning: An Account of Pioneer Work for Moral Welfare* (London: SPCK, 1955), p. 136.

60 Kiernan *et al.*, *Lone Motherhood*, p. 108.

61 *Ibid.*, pp. 102–9; Wimperis, *The Unmarried Mother*, pp. 94–5.

62 Wimperis, *The Unmarried Mother*, p. 266. This point was also made by the MWC secretary Ena Steel ten years earlier in response to Bowlby's criticism of her organisation's policy. Fink, 'Condemned or Condoned', p. 207.

63 Tanya Evans, 'Unmarried Motherhood in Twentieth Century Britain', paper presented at the 12th annual conference of the West of England and South Wales Women's History Network, 'Single Women in History, 1000–2000', 23 June 2006.

64 Fink, 'Condemned or Condoned', p. 58.

65 Kiernan *et al.*, *Lone Motherhood*, p. 109. A study of mother-and-baby Homes in 1968 found that many still aimed to save souls and maintained pre-war regulations and mores.

66 Higson, *The Story of a Beginning*, p. 136.

67 Wimperis, *The Unmarried Mother*, p. 97.

68 Fink and Holden, 'Pictures from the Margins', p. 245.

69 Fink, 'Condemned or Condoned', ch. 7. Key novels she cites are S. M. Edmunds, *Home Tomorrow* (1952); K. Barratt, *The Fault Undone* (1949); Flora Sandstrom, *The Door* (1959); N. C. James, *Over the Windmill* (1954); J. Hall, *Yesterday's Sowing* (1957).

70 Fink notes that the Department of Health asked for annual records to be kept of the numbers of women teachers who approached Moral Welfare associations for help.

71 Celia Fremlin, *The Hours Before Dawn* (London: Virago, 1965), p. 191.

72 John Gillis, 'Marginalization of Fatherhood in Western Countries', *Childhood*, 7:2 (2000), pp. 225–38.

73 Kiernan *et al.*, *Lone Motherhood*, pp. 175 and 286.

74 Susan Musson, 'The Children of Unmarried Parents Bill', *Woman's Leader*, 19 January 1923.

75 Hansard, 165, cols 905–29.

76 Fisher, *Twenty One Years*, p. 11.

77 See Hansard 197 and 200, second and third readings of the Legitimacy Bill.

78 Wimperis showed that out of fathers of illegitimate children in a study undertaken in 1950 in 'Midborough' (an anonymous Midlands town), 44 per cent (96) of the 217 men whose marital status was known were single, but that many of these men were

cohabitees. While only 25 per cent of the mothers in the study were unmarried and not cohabiting, it is not possible to tell whether the fathers of their children were single, or how many single fathers were living separately from the mothers of their children who were married. See chapter 2.

79 Wimperis, *The Unmarried Mother*, p. 123. She compared Britain unfavourably with other countries in this respect.

80 *Ibid.*, pp. 144–5.

81 See Segal, *Slow Motion*, p. 20.

82 Dulan Barber, *Unmarried Fathers* (London: Hutchinson, 1975), p. 23.

83 *Ibid.*, pp. 27 and 29.

84 Letter from Ian to KH, 13 February 2003.

85 Webb, *Precious Bane*, p. 128.

6

'A world clamouring for motherhood':
adoption and fostering

The right thing to do is the simple thing. We have these war-orphaned children and others. And we have women who are childless and may never be able to marry. The problem then is this: What can be done to bring together the childless woman with a mother's nature and the motherless child?[1]

Introduction

IN THE LAST CHAPTER, I focused on the importance of marriage in regulating reproduction and parenthood and the stigma attached to unmarried women who conceived or gave birth to children. Paradoxically, as the passage above illustrates, this meant that it could be regarded as less problematic for unmarried women to foster or adopt other people's children than to rear their own. Accounts of lone women adopting or fostering were common in this period and the practice became a subject of some debate amongst legislators, journalists and psychologists, but it was also a deeply personal issue addressed by many single women as a way of compensating for their childless state.

I examine these debates here as well as fictional and autobiographical stories of single-parent adoption, to explore the ways in which the institution of marriage was used to sanction unmarried women's desires to be mothers. What is most striking about these narratives is the contradictions and inconsistencies they often displayed. On the one hand, child adoption was presented as a way of avoiding the undesirable traits of spinsterhood. On the other, it was regarded as unhealthy for a woman to sink all her emotional needs into a child without an accompanying adult relationship with its father. In both cases, unmarried women's maternal desires were assumed to be central to her identity and judged against the norm of a married mother.

Adoption was rarely recommended and more tightly regulated for unmarried men, and concerns about sexual abuse are suggested by legislation preventing them from adopting girls.[2] It was not often discussed outside Parliament except in fiction, and, even in novels, bachelors who adopted children were rarely their primary carers. Rather, they conformed to masculine stereotypes by relinquishing day-to-day child care to female servants or relatives, or by discovering a lost child and using it as the means to find or replace a wife.

Single parent adoption and the law

Until the passing of the 1926 Adoption Act, there was no clear conceptual distinction between fostering and adoption.[3] Both were insecure arrangements in which rights over the child remained with the natural mother.[4] Where fostering involved payment, the 1908 Children's Act required registration with the local authority, and foster parents were limited in the number of children under the age of seven they could look after. But neither foster parents nor adopting parents who took on full financial and parental responsibilities had any legal redress should the mother decide to take back her child.[5]

The informality of adoption arrangements before 1926 was advantageous to unmarried people wishing to adopt children, since they did not have to convince a court of their suitability as adopting parents. Miss Peto, who gave evidence to the Hopkinson Parliamentary Committee on Adoption in 1920, was in this position. She and her woman partner had adopted seven illegitimate children and from 1916 had also acted as a private adoption agency. By advertising in *The Times*, calling themselves 'The Storks', they had matched twenty illegitimate children and parents of 'the better classes', without inspection or regulation by any outside agency.[6]

The First World War was a particularly important catalyst for adoption. In 1916 the Registrar-General had drawn attention to the higher mortality rate of illegitimate babies (twice the rate of legitimate births), and this coupled with the loss of so many young men during the war gave the idea of 'saving babies' a strong cultural resonance.[7] A letter to Marie Stopes from a midwife in 1920 described the rescue of just such an unwanted baby by an unmarried woman:

> My baby is nearly five. Her name is Marie and she was a little unwanted atom weighing 2lbs 6oz. I looked after her from birth in hospital in 1916, and when her mother said she was going to let her die because she did not want her, I nearly broke my heart. I vowed that I would keep her....

That is my little contribution toward loving Humanity and how proud I am to work for that wee mite.[8]

The war also marked a shift from a position where adoption was regarded as a matter of purely personal and private concern to families towards a much greater degree of state regulation. Interest in legalising adoption was fuelled by publicity about the high number of wartime 'irregular unions', the rise in the illegitimacy rate at a time when the legitimate birth rate was falling, and the pressing need to find alternatives to institutional care for orphaned and illegitimate children. Comparisons were also made with other 'civilised' European countries as well as with the USA, Canada, Australia and New Zealand, nearly all of which had adoption laws.[9] Thus, from 1920, there was increasing pressure for a law that would formalise adoption and transfer parental rights to the adopting parents. This was regarded as desirable by single as well as married adopters, partly because it would remove the fear that the natural parents might reclaim the child when it was of an age to be economically useful, but also because it would counter the stigma of illegitimacy.[10] Miss Peto was concerned about the lack of regulation and had taken pains to ensure that none of the birth mothers knew where her child had been placed. There were also material consequences for adopted children, who remained illegitimate under the law. She had told her adopted 'nieces and nephew' and their schools that they were orphans, fearing that if their illegitimate status was discovered they would be refused a place or expelled.[11]

Questions about the suitability of single people to adopt children arose out of two principal areas of concern. The first was the perceived importance of promoting the nuclear family as the most desirable and natural place for a child to be brought up. With this in mind, adopting agencies generally prioritised married couples who could provide both a mother and a father for the child over all other potential adopters. Yet in the debates and committee proceedings in the years before the 1926 Adoption Act, both single women and men were considered eligible to adopt. The Hopkinson Committee (1920) did not raise any questions about Miss Peto's marital status, and a deputation to the Home Secretary from the National Council of Women of Great Britain and Ireland in the same year made a strong case for legal adoption by unmarried women, whom they described as 'childless mothers'.[12] Some MPs also went as far as to offer spinsters support and encouragement. The Conservative MP Nancy Astor stressed the strength of the maternal instinct: 'It is really one of the tragedies of life. The best work that is being done for children today is being done by childless women'.[13] Labour MP Ellen Wilkinson, herself single, was a rare dissenting voice at this time. Expressing concerns which surfaced much more widely in the 1950s, she pointed out cases where an 'empty headed' childless woman had adopted a young, pretty, 'fluffy-haired blue-eyed' child and got rid of it, usually to the workhouse, when it got 'to the gawky stage of childhood' and was no longer a 'pet to play with'.[14]

A case was made by some MPs for joint adoptions by members of the same sex: 'Then again, I feel an injustice is being done to maiden ladies and bachelors. I do not see why two maiden ladies should not adopt a child, and probably prove the very best foster parents. I have seen cases where such women have adopted a little waif of this description and very good results have followed both to the foster parents and the child.'[15] The eliding of fostering and adoption in this passage shows the fluidity of child-care arrangements at this time, but the fact that this suggestion was not allowed in the final Act suggests that legislators may have had doubts about legalising arrangements which denied the possibility of reverting to more traditional familial forms. A single woman or man might still marry and thereby provide the child with a new adoptive father or mother. This would not be possible for a child who had been jointly adopted by two people of the same sex.

The objection to joint adoptions by unmarried partners was not, however, entirely uncontested in the House of Commons. Mr Palin took a rather different view, feeling it would only be fair to allow two bachelors 'who may have been unfortunate in the marriage market' to be compensated by 'taking the responsibility of training up a boy', and asked for this to be taken in to consideration at the committee stage.[16] There was no specific mention of homosexuality in these debates, but the fact that the committee did not support his suggestion may have been motivated partly by a second area of general concern in relation to single adopters, which was that they might subject children to undesirable sexual influences.

Such concerns were not confined to homosexuality. More overt worries about sexual impropriety (though still not fully articulated) can be found in a clause which prevented single men from adopting girls.[17] And here once again an objection was raised in the House of Commons. While admitting that 'the male sex might not be as good as they might be', Sir Robert Newman asked 'why a man because he happens to be a bachelor or widower should be assumed to be an unfit person or not to have a proper reason for wishing to adopt a female child?' He pointed out the anomaly that a man whose wife had died was allowed to retain custody of an adopted daughter, but was persuaded to withdraw his amendment when it was pointed out that wording of the clause gave the courts some discretion in this matter.[18]

The number of legal adoptions rapidly increased in number after the 1926 Act was passed, rising from 3,000 in 1927 to a peak of around 27,000 in 1968,[19] but subsequent adoption acts were less encouraging to single adopters, continuing rather to uphold the primacy of the nuclear family. The 1939 Adoption (Regulation) Act was introduced as a private a member's bill by Miss Florence Horsbrugh (1889–1969), who had chaired the Departmental Committee on Adoption Societies and Agencies and subsequently became the first Conservative woman to hold a cabinet post, as Minister for Education in the post-war government. Both the report and the Bill were concerned mainly with the supervision and control of organisations which were placing children for adoption without making sufficient checks about prospective adopters' backgrounds. While no suggestion was made that single people should be prevented from adopting children, the report gave as an example of an unsuitable placement a case of an unmarried woman who, despite having two references, one from a probation officer, was found by the NSPCC to be mentally unbalanced.[20]

By the 1950s, doubts were raised more frequently about the creation of single-parent families through adoption. One concern was whether women might be seeking to adopt their own illegitimate children in order to avoid stigma and that to approve this practice would therefore encourage immorality. Applications by unmarried mothers were regularly turned down by magistrates on these grounds, and an appeal court ruling in 1958, which showed that magistrates were confusing illegitimacy with adoption, appears to have made little difference. Although it was pointed out that the primary benefit of adoption was to remove legal disabilities from the child, only eighty-seven adoption orders were made in that year in favour of unmarried mothers adopting their own children.[21]

Magistrates may also have been affected in their decision-making by the increasing influence during the 1950s of child psychologists, such as Bowlby, who argued against policies that would encourage single mothers to keep their babies, believing that the mothers were emotionally disturbed and that their children would have a more secure future if adopted by a family.[22] Bowlby made no mention of single fathers in his influential report to the World Health Organisation, *Maternal Care and Mental Health*, in 1952, and the number of single fathers who legally adopted their own children at that time was very small. But the practice was not unknown. The *Registrar-General's Statistical Review of England and Wales* showed that twenty-five lone natural fathers adopted their own children in 1950 (0.2 per cent of all adoptions), compared with fifty-nine lone natural mothers (0.6 per cent).[23]

The Hurst Report on the Adoption of Children in 1954 gave particular consideration to the issue of single-parent adoption. Although not wishing to exclude unmarried adopters 'in special circumstances', it maintained that 'an unmarried woman who adopts a child cannot provide him [*sic*] with the normal pattern of home life', and recorded a 'firm conviction that, when an adoptive home is being sought for a child who has not formed any attachments to relatives or friends of his family, a married couple is likely to be the best choice'. It therefore recommended that the wording of the next adoption act should be changed from 'applicant' to 'applicants', 'so as to show that normally adoption is by a couple'.[24]

Parliamentary debates and reports on child adoption give no indication of how many single people wished to adopt or how successful they were. Neither is it possible to know the extent of informal fostering arrangements involving unmarried women or men. The Care of Children Committee, chaired by Miss Myra Curtis, reporting in September 1946, noted the difficulties of regulating 'private boarding out or "fostering" now arranged direct between the parent of the child (generally illegitimate) and the foster mother'. While recommending that foster parents should be required to notify local authorities about the placement of children of all ages, whether or not payment was involved, they stopped short of requiring preliminary notification by the parent for fear of widespread evasion.[25]

The Curtis Committee strongly encouraged the expansion of the boarding-out system by local authorities. However, the tensions between working for both money and love are apparent in the recommendation that a foster mother should not be 'paid for her trouble' over and above the child's board and lodging expenses, for fear she might consider financial gain as a primary motive to foster. This had a direct bearing on women wishing to foster who did not have husbands to support them. The committee got round this problem by seeing lone women who fostered children for a living in a different light from married women. They viewed with favour suggestions that 'the methods of placing children in homes should include an arrangement with a woman who has a home of her own but must work to maintain herself, by which she takes a number of children and is paid a living wage'. But the report stressed that there was a very fine distinction between this kind of arrangement and a 'scattered home', where the local authority owned the house and employed a woman to look after a small group of children. In this latter case the woman would be a *full time servant of the authority* (my emphasis) and 'there is of course no objection to remuneration'. The conflict between financial gain and emotional labour was more obvious when the woman owned her own home and could not be classified as a servant. This may help to explain the suggestion that it would work best in cases where 'there were a large group of brothers and sisters who should be kept together and could not be fitted into a single Home forming one of a group'.[26] In such cases, the advantages of being able to recreate a family (albeit a single-parent family) would outweigh other considerations.

Advice literature on adoption by single women

Views in advice literature about the desirability of single women adopting children followed a similar trajectory to legislative debates. In the 1920s, the rescue of a war baby was seen as a possible solution to the 'surplus woman' problem, but by the 1950s the 'lost generation' was ageing. Spinsters had become an anomaly in a society in which marriage rates were rising and more middle-class women were in employment. Psychologists became increasingly insistent that for the sake of the mental and physical health of the child, adoptive mothers should also be wives. There was no comparable literature advising single men.

There was, however, little consistency in the advice offered to unmarried women throughout this period. For example, in *Sex and Common-Sense* (1921), Maud Royden, who had been a witness before the National Birthrate Commission during the First World War, saw adoption as a way for middle-class single women to become mothers without adding to the numbers of fatherless children. Like Nancy Astor, she regarded the rescuing of 'waifs', to whom 'such a home, though imperfect would be a paradise to what it has had', as a proof of real maternal love: 'that so few children are adopted in a world clamouring for motherhood proves the essential selfishness of the claim'.[27] Yet she also offered a warning. From her own experience, as one of a number of unmarried feminists who had adopted children in the late nineteenth and early twentieth centuries,[28] she insisted that a mother, though she 'tries all she can – yes and works miracles of love to make herself all she *can* be to her child', could never make up for its loss of a father, because above all 'a child should have a father and a mother and a home'. Thus single women could provide an essential support system for children in a world where marriages and families had broken down and could save them from being put into Homes, but they should not regard themselves as being able to supersede married parents. Waifs were in *Homes* because they had been excluded from 'normal' families, and the *home* of an unmarried woman could not provide a complete remedy for this exclusion.[29]

Doctors and psychologists were equally ambivalent. The prominent gynaecologist Mary Scharlieb, in *The Bachelor Woman and her Problems* (1929), was concerned that women without children to nurture might wither and become hardened, and considered it a useful way of appeasing 'that incessant aching longing for fulfilment of that primary feminine instinct ... There is one thing essential to her happiness, and that is that she shall have the real care and responsibility of one or more little ones.'[30] However, by the 1930s, developments in child psychology and the increased hostility of some child-care experts to lesbians helped to focus concern on the idea of possible emotional damage to the child.

Psychologist Laura Hutton was one of the few who looked at the problem from the viewpoint of both the child and the would-be mother. Her sensitive analysis of the psychosexual and emotional difficulties experienced by independent, mature single women raised the possibility that they might invest too much in children. She was initially against adoption on the grounds that 'a child adopted because the adopting mother's affections are starved is going to suffer serious psychic damage unless the latter has a very thorough knowledge of herself and her needs and is able to satisfy these by other means besides the care of a child'.[31] Yet in the second edition of her book, published in 1937, she took a more positive stance, recognising that 'if two women lived together, one as a professional and the other as a homemaker, this would be more beneficial for the child and would also improve their standard of living'.[32] Not only did she see that a single woman adopting a child might need emotional and financial support from other adults, but also she recognised the source of this support might justifiably fall outside the boundaries of heterosexuality and marriage, and come from a woman partner.

Attitudes hardened after the Second World War when the nuclear family was reinforced more strongly as a norm. Smith, in *The Single Woman of Today* (1951), who was herself single and who reviewed much of the psychological, sociological and medical literature on singleness from the preceding two decades, saw many unanticipated difficulties in adoption both for the single woman and particularly for the child, emphasising the importance of child psychology in deciding questions of this kind.[33] By 1953, pitying and often quite negative attitudes towards the single woman prompted Margery Fry to offer another insider's perspective in a broadcast talk, subsequently published as a book.[34] Fry, who had been a pioneering figure as principal of Somerville College and influential in developing university women's education earlier in the century,[35] drew attention to single women's maternal yearnings, arguing that 'in many women the desire for children is an instinct at least as profound a the desire for sex'. While accepting that a married couple in full agreement with one another would be the best adoptive parents and recognising that sometimes neurotic selfishness prompted the desire to adopt, she knew of 'so many successful cases where single women have spent their perfectly normal maternal instinct upon the upbringing of adopted children that any general rule against the arrangement would seem [to her] to involve a needless waste of the stores of potential love and care'.[36]

However, few social or child welfare workers by this time would have regarded the single woman as a suitable adoptive parent, principally because she lacked a husband but also, given the supposed psychological and medical causes and consequences of spinsterhood which had been identified over the preceding two decades,[37] because of the probability that she might damage the child. Eyles noted the stringency of post-war adoption laws which made it very difficult for a single women to adopt.[38] In a third, revised edition of Hutton's book, which had been reprinted twice in the 1940s and now had a new title, *The Single Woman and her Adjustment to Life and Love* (1960),[39] the author discussed the influence on adoption practices of social workers who could see little benefit in taking a child from one single women and giving it to another:[40]

> Here one has to point out at once that a single woman will not find much sympathy or help these days in her efforts to find a child to adopt. With the ever growing awareness in Child Welfare workers today of the child's deep need for a normal home environment with *two* parents, the offer of a single woman will not appear very acceptable and in fact at the present time the established Adoption Societies will not accept such women on their registers.[41] (emphasis in the original)

Yet interestingly, while Hutton continued to warn of the dangers of adopting a child to satisfy an unmet need, she qualified her original objection to adoption still further. Provided 'all the difficulties had been foreseen and accepted', she could not 'imagine any step that could bring an unmarried women nearer to complete fulfilment that this substitute for natural motherhood'.[42]

Hutton's changing views on the desirability of single women adopting a child suggest tensions between recognising the desire of an unmarried woman for a child and the need of a child for parents which can be discerned throughout our period. The fact that these two supposedly natural sets of needs and desires conflicted made it difficult for writers on this subject to maintain a coherent position. For example, in *Unmarried but Happy*, the journalist Leonora Eyles seemed unclear as to what should take precedence. She began with an unequivocal claim that the woman with children is more fortunate than the one without because she has 'an anchor in the community', 'something to strive for', 'a reason to be "good"', 'a warm and vital emotional outlet' and 'even without a man she is unlikely to get dried up and selfish'. A few lines later, she backed up this position by stating that from the point of view of a single woman, adoption would be an excellent plan. But she then backtracked because without a man the child might become the victim of a new mother's emotions and posses-siveness, and from this position, Eyles could support the apparently harsh law which made it difficult for a single woman to adopt, which seemed to her 'to work out the best for all'. Yet she could not hold onto this view either, and immediately contradicted it with cases where an unmarried woman had looked after orphans and 'made a wonderful job of it both for herself and them'. Finally, lest single women might think the only way of not becoming dried up and selfish would be to have a child of their own, she warned them against becoming pregnant by a casual male acquaint-ance 'because a child is too serious a responsibility to be brought into the world in so haphazard a way just to gratify a woman's need'. All this in the space of a page![43]

The clue to Eyles' and other commentators' difficulties in maintaining a consistent position lies in the way in which the institution of marriage has been used to sanction woman's needs and desires. As an unmarried woman, if neither her maternal nor sexual desires were fulfilled, there were dangers of her becoming dried up, rigid and selfish. However, if a woman's maternal desires were fulfilled without an accompanying sexual relationship within marriage, she could also be regarded as demanding and selfish. Hutton was unusual in recognising that while it might be unhealthy for a woman to sink all her emotional energy into bonding with a child, if committed adult relationships between women were given the same social sanction as marriage, the outcome for a child might be nearly as good for all parties as it would be for those brought up by hetero-sexual couples.

Adoption and fostering in women's fiction and film

Popular fictional representations of single women fostering and adopting in the 1930s and 1940s generally ignored doubts raised by psychologists and drew upon the trope of a child rescuing an old maid, alleviating her loneliness and maternal yearnings, and offering her an acceptable substi-tute for marriage. In such cases, adoption was often presented as a dual rescue, providing a family for the unmarried woman and a home for the many orphans and children in institutions. What is noticeable in the examples that follow is the use of the language of marriage to describe less socially acceptable domestic relations for the single woman.

In a short story in the magazine *Woman's Friend* (1938), Faith Gardner, the retiring matron of an orphanage who had devoted her life to other people's children 'so dear to her heart she might have borne every one of them herself', asked one of the older boys who had run away from the Home to come and live with her:

> 'Billy' she said eagerly, 'come away with me instead. I'm a lonely old woman who needs someone like you to keep going. We should have quarrels, for we're an awkward, obstinate couple, but we could have fun all right, and show each other what life is.'
>
> 'Gosh Matron, it'd be fine if you'd really have me. I'm handy about the house, when I get the chance, and you should just see what I can lift when it comes to carrying coals and things.'[44]

The parallels with married life are striking, with Faith referring to them as 'a couple' and Billy offering to do the traditional household work of a husband. However, lest readers should suspect her motives for adopting an older boy, Faith shortly afterwards got an offer from a genuine prospective husband who would complete her new family.

A story in *Woman* in 1937 entitled 'Not Wanted' went further, by suggesting that adopting an older child could be a viable option for career women who were unable to marry. It told the tale of a woman doctor who adopted a boy whose parents had been killed in a car crash and who had been rejected by prospective married foster parents. In the final passage, it becomes clear that the title has a double meaning, and that it is not simply the child who felt unwanted: 'How'd you like to live with me John?' she asked. 'Do you think I could be both father and mother? We two Orphs ought to live together, don't you think so? In this house?'[45]

The term 'Orph' positioned the doctor as lonely and friendless. Adopting John enabled her to leave the impersonal hospital flat and go into a house-based general practice considered more suitable for a woman. John's strong interest in medicine and ambitions for the future indicated that he would be her assistant and later perhaps her working partner. Whereas the masculine associations of her job gave her the credentials to be both father and mother to him, her femininity and maternal nature were also evident through his frequent references to her prettiness and likeness to his dead mother. It became apparent then that for the satisfactory resolution of the story it was not coincidental that she had chosen a boy. There is no reference to any sexual feelings, or any unhealthy emotions feared by psychologists, but her offer did carry overtones of a proposal. The ending suggested she would gain a close imitation of marriage and family life, with John standing in as both son and substitute husband. Perhaps most significantly, in this fantasy resolution the woman was not forced to choose between having a career and a family: she could have both.

The Hollywood film *Now Voyager* (1941) (a favourite of the playwright Alan Bennett's unmarried aunts[46]) also showed a child as saviour for an old maid, but its ending was more ambiguous than the stories above. Its heroine, Charlotte, who is tempted into an affair with a married man, maintains respectability by living apart from her lover, Gerry, while taking on the upbringing of his neglected daughter, Tina. The lovers could not consummate their relationship or ever acknowledged it in public, but expressed it through the child who they pretended belonged to them both. The film stoped short of allowing the re-creation of a nuclear family outside marriage, but showed how, by fostering Tina, Charlotte could avoid the twin perils of loveless marriage or dried up spinsterhood. She retained contact with her lover and cared for his child without being married and without suffering the shame of unmarried motherhood. Thus, while on the surface the film upheld marriage, it also exposed the flaws in this institution while at the same time showing fostering as a viable 'third way' for the woman who could not marry.[47]

By the 1950s, such an optimistic view of child adoption in an all-female household would have appeared misplaced by psychologists. Yet women's fiction after the Second World War continued to show the holes in the nuclear family, giving ordinary women reassurance that they were not abnormal in finding marriage and motherhood problematic. In women's novels of the 1950s (like women's film in the 1930s and 1940s), sexual and maternal conflicts were often played out in relation to unmarried motherhood and child adoption. And once again, the central issues were the difficulties unmarried women faced in becoming mothers outside marriage, and whether adoption was in the best interests of the mother and her child.[48]

One novel in this genre from the 1950s which explored the difficulties unmarried mothers had in both acknowledging and adopting their own children is *Home Tomorrow* (1952) by Selina Mary Edwards.[49] Edwards addressed a question faced by magistrates at this time: whether a woman who has a child in an adulterous relationship should be allowed to avoid paying for her 'sin' or, for the sake of the child, be acknowledged as its mother. The book's unmarried heroine, Celia, pregnant by a married man, gave her child to her married sister to adopt at birth but later gave up her job as a teacher and reclaimed him after both adoptive parents died. While Celia did not try to adopt her son legally, she became his guardian, and this pretence that she was fostering him and denial of their blood relationship was shown to have negative consequences. Her child rejected her, and it was only after she admitted her past to her ex-colleagues that he started to call her mother. Unlike Charlotte in *The Old Maid* (discussed in the previous chapter), who for the sake of her child did not allow herself to be acknowledged as a mother, this novel had a happy ending. The merging of blood and adoptive ties was shown to have the best outcome for both mother and child, and, in line with 1950s maternal ideology, the career of motherhood took precedence over all other possible futures for Celia.

It is also possible to find novels with bachelor heroes who rescued or cared for babies, but these stories had much more traditional 'happily ever after' resolutions than those portraying single women with children. *A Bachelor's Baby* was published in 1920, at a time when baby rescue and the perceived need for men to marry women deprived of husbands by the war would have resonated strongly with a contemporary audience. Its plot centred on the acquisition of an abandoned baby by the bachelor hero, Jimmy, who regarded it as an invaluable aid to matrimony:

> In fact he felt rather sorry that it was not the sort of idea one could patent. It was so simple. You merely secured a baby – an unclaimed one for preference – and woman's maternal instinct did the rest ... it reduced the art of love from a complex, heart aching struggle to a mere formula. Business men with little time to spare for courtship, would find it a veritable boon.[50]

Jimmy used this device successfully to entice another older bachelor into proposing to his spinster neighbour, Miss Fisher, thereby creating an instant new family. The fact that the baby unexpectedly turned out to be Miss Fisher's nephew also reflects debates during the 1920s about how far the blood relationship should take precedence and whether it was better for relatives rather than strangers to adopt motherless babies.[51]

A novel with an almost identical title, *The Bachelor's Baby* (1958), published nearly forty years later, used the juxtaposition of a single man and a baby in a similar way: the baby became the means to persuade an apparently confirmed bachelor to marry his childhood sweetheart, a spinster in her early thirties whose biological clock was ticking and who was in danger of being left 'on the shelf'. In this story, however, the importance of fatherly love is the central issue and the plot is less mechanistic. This story spoke to 1950s concerns about men's flight from domesticity and the importance of persuading bachelors to take on the responsibilities of mature manhood, and underlined the linkage between fatherhood and marriage. The hero married his sweetheart because he had learned to love someone else's child and as a result wanted to father one of his own. The baby was the catalyst for him to reject the freedom of the single life and enter into matrimony.[52]

Adoption in children's fiction

Bachelors also adopted children and were saved by them from lonely lives in two classic stories of middle-class childhood written before the First World War which remained popular in Britain throughout the twentieth century. *A Little Princess* (1903), by Frances Hodgson Burnett, has many fairy-tale elements, particularly in its 'happily ever after' ending, where a wealthy bachelor rescues the child heroine, Sarah, from the clutches of a neglectful and cruel spinster teacher and retrieves her lost fortune. The final pages of the book underline the importance not only of the child finding a father figure but also of the part a child could play in making a sick and lonely unmarried man fulfilled and happy: 'He was weak and broken with long illness and trouble, but he looked at her with the look she remembered in her father's eyes – that look of loving her and wanting to take her in his arms. It made her kneel down by him, just as she used to kneel by her father when they were the dearest friends and lovers in the world.'[53] The language of heterosexual love and marriage is particularly striking in this book. By calling Sarah 'little missus' her new foster father suggests she is in the place of a wife, just as the boys became substitute husbands to the spinsters in women's magazine fiction.

Another twentieth-century orphan story beloved of many British child and adult readers is *Anne of Green Gables* (1908), by the Canadian author L. M. Montgomery. Anne was adopted by a single brother and sister, representing a childless couple in need of a child's love. Like *A Little Princess*, this book makes use of familiar bachelor and spinster stereotypes. The sixty-year-old bachelor brother Mathew, who knew nothing about bringing up children, became Anne's confidant, sometimes overruling or softening his sister Marilla's harsher methods of upbringing. However, in this case, although Anne is shown to have brought laughter and love into a rather rigid and joyless household, neither saw themselves as her parents. Marilla refused to be called aunt, insisting that Anne used her first name, while Mathew did little in the way of hands-on parenting: 'Mathew thanked his stars many a time and oft that he had nothing to do with bringing her up. That was Marilla's exclusive duty; if it had been his he would have worried over frequent conflicts between inclination and said duty'.[54]

Marilla, on the other hand, learned to love Ann. The child's affection softened her 'spinsterish' reserve and brought out her maternal qualities. Marilla's greatest reward came at the end of the book, when Mathew died and she was threatened by blindness, whereupon Anne took up the dutiful daughter role, giving up the chance of going to college in order to stay at home and care for her guardian.

The mutual benefits single men and women gained in adopting children are evident in another children's classic, Noel Streatfield's *Ballet Shoes* (1936), a best-seller throughout the mid-twentieth century and the instigator of a genre of girls' career novels.[55] In this story, unmarried women nurtured and educated motherless children but also offered them the possibility of aspiring to futures other than marriage and motherhood. The children were 'collected' by Great Uncle Mathew (GUM), an eccentric professor of geology who was absent during almost the entire progress of the book having bachelor adventures abroad. His great-niece Sylvia became a guardian to the girls and enlisted other unmarried women, including a nanny, a cook, a housemaid, a dancing teacher and two retired university lecturers, to support her in their upbringing and education.

These women gave contradictory messages to the Fossil children. On the one hand, they reinforced the non-materialistic values thought appropriate to middle-class girlhood, whilst on the other they encouraged in them more typically masculine desires to become self-supporting and to develop their own careers. The girls wanted to become women who had made their name in their own right and they rejected ties of blood and family name. Each year on their birthdays, they vowed 'to try and put our names in history books because it's our very own and no-one can say it's because of our grandfathers'.[56] By contrast, Sylvia found it hard to reconcile the conflicts between the middle-class belief that children should not have to work and an economic position that made the children's earnings essential for their survival.[57] And her position as a poorly educated, untrained, middle-class single woman, taking in boarders and bringing in insufficient income to provide for three children, would have been realistic during the Depression years.

The book also sent strong messages about the gender divide in parenting roles and the irresponsibility of bachelors. GUM thought of the children as part of his collection of fossils. He gave Sylvia babies as presents because he thought 'all women liked babies', and without asking her permission assumed she and her nurse, Nana, would look after them. With no knowledge of children and essentially unreliable, he only appeared at the beginning and the end of the book, launching the children into the story but playing no part in their subsequent adventures. When he returned after a ten-year absence leaving no address, he had forgotten about them and thought they were still babies. Because he had failed to provide for them, his niece Sylvia had been forced to take over physical and financial responsibility for them. Yet his neglect was ultimately seen to be beneficial, forcing the children to become self-reliant, and by the time he returned, two of them were on the road to fame and fortune. And when he approved the third child's choice of career as a pilot and offered her a home, he was able to benefit from her companionship as well as retaining the services of cook and housemaid.

In some ways, the book did subvert gender norms, which in the 1930s oriented girls strongly towards giving up work on marriage. By showing the unreliability of men as providers for children and the importance of female self-sufficiency, the book makes careers for women seem not optional but essential. Thus, the book's strongest message was to encourage girls to aspire towards adventurous, glamorous, even masculine jobs, which may explain its popularity.[58] Yet it was also a conservative text, maintaining old class and gender hierarchies which were in reality far from stable in this period. The 'servant problem' was a hot topic in most 1930s middle-class households, but servants in this book are loyal and do not leave families without notice.[59] The nuclear family norm could only be challenged by creating an equally secure family base. This is achieved by portraying their foster mother, nanny, cook and maid as having no career aspirations or lives of their own.

Adoption stories in autobiography and oral history

Turning now to the narratives of women who had themselves adopted children, the autobiography of Rosamund Essex (born 1900) appears to bear out the optimistic picture painted by the fictional accounts above. Essex overcame religious conservatism by becoming in 1950 the first woman editor of the *Church Times*, and also managed to adopt a child in 1939, at a time when single-parent adoption was still considered acceptable by adoption societies. It is a story of struggle against adversity whose form was doubtless influenced by the political climate of the 1970s, when it was published, a period when women were becoming increasingly confident that they could overcome the barriers to women's full emancipation. The narrative hinges on what she described as one of the most fateful moments of her life. Towards the end of the First World War she was informed by her sixth form mistress that it was a statistical fact that only one in ten of her class would ever marry. Essex's chief concern about this forecast was that she might grow into an 'acidulated old spinster',[60] and she was determined to avoid this fate by adopting a child as soon as she had enough money to support it, an ambition she achieved in 1939 while working as a reporter.

Essex had clear criteria for adoption. Like the doctor in the women's magazine story 'Not Wanted', she deliberately chose a son (most adopters preferred girls), and justified her decision to adopt on the grounds that it was better for the many abandoned and unwanted children to have one parent and a home than no parent and an institutional life. She wanted a child who was old enough to talk so that he could tell her if anything was wrong when she went out to work. Anxiety about her vulnerable position as a single mother may have fuelled a determination not to have professional visitors keeping an eye on her, and also her concern that the original mother should not know where her child was.[61]

Despite her son's initial difficulties in the 'transition from a "home" to a home', being a mother had made her intensely proud and happy, and she had from the beginning found it difficult to remember he was not her birth child. Her narrative acknowledges the important part played by her nanny in giving the child security and enabling her to work, yet she still saw herself as the most important person in her child's life: 'Like so much of the rest of my life, it was a struggle to be a mother and a father combined and to hold down a demanding job. In all those early years of my son's childhood, I never went out in the evenings or socialised at weekends except with him. It was a non-stop life. But it was worth everything to me.'[62]

While there is no clear evidence that single-parent adoptions were any more or less successful than those in two-parent families, much depended on the adopter's motives, the degree to which she was able to commit herself to a child, and what support systems were available to her. Martha Vicinus has shown the difficulties experienced by feminists who adopted children in the late nineteenth century and the unhappy consequences for some of the children concerned, pointing out the discrepancy between single women's familial ideology and the reality of their lives, which were strongly committed to campaigns and causes outside the home.[63] Choosing one child over another could also create unforeseen problems, as Pamela Travers (born 1899), author of the Mary Poppins series of children's books, discovered. In 1939, her 'desperate need for someone to love and control' led her into adopting a baby boy because he was better looking than his twin brother, whom she rejected. However, because she did not tell her son he had a brother, she was faced with his unbounded rage when the boys unexpectedly encountered one another at the age of seventeen.[64]

Francesca Wilson (born 1888), an energetic and charismatic teacher, author, journalist and relief worker, tried to assuage similar feelings of emptiness and loneliness by fostering a stream of refugee children and young adults. Francesca said she was not brave enough to follow the example of two of her fellow teachers who had adopted babies:

It is easy to be fond of a baby, but later on the baby might turn into something gross and alien. I felt I wanted to see how the child was turning out, and decided to lessen the risk of adoption by making it temporary.[65] I decided to look for children who longed for education but whom poverty was depriving of it, to whom I could give a year or two of it, or who knows? Perhaps more, perhaps several years.[66]

Francesca's ambivalent feelings towards children, which made her want to build in an escape clause, created problems when she later unofficially adopted two of her protégés. Unlike Essex, she did not provide them with a stable home life, and when in 1936 she was sucked into relief work in the Spanish Civil War, she left Misha,[67] aged fourteen, for long periods of time to be cared for by friends, causing him considerable resentment. Asked many years later to contribute a personal recollection to her autobiography (privately published after her death), Misha admitted he could not write objectively about his 'surrogate mother'. But he did indicate his periodic feelings of loneliness when her work took priority: 'I always knew when Francesca wished to be left alone, mostly when she was writing one of her many articles for *The Manchester Guardian*, or yet another book. She would then have nothing but oranges whilst I ate my heart out in the Housekeeper's room.'[68]

In Misha's story, once again we see the shadowy figure of another woman, in this case the housekeeper, who may have given more physical care to Misha than Francesca did, but who appears in the narrative only to underline the missing presence of his adopted mother. Francesca described her relationship with Misha with a mixture of pride and guilt and, reflecting on his later accusation that she had deserted him, argued: 'Perhaps he was right. But one thing my temporarily adopted "children", many of them grown up, did not realise was that I had made up my mind beforehand as far as I could to be detached from them ... I wanted to be unpossessive, to demand nothing. I had taken them at my own whim because I needed them, or felt I did. I expected nothing in return.'[69]

In fact, this was far from the case, as it was Francesca's jealousy which led her to distance herself from Misha. Hurt by his attachment to the friends with whom she had left him, she admitted:

I knew I had no right to complain. I had neglected him from Spain. I bowed to what I thought was inevitable and detached my heart from Misha as much as I could. Later on I realised how wrong I was to detach myself so ruthlessly. Misha was 14, a period when adolescents revolt almost automatically from their parents or guardians. I should have had more faith and confidence in the strength of our relationship.[70]

Francesca's analysis of Misha's behaviour, written in the 1970s, owes something to the post-war theories of child development and the dangers of overattachment discussed above. In a society which regarded single women's maternal desires as natural but pitied and criticised their child-less condition, and which encouraged them to look after children while forbidding them children of their own, the temptation for her to take in orphans from abroad was strong. But she was also frightened of becoming too attached to her adopted children and worried that they might tie her down. Francesca's fascination with relief work and her love of travel and adventure conflicted with her need to be loved and her desire to fill her 'empty nest'. Her roving life-style made it very difficult for her to provide long-term stability.

Short-term fostering could nevertheless provide a vital refuge for children orphaned and dislocated by war. The BBC radio programme *Home Truths* (2005) told the story of an unmarried woman who ran a tobacconist's and sweet shop in north London. In 1939 she had fostered three Jewish teenage girls from Prague, who came to England on the *Kindertransport* in which Britain granted refuge to around 10,000 children from Austria, Germany, Poland and Czechoslovakia. Although Miss Harder's death at the age of fifty-four meant the sisters were only with her for six months, the 'kindness of strangers' was remembered with gratitude by one of the girls, who described her as an angel and 'a beacon of light in her life'.[71]

Oral history interviews are an important source of autobiographical narratives on adoption and fostering, which give rather different perspec-tives from the written accounts above. Most significantly, they show that the shame of illegitimacy was not confined to birth mothers but could also affect single adoptive mothers. It is clear from their accounts that magistrates' concerns that women might be seeking to adopt in order to conceal an illegitimate pregnancy had a wider currency and that children adopted or fostered by unmarried women were often assumed to be their own. This may also have been the case for Rosamund Essex, whose adopted son introduced her as 'Miss Essex' to a shocked bishop, although it appears not to have affected the child's relationship with his mother in any material way.[72]

Other women in her position found the stigma of unmarried mother-hood so uncomfortable that they refused to be called mother even if they regarded themselves as having fully replaced the birth mother. Health visitor Ellen described her longing to adopt a little 'gypsy' [*sic*] girl during the interwar years, but hadn't enough money. But she was much less relaxed than Essex about how such an exposure would be interpreted.

She told a story about a friend in a similar situation:

> She worked in an orphanage before she became a health visitor, and this
> little girl was always coming in and out, and then the woman [previous
> foster mother] didn't want her after a bit, so she [health visitor] adopted
> her. She called her Penny as she only cost a few pence to have you see.
> She was single and she [the girl] called her mummy, but then she [health
> visitor] said, when she got to about ten, it was a bit awkward, there was
> no man you see, that she must call her auntie. So she called her auntie,
> because you see, it looked as though she were illegitimate, you know.[73]

This woman's renaming of the child in financial terms to reflect the fact
that she was cheap to keep, and her rejection of the term 'mummy', might
indicate the uncertain nature of the bond between them, particularly as
the child grew older. Yet Ellen's explanation that she feared the stigma of
illegitimacy is also entirely plausible.

Similar fears were voiced by Ethel (born 1902), a cab driver's daughter
from a family who set great store by respectability, who had adopted her
cousin's daughter at the age of two in 1926, after the child's mother had
died:

> Of course it was a big ordeal for my parents to let me have her, and course
> some people thought she was my child (laughed). As my daughter said,
> 'they're not your friends because there's no sense in saying you go away
> for three weeks and come back with a child of two, that's she's *your*
> child.' ... I always told her about her mother, so she knew. She wanted
> to call me mummy when I first came and I said 'no'. I said 'I'm not your
> mummy and er call me aunty if you like' ... and now she calls me aunty.
> She's seventy now ... It was hard for my mother because she always bore
> that, that I should have taken a child and people think she was *my* girl,
> but I never bothered about it.

Despite being called aunty, Ethel said she thought of the child as her
daughter and that she was very dear to her. It was a closeness strengthened by Ethel's continuing attachment to the child's father, who emigrated
from England to Canada not long after his wife died. Ethel refused to
accompany him, as she had not wanted to leave her home, but she hoped
for many years that he might return and marry her, and was devastated
when he finally wrote and told her he had remarried out there. There are
some parallels in this account with the film *Now Voyager*, with the child
seen as a partial substitute for the relationship Ethel would have liked to
have with its father, but her romantic ending had no connection to her
adopted child. At the age of seventy, Ethel married a widower, and the
love and companionship she experienced in old age were described as the
happiest years of her life.

The evidence in this chapter demonstrates the difficulties faced by single women who chose to adopt or foster children. While women's and children's fiction show the joy fostering and adopting children could bring to lonely single men and women, personal narratives are more complicated. In a 'world clamouring for motherhood', single adoptive mothers were given contradictory messages about their motivations and suitability to be mothers, limited support, and sometime obstructions by legislators, psychologists and social workers who policed adoption law and practice. These stories also provide further evidence of a deep gender divide in parental roles. Although unmarried men were not barred from adopting boys, the lack of evidence of single men adopting children suggests that this practice was unusual and not encouraged.

Little has changed in this respect. A study of single-parent adoption undertaken by Morag Owen in the mid-1990s indicated that single parents were overwhelmingly women and that they were considered only in relation to children with special needs: 'There is still a presumption that normal, healthy babies should be placed only with married couples, who will give them the type of upbringing they require for social and emotional survival.'[74] In this study only one adopter was an unmarried male, and despite the fact that he had spent several years in the caring profession and was described as having 'an outstanding ability to relate to children', he was told by social workers that he would have to wait a long time for a child, with no guarantee of success.

Owen followed Hutton in recommending that single adopters should have strong social support systems, but also acknowledged their special skills and commitment. Many unmarried women wishing to adopt in the mid-twentieth century could have demonstrated similar qualities. Their widespread exclusion from being considered fit to parent by adoption societies and social work departments in the 1940s and 1950s, often also staffed by unmarried women, suggests a missed opportunity both for the women themselves and for the children who remained in insitutional care.

Notes

1 C. Gasquoine Hartley, *Sunday Pictorial*, December 1917.
2 This was disallowed by a clause in the 1926 Adoption Act.
3 David Kirk and Susan McDaniel draw attention to the frequent exchange of the terms fostering and adoption in 'Adoption Policy in Great Britain', *Journal of Social Policy*, 13:1 (1984), p. 83. The practice of subsidising adoption has blurred distinctions between the two. This was also the situation before 1926 in cases of what came to be known as 'professional adoption' or 'baby farming', where (usually unmarried) mothers gave

a lump sum to someone who would take on the complete care of their baby. Jenny Keating, 'Struggle for Identity: Issues Underlying the Enactment of the 1936 Adoption of Children Act', *Journal of Contemporary History*, 3:1, www.sussex.ac.uk/history/documents/3._keating_struggle_for_identity.pdf, accessed 23 August 2006.

4 See Margaret Richards, *Adoption* (Bristol: Jordan and Sons, 1989); Billy Strachan, *Adoption* (London: Barry Rose Law Publishers, 1992); Mary Kathleen Bennet, *The Politics of Adoption* (New York: Macmillan, 1988).

5 The only exception was pauper children, who came under the jurisdiction of the 1899 Poor Law Act. This enabled Boards of Guardians to 'adopt' and assume legal custody of workhouse children whose parents had died, deserted the home, been imprisoned for offences against their offspring, been judged morally or mentally unfit, or permanently disabled while in receipt of Poor Law aid. George K. Behlmer, *Friends of the Family: The English Home and its Guardians, 1850–1940* (Stanford, CA: Stanford University Press, 1998), p. 286.

6 NA, HO/45/354040, Evidence of Miss Peto.

7 M. P. Hall and I. V. Howes, *The Church in Social Work: A Study of Moral Wefare Work undertaken by the Church of England* (London: Routledge and Kegan Paul, 1965), p. 33.

8 MSP, PP/MCS/A78, Miss KE to MS, 22 March 1921.

9 *Report of the Committee on Child Adoption* (London: HMSO, 1921) Cmd. 1254, paras 4 and 5.

10 *Ibid.*, para. 13.

11 Evidence of Miss Peto.

12 NA, MH55/276.

13 Hansard, 182, col. 735.

14 Hansard, 192, col. 950.

15 *Ibid.*, col. 942.

16 *Ibid.*

17 This was recommended in the draft Bill submitted by the Child Adoption Committee chaired by Justice Tomlin in 1925 and was incorporated into the Act. *Child Adoption Committee, Second Report* (London: HMSO, 1925), Cmd. 2469, para. 2.2.

18 Hansard, 196, col. 2649.

19 Richards, *Adoption*, p. 4.

20 *Report of the Departmental Committee on Adoption Societies and Agencies,* , Cmd. 5499 (London: HMSO, 1937), Section 10, p. 13.

21 Fink, 'Natural Mothers'.

22 Fink, 'Condemned or Condoned', pp. 206–7.

23 By 'lone', I mean natural fathers not living either with their children's mother or with a wife who was not the child's mother.

24 *Report of the Departmental Committee on the Adoption of Children*, Cmd. 9248 (London: HMSO, 1954), p. 47.

25 *Report of the Care of Children Committee*, Cmd. 6922 (London: HMSO, 1945), para. 475.

26 *Ibid.*, para. 471.

27 Royden, *Sex and Common-Sense*, p. 61.

28 Others were Charlotte Despard, Mary Carpenter and Constance Maynard. See Vicinus, *Independent Women*, pp. 43–4.

29 Royden, *Sex and Common-Sense*, p. 61.

30 Scharlieb, *The Bachelor Woman*, pp. 54–5. See also pp. 74–5.

31 Hutton, *The Single Woman and her Emotional Problems*, pp. 137–8.

32 Hutton, *The Single Woman and her Emotional Problems* (second edition 1937), p. 156.

33 Smith, *The Single Woman of Today*, p. 124.

34 The talk was published with some additional material as Margery Fry, *The Single Woman* (London: Delisle, 1953).

35 Dyhouse, *No Distinction of Sex*, pp. 10 and 240.

36 Fry, *The Single Woman*, pp. 11–12.

37 These included symptoms such as frigidity, emotional immaturity and the tendency to regress to childish forms of behaviour, and the likelihood of mental illnesses, such as hysteria, epilepsy, obsessional neurosis, depression, manic schizophrenia and nervous breakdown. Smith, *The Single Woman of Today*, pp. 46–49 and 105–18, Hutton, *The Single Woman and her Emotional Problems*, p. 9. Similar debates in the USA are described by Laura Briggs, 'Mother, Child, Race Nation: The Visual Iconography of Rescue and the Politics of Transnational and Transracial Adoption', *Gender and History*, 15:2 (2003), p. 184.

38 Eyles, *Unmarried but Happy*, p. 33.

39 Laura Hutton, *The Single Woman and her Adjustment to Life and Love* (London: Barrie and Rockcliffe, 1960), p. xiii.

40 This view was still being expressed in a child adoption manual published in 1969: R. Rowe, *Yours by Choice: A Guide for Adoptive Parents* (London: Routledge, 1969), quoted in Morag Owen, 'Single Person Adoption: A Report to the Department of Health', University of Bristol, 1996.

41 Hutton, *The Single Woman and her Adjustment to Life and Love* (1960), p. 111.

42 *Ibid.*, p. 114.

43 Eyles, *Unmarried but Happy*, p. 33

44 Edith Calderbank Lewis, 'No Life of her Own', in *Woman's Friend*, 15 January 1938.

45 Helen Genung, 'Not Wanted', *Woman*, 3 July 1937, pp. 8–9.

46 Alan Bennett, *Untold Stories* (London: Faber and Faber, 2005), p. 60.

47 For further discussion of this film see Fink and Holden, 'Pictures from the Margins'.

48 Niamh Baker, *Happily Ever After: Women's Fiction in Postwar Britain 1945–1960* (London: Macmillan, 1989); Fink 'Condemned or Condoned'. This novel and the others discussed below fall into the category 'middle-brow'. It appeared in G. B. Cotton and A. Glencross, *The Cumulative Fiction Index 1945–60* (London: Association of Assistant Librarians, 1953–9), which listed novels available in circulating libraries, schools and bookshops. The fact that they were often borrowed from libraries rather than purchased makes the readership of books of this kind difficult to assess. See Nicola Humble, *The Feminine Middlebrow Novel, 1920s to 1950s* (Oxford: Oxford University Press, 2001), for a discussion of this genre.

49 S. M. Edwards, *Home Tomorrow* (London: Heinemann, 1952). See Fink, 'Condemned or Condoned', ch. 7, for further discussion of this novel.

50 Rolf Bennett, *A Bachelor's Baby* (London: Odham's, 1920), p. 43.

51 See Janet Fink, 'Private Lives, Public Issues: Moral Panics and "the Family" in Twentieth Century Britain', *Journal for the Study of British Cultures*, 9:2 (2002), pp. 135–48, for a discussion of the debates about blood and adoptive relationships at this time.

52 Gwen Davenport, *The Bachelor's Baby* (London: Doubleday, 1958).

53 Frances Hodgson Burnett, *A Little Princess*, 1903 (London: Frederick Warne, 1975), p. 178.

54 L. M. Montgomery, *Anne of Green Gables*, 1908 (Penguin: London, 1994), p. 234.

55 'Noel Streatfield', in Humphrey Carpenter and Mari Prichard (eds), *The Oxford Companion to Children's Literature* (Oxford: Oxford University Press, 1984).

56 Noel Streatfield, *Ballet Shoes*, 1936 (Harmondsworth: Penguin, 1960), p. 37.

57 *Ibid.*, p. 127.

58 Petrova's desire to be an air pilot or car mechanic was an offshoot of the short-lived adulation that in the 1920s and 1930s was offered to women who become famous as aviators, explorers or engineers. M. Cadogan and P. Craig, *You're a Brick, Angela! A New Look at Girls' Fiction from 1839 to 1975* (London: Gollancz, 1976), p. 288.

59 For a discussion of domestic service in this period, see Judy Giles, *Women, Identity and Private Life in Britain, 1900–50* (London: Macmillan, 1995).

60 Essex, *Woman in a Man's World*, p. 15.

61 Essex asked the judge at the county court to use his discretion not to call the mother to court, *ibid.*, p. 47.

62 *Ibid.*, p. 48.

63 Vicinus, *Independent Women*, pp. 43–4.

64 Valerie Lawson, *Mary Poppins, She Wrote: The Life of P. L. Travers* (London: Aurum Press, 1999), pp. 178–83 and 230–1.

65 Belief in hereditary weakness, fostered by the eugenics movement, may have lain behind the common interwar pattern of late adoption. According to Stephen Humphries and Pamela Gordon, *A Labour of Love: The Experience of Parenthood in Britain 1900–1950* (London: Sidgwick and Jackson, 1993), few wanted to adopt babies in nappies, the most common age being five.

66 Francesca Wilson, *A Life of Service and Adventure* (privately published: ISBN: 09522912.4.x, 1995), pp. 114–15.

67 Misha was the son of a Tsarist officer who lived under her care in England throughout his adolescence.

68 'From Misha Solokov Grant', in Wilson, *A Life of Service*, part 2, 'Personal Recollections of Francesca Wilson', p. 20.

69 Wilson, *A Life of Service*, p. 124.

70 *Ibid.*, pp. 128–9.

71 BBC Radio 4, *Home Truths*, 20 August 2005, programme and website www.bbc.co.uk/radio4/hometruths/20050822_refugee.shtml, accessed 20 August 2005.

72 Essex, *Woman in a Man's World*, p. 49.

73 Midwives who 'took home unwanted or orphaned babies and brought them up as their own' are described in Nicky Leap and Billie Hunter, *The Midwife's Tale: An Oral History from Handywoman to Professional Midwife* (London: Scarlett, 1993), p. 69.

74 Owen, 'Single Person Adoption'.

7

Family romances:
aunts and uncles

I was never in any doubt at all that my appointed path would be single in the world and by the time I was in my teens was quite deliberately looking to Mona and Aunt Flo as role models. Mona knew this and told me not long afterwards that she had left me all her jewellery in her will. In a way that made me feel that I too was part of her circle of single women.[1]

'But he's our uncle' said Nancy.
  'He's our friend' said John.
  And then Titty said something which almost as soon as it was out of her mouth, she wished she hadn't said.
  'It's the same as if it was Daddy' she burst out. 'Think, think. You couldn't learn Latin if you knew your father was a prisoner.'[2]

Introduction

This chapter focuses on maiden aunts and bachelor uncles and their relations with children, through blood, marriage or family friendship, using children's fiction, social surveys, oral history and autobiography as sources. My reason for looking at children's rather than adult fiction to cast light on these relationships is that I was struck by how often unmarried aunts and uncles rather than mothers and fathers appeared as key adult characters in books aimed at young people, and wondered what purpose they served for the child reader. By linking these fictional accounts to experiences of unmarried aunts and uncles recounted in oral history and autobiography, we can also see how similar characterisations and narratives were used in each genre to make sense of relationships which lay outside the nuclear family norm. The nature of my sources means that many of the examples of aunts and uncles I give here are from a child's perspective. But though voices of aunts and uncles are scarcer, they too offer some valuable insights into these relationships.

The stories which children find particularly compelling are those which relate to both their inner world (fantasies and psychic formations) and outer world (familial structures and significant people who surround them). Freud's essay 'Family Romances' is helpful in this respect. He suggested that in their daydreams children often reject their real mothers and fathers and fantasise about having been born to other, usually rich and famous, parents. Such fantasies play an important part, he believed, in helping children deal with conflicts and difficult feelings about their families during their everyday lives.[3] While fictional unmarried aunts and uncles were seldom exalted figures, the frequency with which they replaced parents or were the most significant adult characters in stories suggests that they fulfilled a similar purpose and spoke strongly to childhood fantasies at this time.

The avuncular relationship had a particular salience in mid-twentieth-century Britain, when the weight of expectation on mothers and fathers to fulfil all a child's needs was increasing. Indeed both the theories of Freud, who focused on the Oedipal drama and the importance of a core familial group of mother–father–child, and those of his colleague Melanie Klein, who laid more emphasis on the mother–child dyad, were themselves part of this trend.[4] In practice of course, these expectations could not be fulfilled. In a society torn apart by war and economic depression, the nuclear family core was unstable, and British colonial activities involved the dislocation and separation of many families.[5] As shown earlier in my own family story, fathers were often absent, mothers did not undertake all the physical care of their children, and even if they did, they could never be always emotionally available.

John Hodgson, in his study *The Search for Self: Childhood in Auto-biography and Fiction since 1940*, also offers useful insights into non-parental relationships. He points to the 'major shifts in consciousness about the nature and significance of childhood during the twentieth century,'[6] and draws upon both Freudian and Kleinian theory to help us understand the place in autobiography and autobiographical fiction of 'particularly significant others [who] taken collectively, provide the shaping and nurturing experiences every child undergoes on the journey from dependence to independence.'[7] Although he foregrounds the parent–child dyad he does offer space for 'other adults,'[8] and several of his examples suggest that unmarried women as nannies, servants, governesses or friends played an important part in these autobiographical childhood journeys.

Unmarried aunts and uncles performed similar functions, but their significance was multifaceted. First, in fantasy and in memory, anger and grief about parental absence or unavailability were often displaced onto aunts and uncles who were either demonised or portrayed as wise figures or idealised companions to replace an absent mother or father. Second, as Eve Kofsky Sedgwick has argued, family systems which included an avuncular function gave children their first sense of alternative lives which did not inevitably lead to heterosexual couplings or procreation.[9] As we shall see, aunts and uncles emerge as significant figures in a number of fictional and autobiographical stories, but not always as positively as Sedgwick implies. For these 'other' relationships which fell outside the boundaries of marriage and the nuclear family were fraught with contradictions. Because being unmarried was linked with not having achieved the full status of adulthood, single aunts and uncles were often portrayed as meeting children at their own level. But, perhaps partly because of their assumed youthfulness, it could be hard for children to accept favourite aunts' and uncles' adult friendships and partnerships outside the family.

Third, and perhaps most importantly, the different ways in which the maiden aunt and bachelor uncle were portrayed in these stories offer new insights into gender divisions in parenting roles. For, while aunts and uncles seem to appear with equal regularity in children's fiction, their roles in some important respects were not the same, and bachelor uncles do not appear as 'significant others' in autobiographical accounts as frequently as maiden aunts. This may reflect the lower numbers of single men in the population and the fact that uncles were much less likely than aunts to have replaced absent parents, yet this does not mean the relationship was of no importance. Social surveys show many instances of unmarried uncles living with or near children, and interviews testify to feelings of mutual affection from and towards nieces and nephews.[10]

The scarcity of uncles in male autobiography is symptomatic of a larger absence in the personal lives of men. Men did not generally consider relationships with children to be a subject for discussion in autobiographies because, as Mary Evans has argued, twentieth-century male auto/biographies remained locked into rigid distinctions between public and private, and silenced emotional and sexual life. Thus, the lack of avuncular figures in autobiographical stories written by men reflects a more fundamental denial of the importance of childhood itself. This can be linked to an implicit refusal by many authors of psychoanalysis as the most radical of twentieth-century developments in understanding, and is reflected in autobiographical writings where 'childhood is given almost no discussion and, more significantly, allowed no influence on adult personality or behaviour'.[11]

Finally, it should be noted that although the autobiographical and oral evidence I present is from men and women from across the class spectrum, the fiction I discuss was read primarily by middle-class children. The extent to which the connections I make between these genres could be applied to fiction read by working-class children is therefore less certain.[12]

Maiden aunts in children's fiction

I begin by looking at the maiden aunt, a legendary figure, prominent in many family myths, often associated with Victorian lives of sexual repression and service.[13] Daughters kept at home and prevented from marrying in order to look after parents were also often expected to put financial and material, physical and emotional resources at the disposal of nephews and nieces. They were particularly likely to have replaced the mother when the latter had died in childbirth, and were important in long families where grandmothers had died by the time the youngest children were born, and were therefore unavailable to give care. And, as with my own relatives, they were a significant presence in colonial families who sent their children home from abroad to be educated.[14] The high numbers of young women who did not marry in the late nineteenth century, when families were larger and marriage rates lower than after the First World War, meant that older unmarried aunts attached to families remained ubiquitous throughout the early and mid-twentieth century.[15]

The primary meaning of the term 'aunt' refers to a relationship with a sibling's child, but one of its secondary definitions is 'a woman to whom one can turn for advice, sympathy, practical help etc.',[16] so it is not necessarily connected with families. Being a maiden has very different connotations, suggesting youth, virginity and the absence of children or a sexual relationship with a man, while for a woman beyond child-bearing age being an 'old maid' implies an inappropriate naivety, even eccentricity, indicating that she has not achieved the position of full adulthood conferred by marriage and making her open to ridicule and pity. Connecting 'aunt' with 'maid' is therefore contradictory: as both an insider and outsider in families, she could be invested with power but also with vulnerability.

The maiden aunt was a common character in children's and adult fiction throughout the nineteenth and twentieth centuries,[17] but her role in school stories of the 1930s as maternal substitute is of particular relevance here. Usually written by middle-class unmarried women and read by middle-class girls and young women, this genre of books was a major commercial success throughout the first half of the century. Rosemary Auchmuty sees the popularity of girls' school stories as a response to the shift 'from separate spheres to the compulsory mixing of the sexes', a refuge from an increasingly heterosexual and heterosocial twentieth-century world.[18] However, she concentrates her attention on schoolgirls and their teachers, and ignores the more shadowy figures of maiden aunts.

Although aunts rarely spoke for themselves and were often marginal to the main storyline, they generally had clearly defined roles as deputy or replacement parent figures. They might make parties go with a swing, like the aunt who was always thinking 'of such jolly things' in Angela Brazil's *The School on the Cliff* (1938).[19] However, those who deputised for dead or absent parents could also be transitional carers whose deaths enabled the heroines to move forward into a new stage of their lives. For example, in *Sarah to the Rescue* (1932), by Dorothea Moore, the death of an aunt who had cared for the motherless Sarah prompted her to go out in the world to find adventures, whilst in Irene Mossop's *Una Wins Through* (1935) a rich aunt adopted a child and died leaving her an heiress; in both cases the girls were rediscovered and reclaimed by their original families.[20]

Katherine Moore argues that affectionate, sensible and valuable aunts have been more commonly acknowledged in memoirs and letters, while tiresome, ridiculous, sinister or sadistic ones are more likely to appear in fictional guise.[21] As such, they could be used as external objects upon which children might unload their frustration about unmet needs and desires. In stories with boy heroes, aunts were often restrictive, unadventurous figures, as in Richmal Crompton's ever popular *Just William* stories (published from the 1920s to the 1960s), but they could be equally confining for girls. In *Molly's Chance*, by J. H. Byron Lewis, Molly's aunt was 'a severe figure', a 'rather hard-featured old lady' who looked searchingly through platinum lorgnettes and forbade Molly to do games at school. She swooped on Molly 'in a perfect tornado of management like a wolf from the fold – albeit a best-intentioned one', and Molly felt she had to be grateful. Her friend Gypsy's aunts were equally restrictive, preventing their niece from going on holiday with her exciting Uncle Reggie. These women were represented as interfering but well-meaning outsiders whose hunger for affection was channelled into a form of power and restraint unacceptable to their nieces. Aunts 'don't count' and 'never understand'.[22] Their marginalisation and lack of status reinforced their alienation.

The problematic function of the aunt as substitute parent is particularly well developed in Angela Brazil's *The School at the Turrets* (1935). Here Susie's aunt, Miss Martin, who was both guardian and teacher, prevented Susie from seeing her father. Because of her rather rigid disposition and her uncomfortable dual role, she was unable to be an adequate substitute mother to her niece, resulting in tensions and misunderstandings between them. The dull, worthy, strict Miss Martin was juxtaposed with Susie's absent father, who was living in Australia, contrasting feminine/home/ safety with masculine/ abroad/danger. When Susie was asked: 'Does Miss Martin ever take you away?', she replied with feeling: 'No, thank goodness. The only person I want is my Daddy.'[23]

Valerie Walkerdine draws upon Freud's 'Family Romances' to demonstrate what purpose such representations might serve for girl readers. In her analysis of 1980s British comics *Bunty* and *Tracy* (read by pre-adolescent girls), she noted the overwhelming use of cruel 'surrogate' parents for girls who had been removed from their own families in tragic circumstances.[24] Looked at in this light, the use of an aunt to stand in for the mother as a means to separate a girl from her father may have provided a safe object on which the child could project her anger at having to deny feelings for him which the incest taboo made it difficult for her to express.[25] Walkerdine argued that such representations could be helpful 'because the fantasies created in the texts play upon wishes already present in the lives of young girls', which meant that the resolutions offered related to their own desires.[26] The creation of two mother figures also relates to the Kleinian idea of splitting, in which the 'bad', unacceptable feelings a child has about her real mother's inability to fulfil all her needs are projected onto a substitute, leaving the image of the 'good' mother untarnished [27] (often fictionalised in children's stories as dead or abroad). Such devices allowed girls to fantasise, and play out in their imaginations conflicting feelings about their own mothers.

Because aunts and other single woman were so often used as surrogate parents, the common fictional use of this role can be understood as reflecting reality for many children throughout the nineteenth and twentieth centuries. Yet the significance of the frequency with which they appear in girls' fiction suggests also the ready availability of the maiden aunt image to stand for what is 'other' in women, to represent the part of the mother which was in reality unavailable and had needs which conflicted with those of her daughter.

The ambivalent nature of many maiden aunt characters, in which strength, power and independence were either allied or contrasted with restriction and alienation, also suggests that these characters may have enabled girls to grapple with the benefits and costs of futures outside marriage and motherhood. This was the case in the 'Swallows and Amazons' series of adventure stories by Arthur Ransome, one of the bestselling British children's authors from the 1930s to the 1950s, whose books were read by both boys and girls. His stories, like those of Byron Lewis and Brazil, show a split between bachelor uncles and fathers as adventurous and enabling and maiden aunts as restrictive and confining, suggesting ways in which girls were both socialised into but also could reject normative feminine roles. In *Swallowdale* (1931), Great Aunt Maria was a 'prim elderly lady' who disapproved of virtually everything her nieces did. She did not appear in person, but was depicted mainly through the eyes of the children as a critical outsider, not in this case as a maternal replacement but rather as a negative influence on their mother, compelling her to curtail their freedom. Maria's interference cemented the girls' bond with their seafaring uncle Jim (who was equally intimidated by her), but it also strengthened his authority as a replacement for their absent father. Thus, when in her censure of the children's behaviour she committed the cardinal sin of 'making mother cry', Uncle Jim invoked their dead father in his response: 'Bob would have liked them as they are.'[28]

Ransome's great-aunt was, however, a less marginal figure than the maiden aunts in schoolgirl stories. In *The Picts and the Martyrs* (1943), he gave her a quite remarkable degree of power and authority. Indeed in order to escape her aunt, the child Nancy had to involve most of the local community in a plot to deceive her. Yet she was only partially successful, for, while the great-aunt never discovered Nancy's deception, in one of the closing scenes she triumphed over them all, humiliating grown men and forcing them into submission. And she ended up evoking their reluctant admiration; the police and firemen saluted her with a cheer when she departed, and she was compared favourably with great-niece Nancy.[29]

It is in the figure of Nancy, captain of the sailing boat *Amazon*, that we can most easily perceive Ransome's ambivalence about strong single women. Nancy's boat is well named, as it is in Nancy that the qualities of both her tartar aunt and her adventurous uncle are writ large.[30] Practical, capable and courageous, she seemed to be heading for a very different future from the life of Victorian confinement led by her aunt, yet both characters were in some senses outsiders. Writing in 1960, critic Hugh Shelley tried to imagine Nancy's future, noting uneasily that while she might have been happy in the war and have joined the WRENS, 'as a character one feels she could not be transmuted into a normal, satisfactory adult'. While this comment could be read as casting doubt upon her future sexual orientation, in a way that is characteristic of the homophobia of the period,[31] the direct links made between the spinster aunt and her tomboy niece point to the fact that both figures transgressed gender norms, and suggest that one might ultimately grow into the other.

Tinkler's study of popular magazines for girls in the mid-twentieth century concludes that the frequent portrayal of girl heroines in ways 'inconsistent with prevailing feminine norms' was only acceptable at an age when they were 'deemed to be too young to be entering the marriage market'.[32] However, Auchmuty argues that while tomboys were a stock in trade in girls' school stories, some were allowed to grow up, and while the main heroines may have married, spinsterhood was portrayed as a valid alternative.[33] Returning to the view of the avuncular as offering an alternative to heterosexuality, we can see that Nancy could be viewed as a subversive figure. In a society which saw marriage and motherhood as the only acceptable future, she offered girls a different pathway towards adulthood.

Bachelor uncles in children's fiction

Unmarried uncles did not display their bachelorhood in the same way as maiden aunts. No links were made with sexual innocence or ignorance, nor were there any widespread expectations that bachelors should be closely involved with children. Yet in children's stories, the figure of the unattached uncle is as common as that of the aunt, albeit serving rather different functions in the plot. Like aunts, uncles were often 'split'. A good uncle offered advice and could be the key to exciting adventures; a wicked uncle led children into dishonesty and danger. Where aunts deputised as mothers, an uncle often replaced the father, a scenario not unfamiliar to young readers whose fathers had died, were absent during the wars or lived and worked abroad.

Bachelor uncles were sometimes represented as wise father figures but, unlike most biological fathers, they were in theory at least free from the responsibilities of being the family breadwinner. They were not regarded as the ultimate authority in a child's life and could more easily embody the playful, adventurous aspects of masculine adult–child relationships. Bachelor uncles often signified freedom, lack of commitment and a child-like irresponsibility, and in this guise, they were sometimes, like the absent Uncle Reggie in *Molly's Chance* and Uncle Jim in *Swallowdale*, juxtaposed with overprotective maiden aunts, subverting the norm of the responsible but distant father. For boys, irresponsible uncles could also be presented negatively, offering a standard of behaviour to be rejected as a model for adult manhood, but girls' relationship to uncles was somewhat different. Encountering a playful, irresponsible adult encouraged girl characters to be self-reliant and responsible, but it also engendered in them a positive view of the softer, more nurturing aspects of adult masculinity.

Two of the best-known children's authors in mid-twentieth century England, Arthur Ransome and C. S. Lewis, had bachelor uncles as significant characters in their fiction, which in other respects had little in common.[34] At the time Ransome wrote the 'Swallows and Amazons' series in the 1930s and 1940s and Lewis the 'Narnia' books in the early 1950s, neither author had much experience of living with children. Lewis was still a bachelor and Ransome had left his wife and only daughter,[35] while his second marriage was childless.[36] Yet both authors reconnected with their youth to create books of great imaginative power and appeal to young readers of both sexes.

As a bachelor in his fifties at the time of writing the series, Lewis was on good terms with his godchildren, but they did not play a major part in his life, and his knowledge of children's behaviour and fantasies derived principally from his own childhood.[37] In the 'Chronicles of Narnia', a best-selling series for over fifty years, the key adult characters enabling the children in the stories to discover Narnia were both bachelor uncles. In *The Lion, the Witch and the Wardrobe* (1950), four children were evacuated during the Second World War to the home of a kind, wise but rather remote, avuncular figure, Professor Kirk. The professor mirrored his creator in being an academic with no wife or family of his own,[38] and his insistence on following the rules of logic suggested that, like Lewis, he had spent most of his life in the rarefied atmosphere of Oxford or Cambridge, where celibacy was the norm and marriage discouraged.[39] Yet it was he who provided the magic wardrobe which was the children's entry point to Narnia and encouraged them to believe it was real.

It has been suggested that Lewis wrote *The Lion, the Witch and the Wardrobe* partly as a means of retreat from a troubled period and that he had himself escaped through the wardrobe door into a world of childhood reading.[40] In a sense, the Narnia stories were the childless Lewis's metaphorical 'children',[41] and the character of Kirk mirrored his creator's relationship both to his books and to his young readers. For unlike parents with their children, authors have little influence on what happens to their books after their 'birth' on the day of publication. Both Lewis and Kirk had helped to launch children (real and imagined) into a world of magic and adventure, but took no part in or responsibility for what happened to them afterwards.

The links between bachelorhood and childhood are also apparent in *The Magician's Nephew* (1955), which depicted the origins of Narnia. Here Professor Kirk reappeared as the child Digory, and we learn that he had first discovered Narnia through the actions of his mad bachelor uncle Andrew. Andrew's qualities of dishonesty, vanity, laziness and irresponsibility are contrasted with those of his spinster sister, the sensible, practical Aunt Hetty. Uncle Andrew gave Digory and his friend Polly the magic rings to get into Narnia, just as Digory (as Professor Kirk) was to provide the magic wardrobe for a later generation of children. But as a stereotypical 'wicked uncle' Andrew had little else in common with the wise professor. Rather, his effeminate appearance and dishonourable, cowardly behaviour provided a standard of unmanliness for Digory to despise and reject. Like a naughty child, Andrew was eventually caught, and was then infantilised, treated like a pet and nicknamed 'Brandy'.

What makes the role of bachelor uncles in Lewis's fiction particularly interesting is their liminal status on the borders of childhood and adulthood. Grownups were barred from entering Narnia and Lewis's adult characters seldom had children. Indeed very few married characters appear in any of the books. Professor Kirk stayed in touch with the magic because he remained unmarried and, despite his belief in logical thinking, by remaining open to childhood fantasy he was in an important sense not fully grownup. It was only a few months before writing the last Narnia book, *The Last Battle*, in 1952 at the age of fifty-three, that Lewis met Joy Greshham, the woman who was to persuade him to enter the grownup world of marriage and step-parenthood. But, like Lewis Carol creating *Alice in Wonderland*, it was as a bachelor that Lewis had opened the door to a fantasy world beloved of millions of children, a feat only a handful of other English authors have achieved.[42]

Arthur Ransome had an equally complex, though somewhat different relationship to childhood and adulthood. By the late 1920s, he had become estranged from his only child [43] and, although he had an ambivalent attitude to children, whose company he sought but also often wished to escape,[44] he may have been partly compensating for his loss as a father by writing children's books. A pivotal figure in many of these stories is Nancy's bachelor uncle Jim, also known as Captain Flint and widely regarded as one of Ransome's 'alter egos'.[45] Uncle Jim had a very different level of engagement with children in his stories from that of Lewis' wise professor or wicked magician with the Narnian children, yet he too was not fully grownup. As the 'black sheep' of the family, Jim Turner had been sent to South America when young and had subsequently travelled the world.[46] Returning home in *Swallows and Amazons* (1930), he initially behaved like an adult, excluding his nieces from his houseboat, and he only regained the status of uncle when he renounced grownup behaviour. This was achieved when he had returned to the children's level by engaging with them in a mock battle and submitting to the ultimate humiliation of walking the plank.[47]

Nicholas Tucker argues that 'some of the most attractive characters in children's fiction have always been those loyal companions who accompany the young hero or heroine, or indeed make such adventures possible in the first place',[48] but he also shows the dilemmas these characters pose.

Young readers may desire the security of a wise adult figure to help them out of difficulties but, in their private fantasy worlds, they also wish to escape from adult authority and take charge of their own destinies. Captain Flint solved this difficulty by never upstaging the children, and sometimes the adult–child dynamic was reversed. Although he represented security for the children, being a bachelor meant he did not always have to behave responsibly and, like Lewis' wicked Uncle Andrew, he sometimes got the children into difficult situations which they had to use considerable courage, resourcefulness and initiative to escape. In a later book, *Missee Lee* (1941), set in China, the Captain is shown to be irresponsible and a trifle incompetent. Yet despite his failings, the Captain's nieces and their friends John, Susan, Titty and Roger Walker were unfailingly loyal to him. As the quotation at the start of this chapter shows, when the Captain was in danger the children appealed for mercy, describing him as an uncle, friend and substitute father in order to secure his release.[49]

Yet we should not be led into thinking that an uncle was a straightforward replacement for a father any more than aunts were simple deputies for mothers. The difference between the Walkers' absent, godlike father and their all too human uncle is brought out more clearly in a third book, *We Didn't Mean to Go to Sea* (1935). Here, when Captain Walker unexpectedly encountered his children on a boat, he seemed strangely remote, offering them no comfort or physical affection, despite the fact that they were visibly upset. Titty reflected:

> Daddy was certainly very unlike anybody else. Captain Flint could be counted on in the same sort of way, but even Captain Flint, if he had met them all in some place where he had least expected them, would have called them by name, Captain John, Mate Susan, Able-Seaman Titty ... and then would have been in a hurry to know all about it, and how it had happened and so on. But Daddy ... was asking no questions at all. He had come aboard as if he had left them only for a few minutes instead of being away in the China Seas for ages and ages.[50]

The 'split' between two different kinds of masculine hero figure, the infallible but remote father and the warm, fallible uncle,[51] has a different effect from replacing a mother with a maiden aunt. Captain Flint's masculine failings meant he could never be a perfect father, but his interest and involvement in the children's exploits showed that adventurous men could still have a feminine, caring side. And, as with the mother–aunt split, this may have been helpful for readers who had fathers who were either physically or emotionally absent, particularly in a period when tears were seen as a regrettable weakness to be hidden and keeping a stiff upper lip was a marker of upper- and middle-class Englishness.

Aunts in autobiographical stories, social surveys and oral history

Autobiographical stories, told by women cared for by maiden aunts as children, often reproduce similar splits and projections to those discussed above. Aunts who became substitute mothers could be idealised and portrayed very positively, but they could also be demonised and become the object of negative projections. Yet, perhaps because these stories were told with hindsight from an adult perspective, these images are less polarised than in children's fiction, showing a greater degree of ambivalence alongside some recognition of the aunt's own point of view.

Jane Reid, another colonial child whose parents left her with relatives in the 1930s and 1940s when they were in Sudan, found the strongest memories of her childhood related to her unmarried aunts. In her autobiographical essay, she described one of these aunts, 'Kate',[52] who was her legal guardian, as a 'second mother' and the most important person in her life. The eldest of five children, Kate was 'plain', had spent her whole life as a daughter and 'in the man-short aftermath of the War can never have had any real hope of marriage'. The special charge she had of her niece must, Jane believed, have made 'a world of difference'. Kate's lack of a husband was viewed as having both positive and negative outcomes for their relationship. While Jane appreciated her aunt's love and care, she also experienced it as too intense, a concern that, as we saw in the previous chapter, was also being expressed at this time by psychologists and social workers who opposed the idea of single women adopting children. But it was her other aunt, 'Nelly', nine years younger and better looking than Kate, whom Jane had found particularly difficult.

Nelly had prevailed upon her parents to be allowed to go out to work, but the only job she was allowed was to become a Norland Nurse, where she would be 'safely chaperoned in nice households'. She had a sadistic streak and used to crunch Jane's bones when washing her hands. Jane sensed that the children Nelly looked after in her work were much more important than she was, a belief confirmed by the fact that Nelly's room was covered with pictures of her charges but contained none of Jane. When Nelly went to Sudan, she 'was entirely unresponsive to the hordes of sex-starved young men who crowded around her' and seemed concerned only with completing the knitting for the children in the family she was to work for in Kenya. Yet she was not good with children: 'She demanded love from them, and there is nothing that children shy away from more.'[53] The main points of tension that emerge in this story were the difficulty aunts had in leading lives outside the family and their overidentification with children, while the lack of men in their lives was seen as intrinsically problematic. Thus, although she knew that she came first with Auntie Kate and loved her, Jane found the idea that all her aunt wanted to do when she was old was to live in a cottage near her a little unnerving.

My mother, Joan E., felt even more disturbed when her aunt Lilla's companion Nona tried to persuade her to become a replacement for Lilla, after the latter's death in the mid-1930s. It was hard for women in Lilla and Nona's position to claim rights to adult friendships and partnerships with other women, and jealousies and divided loyalties are often apparent. Nona's request was particularly unwelcome because as children Joan E. and her siblings had disliked her. Letters written by Nona to Joan describing happy memories of the Christmases they had spent together stand in striking and somewhat chilling contrast with the children's view of her, voiced by Joan E.'s younger sister Noreen in her autobiography:

> None of us liked Nona … She used to call us 'dearie' which made us cringe and she had the most horrible rasping voice which hurt one's ears. Although she never in any way ill-treated us, in my eyes she would have been a good candidate for 'the wicked step-mother'.[54]

How far Nona really did act like a wicked stepmother is more questionable. Noreen's tendency to split Lilla and Nona into good and bad mother figures may have enabled her to endure her birth mother's absence, but it also ignored the importance of their relationship, a partnership whose validity she and Joan E. were able to recognise only later in life. Yet while Joan E. understood that Lilla must have needed Nona because she had nothing in her life and wasn't strong enough to train for a career, the sisters still tended to categorise their aunts as either angelic or miserable and sex-starved. Thus Nona was described as having been badly treated by her parents, kept completely ignorant of sex and men, and saved by Lilla, who was 'very sweet and gentle and had more or less rescued her from a life of utter misery'.[55]

A similar story was told by Susan about her childhood relationship in the 1950s with her beloved aunt 'Alice', whose personal papers and photos she had carefully preserved. Alice (born 1889) had formed a lasting partnership with Betty, whom she had first met during the 1930s while she was working as a domestic bursar at a teacher training college. Susan said she had disliked Betty (or B. J., as she was known) because she could not cope with children and thought of them as rivals for Alice's affection:

> I think there was probably always a bit of jealousy. I know B.J. although she enjoyed our company felt that we were taking Alice away from her, which we were. I didn't like the way she … you don't like the smell of people's houses do you. B.J. was a sort of smotherer.

Susan's insight into the rivalry and jealousy between her younger self and Betty owes much to hindsight, as does Jane's recognition of her aunt Kate's restricted employment opportunities and sexual frustration. Only as adults had their nieces seen these women's vulnerability and recognised that their caring responsibilities conflicted with work opportunities and adult relationships.

Some published memoirs from this period telling the stories of significant maiden aunts show clear contrasts between aunts and mothers. For example, as a child Mora Dickson's 'yardstick of acceptable behaviour was often a mental reference' to her maiden aunts, because of their intense privacy and propriety. One aunt had brought up four children after her brother's wife died in 1919, and stayed with them for thirty-two years, but was always known as 'Aunt Evelyn', never 'mother'. Mora saw this aunt's identity, as Jane did her aunt Kate's, as having been shaped by the tragedy of not having married: 'In a very real sense, Aunt Evelyn was a widow, but the dignity of widowhood, even the comfort of widowhood, were denied to her'. Ida Gandy stressed the gap between her freethinking mother and her father's five conventional, religious, unmarried sisters, who lived together and with whom she and her sister stayed as children. Not only did these aunts present their nieces with a very different kind of household and way of life from that of their parents, but they also offered a variety of 'auntly' relationships and ways of demonstrating their affection and love.[56]

The provision of an alternative to rather than a substitute for a parental relationship is also reflected in the image of godmother. In fairy stories, godmothers were often portrayed as wise women outside the immediate family circle who offered the unloved child support, love and good fortune, the antithesis of the cruel stepmother who had taken away the love of the father. Although for fairy-tale heroines 'happily ever after' invariably meant marriage, the fact that the bestower of such gifts was not married and had no visible attachment to men contradicted the dominant narrative. Retaining power meant remaining single.

In her 1960s study of maiden aunts, Moore reclaimed them as 'the fairy godmothers of real life', and several lifelong single women interviewed in the 1990s remembered unmarried aunts or godmothers in this light from their childhood. They were 'fun', 'interested in what we were doing', 'would come down to our level' or 'treated us rather like grown ups'. Alan Bennett's aunts were more glamorous, dashing and adventurous than his mother, 'always on for what they see as a lark'. He saw unmarried aunts serving 'in the family set-up as ladies of misrule'. As 'sisters of subversion', they could be blamed by his parents for getting their nieces and nephews overexcited or 'putting ideas in their heads'.[57]

Having a figure outside the immediate family who could act as a friend and counsellor could also be significant for girls and young women in choosing their career. Millicent (born 1906), whose aunt was a domestic science lecturer who wrote cookery books, had been persuaded by her to follow her example:

> She was very much a Scot, died at the age of 100, five years ago, and she was wonderful to me ... I didn't know what to do and she sort of got me to say I'd go in for teaching cookery. That aunt was at Queen Elizabeth College in London and some of the people she'd got used to go round visiting, and she came to this school that I was at and then she came and said would I like to apply for a post at Kilburn High School, which I did and of course I got the job. I don't think they even advertised for it.[58]

Anne, born in 1932, wrote about the importance of her spinster aunts when she was growing up, including a single friend of her mother's whom she called 'aunt'. Flo, a tailoress (and aunt on her father's side), and Mona, a pharmaceutical chemist (on her mother's), who had her own shop and became 'a kind of medical guru to the area', had both lived with and supported sick mothers and single elder sisters with disabilities. Anne commented:

> I grew up surrounded by both negative and positive examples of single-ness, but there was never any question of the legitimacy of this way of life whether chosen or not. I was very aware of the advantages of independence of action, financial independence and all the women I knew had their own homes which I loved to be in. I don't think I fully realised the burden of nursing, but the idea of caring for others was attractive, reinforced by my religious upbringing. We were constantly told that there are three vocations, you can be a nun, you can be married or you can be single in the world ... I was never in any doubt at all that my appointed path would be single in the world and by the time I was in my teens was quite deliberately looking to Mona and Aunt Flo as role models. Mona knew this and told me not long afterwards that she had left me all her jewellery in her will. In a way that made me feel that I too was part of her circle of single women.[59]

Elizabeth, born 1947, showed me photos of a similar circle of her mother's women friends who never married, whom she had always thought of as aunts even though they were unrelated, and she felt a continuing sense of responsibility to some of them in old age. Such strong role models in childhood enabled women like Elizabeth and Anne to see singleness as a positive choice in a society which favoured marriage. The gift of jewellery from a single aunt to a niece can be seen as symbolic of a different kind of inheritance strategy, both in material terms and as a model for living,[60] offering an alternative to the more usual intergenerational transfers of money, goods, and traditions of marriage and motherhood between parents and their daughters. That the aunt function also straddled the divide between family and friendship is suggested by the common mid-twentieth-century practice of giving older family friends the courtesy title of 'aunt'.

Aunts' own perspectives are harder to ascertain, with nieces and nephews rarely mentioned in professional women's autobiographies.[61] However, letters from my Aunt Norah to my mother show a strong continuing interest in her nieces even after they married, and she did not shirk from giving her opinion about their children's upbringing. For example, in 1954, she diagnosed my illness at the age of two immediately after the birth of my younger brother as symptomatic of my need for attention, and recalled her sister Lilla's 'cure' for their niece Noreen as a child:

> Noreen badly wanted music lessons and Lilla gently suggested to her that it was impossible to find money for music and doctors bills. It is I believe a fact that there were no more doctor's bills at all – a great relief and Noreen had her music lessons. You will manage your little Tink all right – tho she may play you up a lot, and the trouble is that the illnesses are real, they are brought on and caught – may be [even such things as measles], because they are desired.[62]

Peter Townsend's interviews show similar levels of involvement and interest from older working-class unmarried women with nieces and nephews, and in some cases financial support. Two unmarried sisters in their seventies regularly looked after their married sisters' children in times of illness, and described themselves as 'weekenders' who 'took them out to the park to give their mother a rest'. This closeness with nieces and nephews continued into adult life, providing these sisters as it did my aunt Norah with regular contact and an important channel for their affections.

Being in this position, however, could also be oppressive for women who resented being treated as if they had no life of their own. Etta Close, a woman traveller who published accounts of her journeys in Africa in the 1920s, made this point:

> It is hard ... to find it sufficient to be useful to relations, to meet Tommy at the station ... to take care of darling Elsie at the dentists ... and hardest of all to realise that these things are taken for granted, that the relatives are simply saying to one other, 'A single woman, you know with nothing in the world to do, of course she should be glad to be of use to others.'[63]

Records from the New Survey show a number of unmarried older aunts or female lodgers (who may have been treated as aunts) living with families, but the variations in age, employment and generational patterns suggest considerable differences in how these relationships would have been experienced. For example, a forty-year-old Deptford man (who may have been widowed, divorced or separated) with a fifteen-year-old son was supporting his sixty-year-old aunt, who appears to have been in a maternal position within the household. This woman would have had a very different experience from that of another family where a sixty-year-old wife with three working daughters aged between twenty-four and thirty was at home caring for her five-year-old grandchild. These daughters might all have been treated as the child's aunts but would not have been its primary carers, even though one daughter may well have been its (unmarried) mother.

My own oral history interviews with single women show considerable variation in closeness and the degree of confidence shown in relationships with nieces and nephews, depending on the amount of time spent together and what other household and family dynamics came into play. For example, Dora, whose principal identity was as a dutiful daughter to sick and ageing parents, had brought up her brother's daughter from the age of ten after the child's mother had died. Yet she felt that her niece Jean was more like a sister. This may have been partly because of the age gap between them, but it also reflects Dora's mother's continuing maternal position within the household, even though she was in poor health and needed ongoing nursing care from her daughter.

As we saw in chapter 3, health visitor Ellen identified herself strongly as an aunt. She also lived in a three-generational household and shared child care with her sister-in-law, who had been a close friend and housemate since their college days. After her friend married her brother, Ellen had become an additional parent to the children and she presented this as a duty imposed upon her by her family, one of a number of reasons why she hadn't married. However, single women who had not lived with nieces and nephews during their early childhood could be less confident about this relationship. For example, Mildred got to know her only niece well in the latter's adolescence, but did not see herself as a role model. Rather she compared the adventurous demeanour of her niece with her own lack of confidence. Her low self-esteem extended to her position as an aunt, emerging in a comment that her niece had been 'exceptionally kind to her aunt', which seemed to imply she had no right to expect this.

Bachelor uncles in social surveys, autobiography and oral history

Bachelor uncles are easier to trace in mid-twentieth-century fiction than in life, but this does not mean that uncles were necessarily unimportant in families, rather that they were less visible than aunts. The commonest ways in which single men developed avuncular relationships with children were either through co-residency or as family friends. Uncles were a particularly significant presence in children's life in cases where a child lived with grandparents whose unmarried sons were still living at home, a frequent occurrence in working-class households. Of the forty-one single men over the age of thirty in Deptford investigated by the New Survey, seven (usually the wife's brothers) were living with married siblings and their children, and at least two more lodging with families with children under ten where they would probably have played similar avuncular roles, and many more younger men were in similar situations. Young and Willmott also found that the great majority of their single respondents lived with parents, siblings or other relations,[64] with only ten men out of the 137 unmarried people in their general sample living apart from relatives. However, uncles do not always appear in sources of this kind. In large families where an older daughter had a child outside marriage, the child was often passed off as the grandmother's youngest child, and uncles would therefore have been recorded as elder brothers. Yet even in these circumstances, an avuncular relationship could develop if there was a sufficient gap between the child and his or her uncle's ages.

Peter Townsend's interviews with elderly unmarried men show frequent contact with nephews and nieces, with those who had lived with family members most likely to remain in contact in old age. One informant aged seventy-six, who lived alone in squalid conditions, had until three years before lodged with his sister-in-law and her children. The importance of being an uncle for this man is suggested by the fact that he had spent one eighth of his one pound weekly income for food, clothes and household sundries on a gift for his fifty-year-old nephew, who visited him on Christmas day (the only present he gave), and that without this visit, he would have been left entirely alone. Yet these kinds of relationships with children were often perceived as provisional and could not always be relied upon. Another sixty-six-year old unmarried man interviewed by Townsend had lived for forty years with his married sister and two unmarried nieces aged forty and forty-two, but 'despite his strong bond with his sister and her husband and children', Townsend believed 'he was anxious about the strength of those bonds when he in fact becomes old and infirm himself'.[65]

My interviewee Dennis had also kept in touch with a niece whose family had shared his house, but felt that he was closer to his godchildren, who were the offspring of friends. As single men, his and his close male friend's chief contribution was as babysitters:

> I mean we were always there babysitting while they were out … so I mean there's that way you are *useful*, you are single and you can do it … We used to go and play certain games with them and tell them to go to bed and wash behind their ears which they didn't like – come up and give you a scrub if you're not careful.

The importance of uncles particularly for children without fathers is shown in an autobiographical essay by Tony, born in 1920, who had grown up in his maternal grandparents' house never knowing his father, and whose male relatives 'consciously or unconsciously filled the absences in his life which his missing father had created'.[66] His mother's brother was especially generous, providing him with pocket money, helping to pay for his education and introducing him to the masculine world of sport. Tony argued that the presence of his bachelor uncle and grandfather as surrogate fathers had been important in his formative years and he questioned the extent to which not having a proper live-in father had affected his development, feeling rather that it was the secrecy that surrounded the circumstances of his birth and lack of genealogical knowledge about his father's family that disturbed him most.[67]

It is difficult to know how commonly unmarried uncles offered alternatives to relationships with fathers, since we have little other than anecdotal evidence, and their significance has never been considered in any depth. My own experience of my mother's unmarried brother Pat was that he not only played with me, but took me seriously as though I was an adult. Pat lodged with my family intermittently when I was a young child in the mid-1950s, at a time when my father was often absent from home. He was a scientist and, like Professor Kirk in *The Lion, the Witch and the Wardrobe*, called on logic to answer my questions. My strongest memory is of him reading long passages out of the newspapers, which I loved even though I understood little of what he read.

In fact, Professor Kirk was himself modelled on a real avuncular relationship between C. S. Lewis and a family friend. William Kirkpatrick became Lewis's tutor and mentor during a period of alienation from his father. But in this relationship, it was the uncle figure rather than the father who represented the stiff-upper-lip model of masculinity. After the death of his mother when he was only nine, Lewis had been unable to cope with his father's emotional outbursts and was given no help to express his own grief. This resulted in an ingrained hatred and fear of emotional display, especially in men. In contrast to his father, whom he constantly ridiculed and denigrated, Lewis regarded Kirk (who like his namesake insisted that every statement be subjected to the rules of logic) as one of his greatest teachers, a man he revered and to whom he felt deeply indebted. [68]

These accounts suggest that childless unmarried uncles and family friends could form valuable relationships with children, but these were not always unproblematic. Another bachelor family friend from my childhood (whom I later interviewed when he was in his eighties) offered me a more ambivalent viewpoint. David was a probation officer who worked with young offenders and became a close friend of my father. My memory of our visits to his house when I was a child was his unusual ability to meet us at our own level and to devote himself entirely to giving us a good time. Yet as was the case with several other men I interviewed, he was very negative about his suitability as a parent and made much of his bad temper:

> If they were here for a week, rather than for two or three hours, I'd probably be strangling some of them ... I liked children but I don't think I'd have made a very good parent. I think I'd have been a ghastly parent, unfair and irritable and not even-handed. I'd probably have hit them too, I'm pretty sure of that.

David's confrontation of his negative feelings is not only suggestive of pain in this area of his life, but also speaks to the fears many of us have about the frustrations of parenthood and inequalities of power between adults and children. These fears are often connected with single men. A respondent to the 1949 MO 'Little Kinsey' survey who identified himself as homosexual casts further light on the more troubling aspects of single men's relationships with children. During the time he was a teacher he had 'trained himself to be completely negative in presence of unwilling or innocent boys', and he argued that his restraint meant that he was unlikely 'to commit a moral crime' (even though his statement suggests that he regarded some boys as willing and/or guilty). His consequent exclusion from fatherhood was a source of great disappointment to him: 'I am fond of children (no sexual feelings enter here at all, I must emphasise) and I know I would be a good father, just as I am a good uncle.'[69]

The autobiographical and fictional stories discussed here show that bachelor uncles (both in fantasy and in reality) could offer children different views of masculinity. When uncles treated children like grownups they offered them a level of equality which parents usually denied them, and those who played with children were often more adventurous because they did not have total responsibility for them. Although in their dealings with children they might be perceived as wise and generous, not having the authority of a father they could act in ways a father could or should not. In this respect, their presence in children's stories may be a reflection of both the absence of breadwinner fathers and the uncertainty of men's place in family life.

Malcolm Muggeridge's claim that Arthur Ransome wrote good books for children not because he liked them but because he was himself child-like,[70] may be relevant here. Perhaps Ransome put his own child-like qualities into the character of a bachelor because he did not want to associate them with his own failures as a father. For there was also a shadow side to these images of bachelor uncles, portrayed by Lewis in the character of Uncle Andrew and recognised by David in his doubts about his suitability as a parent. It is easier to invest uncles with negative qualities, to portray them as wicked men who abuse or lead children astray, than to admit that fathers might also be inadequate or that parents might have abusive feelings towards children.

Maiden aunts were less likely to be represented as childish or on an equal level with children, characterised rather as warm, loving replacements for mothers or as dominating, restrictive and generally unsatisfactory stand-ins. I suspect this gender split may reflect the view that mothers should place their children's interests above their own, a belief which increased in strength during the early and mid-twentieth century. Maiden aunts often had to stand in for but couldn't always be 'good enough' mothers and were often the recipients of negative projections. But they also challenged heterosexual norms, offering girls relationships and futures in adult life beyond marriage and motherhood. This challenge will be explored further in the next chapter, where I look at unmarried men and women's professional relationships with cildren.

Notes

1 Letter from Anne to KH, 4 February 1995.
2 Arthur Ransome, *Missee Lee*, 1941 (Harmondsworth: Penguin, 1971), p. 205.
3 Sigmund Freud, 'Family Romances', 1909, in *Standard Edition of the Complete Psychological Works of Sigmund Freud*, 9, trans. James Strachey (London: Hogarth Press/Institute of Psychoanalysis, 1959).
4 Davidoff *et al.*, *The Family Story*.
5 See Buettner, *Empire Families*.
6 John Hodgson, *The Search for Self: Childhood in Autobiography and Fiction since 1940* (Sheffield: Sheffield Academic Press, 1993), p. 13.

7 *Ibid.*, p. 55.

8 *Ibid.*, p. 51.

9 Eve Kosofsky Sedgwick, 'Tales of the Avunculate: The Importance of Being Earnest', in Eve Kosofsky Sedgwick, *Tendencies* (London: Routledge, 1994), pp. 63–4.

10 Both my own and Peter Townsend's interviews show this to have been the case.

11 Mary Evans, *Missing Persons: The Impossibility of Auto/Biography* (London: Routledge, 1999), pp. 91–2, 79 and 135.

12 Kelly Boyd has noted the frequent appearance of male non-parental figures such as teachers, tutors and guardians in story papers aimed at working-class boys as agents of socialisation, encouraging obedience to parents and other authorities during the interwar years in Britain. See Kelly Boyd, 'Knowing Your Place: The Tensions of Masculinity in Boys' Story Papers, 1918–39' in Roper and Tosh, *Manful Assertions*.

13 See Nina Auerbach, 'Old Maids and the Wish for Wings', in *Woman and the Demon: The Life of a Victorian Myth* (Cambridge, MA: Harvard University Press, 1982), quoted in Laura Doan (ed.), *Old Maids to Radical Spinsters: Unmarried Women in the Twentieth Century Novel* (Urbana, IL: University of Illinois Press, 1991), p. x.

14 Leonore Davidoff, 'The Decline of the "Long" Family: Context and Consequences', paper presented at Radboud University, Nijmegen, The Netherlands, 20 May 2005.

15 This offers one answer to Nicola Humble's question as to why mid-twentieth-century novels focus on large families at a time when two children had become the norm. Humble, *The Feminine Middlebrow Novel*, p. 150.

16 *Chambers English Dictionary* (Cambridge: W. R. Chambers and Cambridge University Press, 1988), p. 90.

17 Katherine Moore, *Cordial Relations: The Maiden Aunt in Fact and Fiction* (London: Heinemann, 1966).

18 Rosemary Auchmuty, *A World of Girls* (London: Women's Press, 1992), pp. 3–4.

19 Angela Brazil, *The School on the Cliff* (London: Blackie and Son, 1938), p. 155. Brazil was the best-known writer in this genre, and very prolific.

20 Dorothea Moore, *Sarah to the Rescue* (London: Nisbet, 1932); Irene Mossop, *Una Wins Through* (London: Frederick Warner, 1935). I have no biographical information on either of these two authors, but both published extensively in the interwar years. Dorothea Moore was particularly well known for her girl guide stories. See Cadogan and Craig, *You're a Brick, Angela!*, ch. 9.

21 Moore, *Cordial Relations*, p. 118.

22 J. H. Byron Lewis, *Molly's Chance* (London: Thomas Nelson, 1926). pp. 21–2. This book's enduring popularity is suggested by a further edition in 1950.

23 Brazil, *The School at the Turrets* (London: Blackie and Sons, 1935), p. 65.

24 Valerie Walkerdine, *Schoolgirl Fictions* (London: Verso, 1990), p. 92.

25 See Juliet Mitchell, *Psychoanalysis and Feminism* (Harmondsworth: Penguin 1975), pp. 370–3, for a discussion of the incest taboo. The danger of those feelings between father and daughter is shown in an earlier Brazil story, *The Fortunes of Philippa* (1907), where an intense father–daughter relationship is ended by the girl's removal to another household at the onset of adolescence.

26 Walkerdine, *Schoolgirl Fictions*, pp. 91–3.

27 See Juliette Mitchell (ed.), *The Selected Melanie Klein* (Harmondsworth: Penguin, 1986).

28 Peter Hunt, *Arthur Ransome* (Boston, MA: Twayne 1991), pp. 81–2 .

29 Arthur Ransome, *The Picts and the Martyrs*, 1943 (London: Random House, 1993), p. 385.

30 Ransome's admiration for Nancy as a character is suggested by the fact that he named his own boat after her. Christina Hardyment, *Arthur Ransome and Captain Flint's Trunk* (London: Jonathan Cape, 1984).

31 Hugh Shelley, *Arthur Ransome* (London: Bodley Head, 1960), p. 18.

32 Tinkler, *Constructing Girlhood*, p. 87.

33 Auchmuty, *A World of Girls*, p. 103.

34 My thanks to Jo Beedell for pointing out the significance of uncles in the 'Narnia' books.

35 Hugh Brogan (ed.), *Signalling from Mars: The Letters of Arthur Ransome* (London: Pimlico, 1988).

36 Hunt, *Arthur Ransome*, pp. xv–xvi and 20.

37 Walter Hooper and Roger Lancelyn Green, *C. S. Lewis: A Biography* (London: William Collins, 1974), p. 241; A. N. Wilson, *C. S. Lewis: A Biography* (London: Flamingo, 1991), p. 220.

38 Walter Hooper, *C. S. Lewis: A Companion and Guide* (London: HarperCollins, 1997), p. 427.

39 Wilson, *C. S. Lewis*, p. 65.

40 *Ibid.*, pp. 220–3.

41 My thanks to Helen Kendall for this insight.

42 John Cooper and Jonathan Cooper, *Children's Fiction, 1900–1950* (Ashgate: Aldershot, 1998), p. 205. The authors claim that the 'Narnia' books are amongst the most popular ever written for children.

43 Brogan, *Signalling from Mars*, pp. 148–9, 155–8, 160 and 183.

44 Hugh Brogan, *The Life of Arthur Ransome* (London: Jonathan Cape, 1984), p. 299.

45 Shelley, *Arthur Ransome*, p. 18.

46 Like many of its sequels, this drew upon Ransome's experiences as boat builder, traveller and sailor. *Ibid.*, p. 31; Hunt, *Arthur Ransome*, p. 6.

47 Arthur Ransome, *Swallows and Amazons*, 1930 (London: Jonathan Cape, 1958).

48 Nicholas Tucker, 'Finding the Right Voice: The Search for the Ideal Companion in Adventure Stories', in Charlotte F. Otten and Gary D. Schmidt (eds), *The Voice of the Narrator in Children's Literature* (Westport, CT: Greenwood Press, 1989), p. 143.

49 Ransome, *Missee Lee*, p. 205.

50 Arthur Ransome, *We Didn't Mean to Go to Sea* (London: Jonathan Cape, 1935), p. 279.

51 Hunt, *Arthur Ransome*, p. 4. Hunt relates this split to Ransome's ambivalent attitude to his own father. Brogan, *The Life of Arthur Ransome*, pp. 356–7, sees it as a fictional resolution of his need as a child to gain his father's approval.

52 Not her real name.

53 Unpublished autobiography of Jane Reid, 'A 1930s Childhood' (1998).

54 Unpublished autobiography of Noreen Torrey (1995).

55 *Ibid.*

56 Mora Dickson, *The Aunts* (Edinburgh: St Andrew Press, 1981), pp. 8 and 90–3; Ida Gandy, *Staying with the Aunts* (London: Alan Sutton, 1989).

57 Bennett, *Untold Stories*, pp. 56–7.

58 Millicent also went on to lecture, and published books on domestic management

which sold well for many years.

59 Letter from Anne to KH, 4 February 1995.

60 Personal communication from Wren Sidhe. My great-aunt Norah gave me her mother's and father's engagement rings on my eighteenth birthday with a letter which tried rather inarticulately to express how much I meant to her. An example can be found in the late eighteenth century when two spinster cousins built Á La Ronde, a house near Exmouth. The elder stipulated in her will that it could be inherited only by (preferably older) unmarried female relatives.

61 The memoirs of a civil servant, two teachers and the editor of *Good Housekeeping* give very little space to family life beyond childhood. Martindale, *From One Generation to Another*; Amy Barlow, *Seventh Child: The Autobiography of a Schoolmistress* (London: Gerald Duckworth, 1969); Mary G Clarke, *A Short Life of Ninety Years* (Edinburgh, privately published by Astrid and Martin Hughes, 1973); Alice Head, *It Could Never Have Happened* (London: William Heinemann, 1939).

62 Letter from Norah Lea-Wilson to Joan Holden, 23 June 1954.

63 Birkett, *Spinsters Abroad*, p. 30.

64 Young and Willmott, *Family and Kinship*, pp. 181–2.

65 *FLOP*, Peter Townsend's interviews with HE and HB.

66 Tony Foley, unpublished autobiographical essay (1997), cited in Davidoff *et al.*, *The Family Story*, p. 261.

67 *Ibid.*

68 C. S. Lewis, *Surprised by Joy: The Shape of My Early Life* (London: Geoffrey Bles, 1955), pp. 25, 38, 128, 131 and 141.

69 MO, Sexual Behaviour 1939–50, Box 12, Form A9/2, Questionnaire (Panel D94/3) 1949, 12/12/B, ref. 440, index no. 4215.

70 Brogan, *The Life of Arthur Ransome*, p. 299.

8

Interest and emotion:
professional and paid work with children

Other People's babies and that's my life! Mother to dozens and nobody's
wife ... Other people's babies, Nothing to show – twelve months trouble
and out I go.[1]

I think there's something about a nanny. She probably would put a
lot into it because she hasn't got children of her own, because if I had
children I couldn't love or give or feel any different about them at all.
(Interview with Emily)

Introduction

THIS PENULTIMATE CHAPTER GOES to the heart of the issues I
have been exploring throughout the second part of this book. As
I showed in chapter 2, for men and women who never married,
work, as well as being a means to survival, was often central to their
identity and feelings of self-worth. For childless people who actively
chose to work with other people's children in many different fields, for
example as teachers, social workers, psychoanalysts, probation officers,
matrons, house mothers, nannies or nurses, it was also their legacy to the
future, a material and emotional investment in the next generation that
helped to compensate them for not having had children of their own. For
children such an investment could be equally significant, offering, as with
aunts and uncles, valuable role models which were different from those
of parents.

Yet there were also costs to these relationships. Strong attachments
could be formed which resulted in painful partings when workers left
their jobs. And it was not only the children who suffered. Financial
and emotional exchanges between parents and professional workers
or carers could be difficult for all parties. Unmarried people who felt
frustrated because they had been unable to have children of their own

were particularly vulnerable. As suggested in the last chapter, it was easy to invest too much in these relationships and become rivals to parents, leaving children with divided loyalties. This was especially likely in cases where the adults did not have strong social support systems or other satisfying emotional relationships. Rivalries could also occur between professional workers who sought to impart advice and expertise to mothers or take control of children in ways that might or might not have been in their best interests. Finally, children were sometimes neglected in jobs where carers were undervalued and underpaid or where workers were in an ambiguous position, employed to take the place of parents but without the same authority or long-term commitment. This could occur when women who disliked or were indifferent to children felt obliged to enter child-related work on the grounds of their gender or for lack of other employment opportunities, with unhappy consequences for all parties.

The conscious and unconscious motivations that led many unmarried childless people to work with children will be examined here and links made between psychic formations and material conditions. While my main focus is on unmarried women's work with children, circumstances in which unmarried men have been influential in young people's lives are also discussed, particularly in schools and the youth and probation services.

Social motherhood

The assumption that the most appropriate occupation for unmarried women lay in work connected with children has a long history. Most pertinently for this period, it can be linked to eugenicist fears about racial deterioration which found expression in legislation aimed at improving the health of babies and school children in the early years of the twentieth-century, and also to social maternalist ideals which emerged in the second half of the nineteenth century, in which women's special interest in family policies gave them a claim to citizenship.[2] Building upon the pioneering work of an earlier generation in areas such as education, nursing and social work, in the years before the First World War increasing numbers of middle-class women (both single and married) moved into philanthropic and voluntary work with the principal aims of rescuing children and monitoring their welfare.

While many voluntary organisations dealing with children remained active until after the Second World War, often working in tandem with the growth of statutory social, welfare and educational services, during the interwar years these areas of work were increasingly being seen as the province of professional, paid workers.[3] With the exception of boys' secondary schools, youth groups and the probation service, it was work most frequently undertaken by unmarried women, although senior positions and places on managing boards were still often filled by men. College-based qualifications became necessary in areas such as teaching,[4] in midwifery (following the 1902 Midwives Act), and in health visiting. These latter developments saw the replacement of untrained district visitors and handywomen, usually married women with personal experience of childbirth and child care, with professional, unmarried experts. The shift from voluntary to professional work took place in an economic climate in which married women were being discouraged from paid work to avoid supposedly unfair competition with men and where marriage bars were widely imposed, particularly in teaching. Increasing length and costs of training also excluded most working-class as well as married women from these professions until the 1950s.

An economic climate in which so many unmarried women were employed in child-related occupations must also be linked to an ongoing concern about the plight of women affected by the 'lost generation' of men, and the view that to work with children was an effective way of sublimating celibate women's sexual and maternal drives. Stopes took this line by advocating occupations such as maternity nursing for women unable to marry as a means of satisfying 'sex hunger'.[5] The psychiatrist William Sargent made a similar point. He differentiated between biological, parental and intellectual features of the sex instinct and did not regard child-care occupations as helpful for women in whom the biological or intellectual urges were dominant. However, for those in whom the parental feature of the sex instinct was strongest, 'instead of growing bitter and resentful because they lack the opportunity to have babies of their own, they retain their charm and the sweetness of their personalities by caring for children whose parents are too poor, too weary or too uneducated to give them real pleasure and proper guidance'.[6]

By the late 1940s, writing in the midst of the post-war labour shortage, Eyles offered a wider range of suggested jobs to unmarried women, including science, music, literature and business. Yet she too saw work primarily as a means of sublimating the reproductive instincts in the absence of 'natural parenthood'.[7] Thus in *Unmarried but Happy*, she gave a long list of opportunities to work with children, including a range of suggestions for informal care, in schools, playgrounds and girls' clubs, or in child welfare work, child minding and baby sitting.[8] Responding to the acute shortage of domestic labour and the demise of living-in service after the war,[9] Eyles tried to convince single women that they should be plugging a gap (previously filled by servants) which was largely unrecognised by state, despite the post-war government's stated objective of 'rebuilding the family'.

While many of the women who followed advice of this kind might in other circumstances have chosen not to work with children, demonstrating their expertise in the business of mothering could be important for psychological as well as practical reasons, offering a way of claiming authority over mothers. Yet this strategy was not entirely successful. As we shall see, it often produced the kinds of splits discussed in earlier chapters, in which childless women who became involved with children could be perceived either as selfless ministering angels or as interfering, rigid and restrictive. Some women's anger and pain about not having their own children was also projected onto mothers, who in turn resented interference and often projected their own discontents onto women who appeared to have greater freedom.

Child-care experts

The role of single middle-class women in advising, monitoring and regulating working-class mothers and children has been examined by a number of feminist historians, particularly in the context of the late nineteenth and early twentieth centuries.[10] But there has been much less consideration of the psychological motivations behind these women's work and the personal satisfactions and frustrations they experienced.

The pleasure unmarried women gained from displaying their professional knowledge about children can be discerned in advice books and manuals for mothers published during this period by nurses and midwives. One well-known author in this field was Elizabeth Morrison, who advised on baby care for the magazine *Nursery World* throughout the 1930s and 1940s, and in 1949 published a collection of letters from mothers together with her replies to them.[11] Morrison followed the methods of the world-renowned New Zealand child-care expert Frederick Truby King, whom she met when he came to England with his unmarried daughter Mary in 1928. Mary was equally energetic in publicising her father's work during the 1930s, making it available to a popular audience in a handbook for mothers and nurses entitled *Mothercraft* (1934).[12]

The main emphasis in these books and other similar manuals was on the mother's and child's physical health, reflecting wider concerns about infant mortality and the belief that this was principally a result of inadequate maternal care, particularly contaminated milk, dirty bottles and the failure to breast feed.[13] In pre-Second World War war manuals, little attention was given to babies' emotional relationship with their mothers or primary carers. Indeed, mothers could be discouraged from kissing and cuddling babies for fear of spreading germs. There were also warnings against demand feeding, with a strict four-hourly feeding schedule allowing only two hours' daily interaction between mother and baby. Truby King's timetable assumed that a normal healthy baby would sleep almost continuously between feeds and warned mothers to beware of the "'spoilt" cry', insisting that 'a baby who cries simply because he wants to be picked up and played with must be left to "cry it out"' and 'should not be treated as a plaything, made to laugh and crow and "show" off to every visitor to please his parents' vanity'.[14] Morrison's post-war baby advice book was less prescriptive and uncompromising in tone, giving more credit to a mother's innate knowledge and wisdom, reflecting shifts in understanding about childhood during the 1940s. The influence of the psychology and psychoanalytic theory popularised by John Bowlby and Donald Winnicott after the war probably led her to lay more emphasis on the value of motherly love and to stress the 'demonstrative affection and cuddling and very special attention' children required after the birth of a new baby.[15]

However, for both these women, an unimportant motivation for publishing these books appears to have been the pleasure they gained from being baby experts. Truby King's pride in the success of her father's methods shines out of her book, while Morrison laid stress on her long experience of looking after children and selected letters which showed how grateful mothers were for her advice. It is hard to know how representative these letters were. A personal account from Joyce Nicholson described the 'universal agony' experienced by mothers of her generation who had to listen to their babies crying, but for some busy working-class mothers adherence to strict feeding and sleeping regimes may have helped them manage their workload.[16]

Oral testimony from a midwife throws further light upon the satisfaction that could be gained in giving this kind of advice, but also exposes tensions between working-class mothers and middle-class unmarried baby experts.[17] Muriel was attached to an East End maternity hospital in London during the late 1930s, and as one of only two qualified midwives had supervised pupil midwives and medical students. She maintained that mothers in the poorer urban districts had been glad of her services and had few doubts about her ability to take charge of a birth, laying great stress on her authority:

> I mean sometimes they had them before we got there; not very often, 'cos if they did they got well told off you see because that wasted a pupil's

case ... They always sent in good time 'cos they knew they'd be told off
if they had the baby beforehand.

Yet when she moved on to become a health visitor in a country district,
Muriel had more problems. Rural women were less willing to accept the
dictates of an outsider. They didn't like 'new-fangled ideas like immunisa-
tion and taking the baby to the clinic', and the influence of grandmothers
'mucking about in the background saying "you don't want that done
dear"' undermined her authority.[18] While this testimony gives a one-sided
picture, it does suggest the conflicts of opinion that arose between professional childless experts and mothers for whom child-care knowledge
came through their own and their family's day-to-day experiences.
Against their traditional knowledge, Muriel had the weight of the scientific, male-dominated, medical authorities behind her and could if necessary take refuge in a professional identity. Still, she found it easier to deal
with women who could not confront her with this kind of knowledge,
and to maintain her professional superiority had labelled compliant but
ignorant mothers as 'good', whilst those who challenged her authority
were 'difficult'. Carolyn Steedman gives an insight into how such inter-
ventions might be received. Steedman never forgot her mother crying
as she watched the retreating figure of a health visitor who had just told
her 'this house isn't fit for a baby',[19] and the memory shaped Steedman's
understanding of class and gender relations in this period.

Tensions between mothers and child-care experts are also evident in
Our Towns, a report commissioned and written in 1940 by the Hygiene
Committee of the Women's Group on Public Welfare, which was seeking
explanations for the complaints lodged against urban evacuees. The great
majority of serving members on this committee were unmarried, including
the chair, the secretary and the main writer of the report. So also were the
authors of several appendices and three quarters of the witnesses representing a range of different interest groups, while its preface was written
by Margaret Bondfield, a prominent unmarried Labour MP who chaired
the Women's Group (see appendix 3 at the end of the book).

These women's investigation of the conditions of the towns from
which the evacuated children originated[20] was critical of working-
class women's poor parental control, which they said 'appears in every
section of this work with the inevitability of King Charles's Head'. Their
superior knowledge and expertise about childrearing allowed them to set
themselves up as rivals to parents. For example, children's propensity for
eating sweets could be overcome, it was argued, by bypassing the parent,
catching the child young and training it as an 'enlightened despot', so that:
'it will insist, not upon a toffee apple but upon something more like a raw

carrot or an apple without the toffee. Its family must be encouraged to follow suit, and it will some day make a carrot conscious parent.'[21]

But while middle-class women with interests in child care and child health saw themselves as agents of reform, their professional identities in this area of work were far from stable or secure, and this kind of advice could provoke cruel caricatures. A good example of this can be found in a children's story by Eleanor Graham (1896–1984), founder of Puffin Books. *The Children who lived in a Barn* (1938) shows the district visitor, Miss Ruddle, who was 'thin, sharp featured and of a most interfering nature', trying to take a family of children into foster care. But the children remained implacably opposed and allied themselves with the village mothers, who also hated her because 'she poked her nose inside their cottages and tried to discover things that were nothing whatsoever to do with her. She had a passion for "showing them how". She showed them how to keep house, how to look after their children ... in fact there was no end to the things she showed them'.[22]

Similar criticisms of working-class women, seen from the viewpoint of the professional woman, appear throughout *Our Towns*, including an appendix on bedwetting. Miss A. M. Maynard, who worked in a Surrey hospital, discussed treatments which involved removing children from their homes, curing and re-educating them in hospital and ensuring that they had a clean record for a month before leaving. Yet Miss Maynard does not represent herself as an interfering 'Miss Ruddle'. Rather, she shows her strong identification with and attachment to the children she had 'rescued', a belief in their mutual interdependence and also in the benefits for the child that could follow from such a relationship:

> You must first win the battle and they want you to; no one will follow weakness, and no one is so whole-heartedly loyal when once you have their respect as those rescued children. Then you will cure not just one symptom, but the whole child, and from his belief in you and your belief in him, he will come to believe in himself.[23]

The idea that children with these kinds of difficulties needed to be believed in, and must be 'rescued' because they came from 'problem families', was a powerful narrative. And both unmarried women and men were inspired to answer this call, motivated by genuine concern for children's welfare as well as by corresponding needs of their own. Contemporary novels, films and personal testimony from teachers and probation officers offer us very positive views of these kinds of relationships which suggest that childless men and women made important contributions to the lives of other people's children. Yet here too there were contradictions, particularly in the case of unmarried teachers, who as we have seen were sometimes portrayed as sexual deviants and a source of contamination. And perhaps because of this perceived danger, as we shall see, unmarried people's own need to love and be loved by children could not always be directly expressed.

Child-care practitioners: teachers

Oram in her study of women teachers has argued that women in this profession occupied an ambiguous position. Their work lay within the maternal sphere in its concern with the care and upbringing of children, yet it was also masculine in that it was well paid by the standards of other female occupations, offered a lifelong career in public service and required intellectual ability and training. Their marital status complicates the picture still further. The links between femininity and marriage made their spinster status appear anomalous, and any feminist activity which sought to improve their position in relation to men, such as demands for equal pay or an end to the marriage bar, could easily be turned against them. In the context of high unemployment during the 1930s, they could be perceived as affluent, selfish spinsters, depriving the family bread-winner and his family of a job, and also less well qualified to teach than married women because they were sex-starved and unfulfilled and as such unable to understand children or deal with difficult adolescents.[24] These arguments were employed in support of the lifting of marriage bars, finally achieved by the 1944 Education Act and justified by rising marriage rates in the 1940s and 1950s and a post-war labour shortage. Concerns about women without men being in authority over children may not always have been fully articulated, but they were enacted in the common practice of putting a man in overall charge in mixed sex schools.

Kay Whitehead illuminates this anomaly further in a study of English unmarried teachers applying for jobs in Australia in 1947, at a time when married women were entering the profession in larger numbers. This was also a time when psychologists were beginning to stress the importance of the relationship between teachers' personalities and their students' emotional wellbeing. Whitehead argues that the picture given of these applicants in testimonials written by head teachers was in direct opposition to the embittered spinster stereotype, but nevertheless did not show them in a nurturing, maternal role. Rather they were perceived as 'emotionally distant, firm but kind teachers who were assertive rather than passive in their relationship with students'.[25]

This calm, capable, professional image was typical of portrayals of women teachers in English rural schools. Yet social maternalist ideals had by no means disappeared. Rather, teachers' roles were often shown to stretch both within and beyond the school gates, with the implication that their work was a substitute for not having had children. This is apparent in the wartime Ministry of Information documentary film *Village School*, described as 'a tribute to England's women teachers, standard bearers of an education Nazism would destroy'. The film follows the day of an unmarried schoolmistress, showing her to be central to community life as she visits her evacuated pupils' billets, finds replacements for their worn-out shoes and solves problems thrown at her by village foster parents. This work was justified on the grounds that 'children must come through [the war] unscathed in mind and body'.[26] Such close personal involvement was by no means confined to wartime teachers. The aim of Beatrice Chambers, who founded and ran one of the first progressive girls' boarding schools from 1918 to 1944, was to preserve close contact with her 'family' of seventy-five girls and for 'the school to provide as nearly as it could the circumstances of family life with all that implies'. Her success in this respect may be inferred from the fact that she was commonly known as 'Ma' by both staff and students.[27]

In oral history interviews and autobiographies, teachers often represented work with children as a replacement for an absent family. For example, Maud (born 1907), headmistress of a West Country girls' grammar school, described how her staff would often become more dedicated to their work when they reached the age when they were unlikely to marry and have children. However, anecdotes from Mary Clarke (1881–1976), headmistress of Manchester High School for Girls between 1924 and 1945, suggest familial identification with pupils could become a sensitive issue. A mother called in because her daughter had written obscene verses 'put her head in her hands and moaned, "Oh Miss Clarke, to think that one of *your* girls should have done such a thing"' (emphasis in original). But when another pupil's mother accused her of not being able to 'understand a mother's feelings', she declared: 'This got me on the raw and I retorted angrily: "You have no right to say such a thing. I might have half a dozen children for aught you know".[28]

Gwen, a domestic science teacher who taught working-class girls in Vauxhall, gives further insight into this relationship. She saw her gift for teaching and empathy with children as offering full compensation for the lack of her own children. A major satisfaction was her concern for individual children, particularly the more disruptive and difficult girls. It was a role she had taken on early in her life, dating from her first experience as a Sunday school teacher at the age of fifteen. By taking a special interest in children who had particular problems she saw herself as building up relationships of trust which were of mutual value to her and the child. For example, she once asked a child who had thrown a sponge cake across the room to do her accounts for her each evening:

> She used to come after school and do my accounts and I never had any more trouble with her. And I learned a lot about her, she was a child of a broken marriage and there were younger children and she had to look after these younger children and ugh. Well when you feel like that for a girl or take that sort of responsibility it takes the place of having your own children ... I often think of that little girl. I wish I'd done more for her.[29]

This kind of special attention could be of lasting value to children. Janet Hitchman (born 1916) detailed her life in a series of foster homes in her autobiography *King of the Barbareens*. Hitchman claimed that any worthwhile action she had performed and whatever small amount of goodness and decency she possessed were entirely due to the efforts of two unmarried women educators.[30] The writer P. D. James (born 1920) also expressed gratitude for the dedication and devotion of her teachers, most of whom did not leave the school until retirement, and stressed the benefits of an education 'which wasn't circumscribed by the demands of the teacher's husband and family'.[31]

Teachers in this position often sought to influence the career prospects of succeeding cohorts of young women, but their mission to recreate women in their own image alienated some pupils. Summerfield's study of five interwar secondary schools in Lancashire concluded that the programme of these single-sex schools was to reproduce a new model of middle-class femininity in the image of the professional spinster, in opposition to that of the dependent housewife.[32] Yet teachers' visions of working women were narrowly defined within class and gender boundaries, with higher education and teaching seen as the primary and most desirable alternative to marriage. Grammar school girls going straight from school to work even in such respectable female employment as secretarial work or the civil service were frequently despised or ignored. Evidence from interviews at all five schools suggests 'the only career they ever came up with seemed to be teaching'.[33] One of Maud's former pupils had a similar experience in the 1950s and described her former head teacher as unimaginative, rigid and critical.[34] Teachers might dedicate their lives to children's education, but the children they rejected could be left a legacy of feelings of failure.

After the marriage bar was lifted, some unmarried teachers adopted a more defensive position. Maud remembered resentment being expressed towards married teachers (which may have been rooted partly in jealousy) because they were not prepared to dedicate themselves in the same way or put in such long hours.[35] Yet this kind of dedication sometimes backfired on pupils if a teacher did eventually leave to get married. Two girls growing up in the 1950s felt hurt when their junior school teacher, who had taken them away on holiday and treated them as her special 'pets', left her job and withdrew all contact, and this separation remained a source of sadness and puzzlement to them even in adult life.[36]

The bachelor teachers I interviewed also saw themselves as making special contributions to their pupils' progress, and some regarded them as family substitutes. Peter, who taught at a boys' boarding school during the 1950s, expressed pride that he had been the first to suggest that all children should learn a musical instrument, an idea which had spread to other schools. He echoed the schoolmaster Prendergast in *Decline and Fall* in his description of the disapproval expressed by colleagues when bachelor teachers contemplated marriage (see chapter 2). A letter to *The Times* in 1950 from the headmaster of a boys' grammar school made a similar point, arguing that 'it is well known in the profession that bachelors give better service than married man'.[37]

Lionel, who taught in a mixed comprehensive school in the late 1950s and kept the same class of children for three years, many of whom remained in touch with him, described his deep sense of loss when they left or moved on into the sixth form. He became so attached that he felt it was like losing his own family. He connected these feelings with a recurrence of clinical depression, which was associated by doctors with his homosexuality and had previously been treated with electroconvulsive therapy. In such circumstances, as an unmarried man, he was more vulnerable to accusations of abuse than were unmarried women and did not express his sense of loss so clearly. Thus, he was much more circumspect than was Gwen in talking about his relationship with a 'special' pupil who did a paper round and brought him a newspaper each day, commenting 'clearly of course one shouldn't do that'.

While close relationships between adolescents and adult single men are now widely regarded with suspicion, John Bridcut takes a much more positive stance. In his award-winning TV documentary and subsequent book, *Britten's Children* (2006), he showed the importance of a series of close friendships between adolescent boys and the composer Benjamin Britten, both in his personal life and as an artistic influence on his music. Bridcut repudiates the view that these relationships were abusive, arguing that 'almost without exception [Britten's] tenderness brightened the lives of these teenaged boys, and today their faces light up as they recall a unique friendship'.[38]

Child-care practitioners: social welfare workers

Similar concerns surrounded bachelors engaged in social welfare work with young people (including voluntary and paid youth and probation work). This kind of work seems to have occupied proportionately more unmarried men over thirty than other professions, in which younger single men generally predominated.[39] Those in positions of responsibility in, for example, boys' clubs, brigades or scout groups had a duty of care to the children in their charge which at times sat uneasily with their marital status. Being male and single might signify freedom and adventure, but such men were also perceived to be more likely to harm children because they were not fathers and their relationship was non-familial. Robert Baden-Powell, leader of the scout movement, was faced with this anomaly when, in 1921, he responded to a charge of indecency against a scout master whose behaviour he believed had been caused partly by the brutalising effects of the war. Writing in *Boy Scouts' Association Headquarters Gazette*, he made it clear that he had 'no intention of glossing over or hushing up such a crime' and advised local associations to scrutinise the character and past of all new recruits. But while it was the duty of scout masters also 'to prevent the recurrence of this evil in the oncoming generation', he did not suggest that they should preserve a greater distance between themselves and the boys in their charge or take refuge in their professional status. Rather, he advised them to take the place of family members in giving boys the right advice:

> If we are rightly prized as 'elder brothers' rather than as officers or 'teachers' we can quite easily do it, but I think many scoutmasters scarcely realise how much their help is needed nor how much they can do if they will, at this critical period, to see a boy straight for the rest of his life.[40]

Geoffrey Eyles, a scout master who edited the *Gazette*, made it clear that he was following Baden-Powell's guidance in viewing his readers as a substitute family. 'And they nearly all follow the lead of the Chief, I am glad to say in calling me their "uncle". Never, I imagine had an uncle so many nephews as I have and a good many nieces too.'[41] And he continued this theme in the next issue: 'How is a poor editor to write his notes when he has so many boys? I feel more and more like the historic old woman who lived in a shoe. For I have so many boys I don't know what to do.'[42]

It is less easy to tell how far these tensions were experienced by unmarried men and women drawn to work with disadvantaged children and young people in the social, probation and prison services. Most of the published sources offer little sense of a darker side but rather stress the value of this work and the dedication particularly of unmarried women. Social work pioneers Eileen Younghusband and Geraldine Aves, whose work with children from the 1920s to the 1950s culminated in the influential 'Younghusband Report' (1959), fall into this category. Their report, whose recommendations were implemented by the government, insisted that preventative work with families should be the main concern of social workers, across all government departments.[43] Lillian Barker and Cicely McCall were similarly influential in youth custody work during the 1930s, bringing to public attention and working to change the conditions in girls' borstals and approved schools.[44] A history of the London Probation Service pays tribute to the work of many unmarried women. For example, Miss Croker King, based at Westminster juvenile court from 1921 to 1929, visited her young probationers in their homes and invited them into her own home, which she shared with an unmarried friend, This was a 'club' to which some boys reported as late as 10 p.m. And Miss Blythe's effectiveness and influence as a probation officer are suggested by her Saturday reporting book for 1923, which recorded visits from 421 old boys and 60 old girls in addition to those from her current clients and their families.[45]

Important work done by male probation officers in London was also highlighted. This was celebrated in *Court Circular* (1950), a book by the film and theatre critic Sewell Stokes based on an account of his own experiences as a temporary probation officer at Bow Street Court for four years from 1941. In 1952, this book was made into a film, *I Believe in You*, which showed the emptiness of an unemployed bachelor's life and contrasted it with the demanding but ultimately fulfilling work he undertook in the probation service. Most importantly, as the title suggests, the film showed the difference a probation officer's 'belief' in his clients could make to their future lives.

Such a belief inspired my father's friend David to devote his life to improving the lives of young people in London's East End, both through his probation work and also by setting up a youth club in Hoxton in the 1950s.[46] My interview with David offered important insights into his motivation for this kind of work. It appeared that his determination to help young offenders feel that 'someone in the establishment had a good opinion of them' stemmed partly from his parents' denial of him as their son, and society's refusal to acknowledge him as legitimate (see chapter 5). Prickly and often cantankerous with adults, his strong empathy with children remained into old age. So did his lasting influence on a generation of young Hoxtonians to whom he had offered friendship and protection. A story recounted at David's funeral in 1998 by one of his Hoxton clients shows his dedication to his work. Bernie told how David had once turned up at a family funeral in order to prevent him killing his brother. But although David managed to prevent the murder, in the ensuing fight he had himself ended up in the grave!

As a bachelor, who was not expected to have a particular interest in children, David's profession and voluntary work offered him opportunities for close, caring relationships that would have been more difficult to find elsewhere. Unlike many unmarried women, he was not pushed into doing rescue work simply on the grounds of his gender but had made a positive choice. This was not the case with Patience, who had joined the Church Army with a view to becoming a Church Visitor, but had also been expected to do a moral welfare training for which she felt unsuited. As a result, she had been compelled to spend part of her training during the 1920s working in a hostel for young women defined as 'problem girls'. Not only had she had felt threatened by these girls, one of whom had managed to escape her chaperonage and had presented herself at the employment exchange, but she was also horrified that she, a middle-class woman, was expected to do 'menial' work which she felt should have been delegated to the residents.

For unmarried women working in Britain's colonial territories, their recruitment to child rescue also often had little to do with any previous experience or aptitude for work with young people. These women had been inspired by missionary societies (who often tried to recruit them as children) to rescue black babies and convert them to Christianity.[47] Not only, in the context of Empire, was the idea of 'woman's mission' linked to theories of 'racial' and religious difference which justified white women's superior knowledge, but unmarried women's nurturing role could also be invoked, as in the following passage appearing in a history of the Girls' Friendly Society alongside a picture of a white missionary joining hands with a group of black children:

> In Zanzibar the Society has its own Missionary, Miss Bridges Lee, working under the U.M.C.A. Her chief work is done among children, visiting schools in Zanzibar and in the neighbourhood. How happy these little Christian children are in the schools may be guessed from the fact that during an epidemic of chicken pox Miss Bridges Lee was kept busy 'shooing spotty babies away'. 'They will come, they love school so.'[48]

In practice, however, whether they were working at home or abroad, unmarried women often found themselves unprepared for this kind of work, as Patience found during her time in a mother-and-baby holiday Home:

The mothers were on holiday, therefore they had to have their meal alone so that they were relieved from their children, and also, which I wouldn't like the medical profession to know, I suppose, I was responsible for the babies' *feeds* (said in tones of amazement) and I knew *nothing* about babies' feeds *whatsoever* ... Poor little dears, I knew nothing about it at all. But most of them survived ...

Child-care practitioners: residential work

Unmarried women formed the bulk of the residential care workforce, not only in holiday homes, but also in longer-term institutions such as workhouses, children's Homes, orphanages, and reform, industrial and approved schools. As with missionaries, the sense of vocation which pushed many into this kind of work went hand in hand with their religious faith. For both Catholic and Protestant single women, becoming a nun or sister in a charity-based religious community offered a professional status as well as 'enhanced spiritual benefits'.[49] And, in the case of Catholic orders, it was not only English single women but also Irish migrants numbering in their thousands who answered the call.[50] The growth in numbers of children's Homes managed or staffed by Catholic nuns during the early twentieth century continued into the late 1930s (see appendix 4) as did the expansion of Homes run by Protestant sisterhoods.[51] For example, the National Children's Home (NCH), staffed by a Protestant interdenominational sisterhood, expanded and became increasingly professional in outlook during the interwar years. By the early 1930s, it had thirty branches, a purpose-built staff training school, about 350 serving sisters and more than 3,000 children in its care.[52]

The Second World War focused unprecedented attention on these institutions. Not only were children appreciated as an important national asset, but evacuation surveys and Anna Freud and Dorothy Burlingham's study, *Infants without Families* (1943), showed the effects of evacuation and war-related dislocation and disruption. Such studies drew attention both to the larger numbers of orphans and displaced children who would be in need of care after the war and the possibility of psychological damage which might result in later maladjustment.[53] As a result of these concerns, which were articulated first in the Curtis Report (1945) and subsequently in the 1948 Children's Act, local authorities and voluntary institutions were encouraged to set up or convert larger institutions into cottage Homes. These contained small, mixed age 'families' for children who could not be fostered or adopted, headed by a house mother and ideally also a house father as a replacement for absent parents.[54]

In practice, however, these familial ideals were seldom realised. Low wage rates, lack of appropriate accommodation and an expanding job market meant that although a married couple might be in overall charge, hands-on child care in many cottage Homes remained the province of unmarried women. However, the degree to which house parenting was a viable and fulfilling career for these women depended upon their motivations for going into such work and the kinds of support systems available to them. A comparison between records of the Star children's Home in Bristol[55] and those of the NCH during the 1940s and 1950s is revealing in this respect. Both organisations employed predominantly unmarried women, adopted hierarchical work structures which separated domestic work from child care, and encouraged (though were not always successful in recruiting) educated women from middle-class backgrounds to become house mothers.

In other respects, however, there were some important differences between the two organisations. While no lifelong vows were expected from the NCH sisters and they could resign on marriage, they were expected to have a sense of religious vocation and offer long-term commitment.[56] They received in-house residential training in child care, a clear career structure and pension arrangements, and by the 1940s provision had been made for retired sisters to remain living within the community, either within the Homes or in a purpose-built retirement Home.[57] As a result, records from 1934 to 1959 suggest that (with the exception of the final year of the Second World War) they had little difficulty in recruiting staff. From the early 1940s, the Home also responded to the call for children to be brought up in more familial-type settings by creating smaller, mixed age and sex groups under one house mother, which would give the children more individual attention, reduce the amount of regimentation and 'provide a more intimate and homely background for the child'.[58] In 1959, the superintendent of one branch of the Homes made much of the success of his Home, in which eleven sisters had worked for between twenty and thirty-eight years. Each sister had been in charge of her present family for at least seven years and in one case for thirty-two years. Using these figures as evidence, he argued that with rare exceptions, children stayed in the same family group and had the same person in charge of them throughout their entire stay.[59]

Yet it is evident that many sisters who had completed the training did leave the Homes, and not only to marry. In 1938 sisters were required to sign a statement saying that they would remain in the work for at least three years, but out of 329 sisters who resigned over a ten-year period between 1945 and 1954, only forty-eight (15 per cent) retired, with fifty-five

(17 per cent) getting engaged or married and 129 (39 per cent) going into other work. For some of these women, what their principal John Litten described as 'the difficult task of mothering other people's children'[60] had probably become too much. While the NCH rarely recorded thanks to sisters who left to go into other work, the decision made in 1938 that those reaching the age of sixty should not automatically have the right to continue working shows some recognition of the stressful nature of their duties. Staffing difficulties are also evident in May 1946, when seven sisters resigned (or may have been asked to go) after a leave of absence.[61] Thus, it seems that although some NCH Homes did offer children continuity of care, others had a more chequered history. Frequent departures or transfer of staff between Homes are recorded, with several sisters moving four or five times over a period of ten to fifteen years, and some long-serving sisters suffering recurring bouts of ill-health or mental instability.[62]

House mothers at the Star Homes were much more likely to see child care as short-term work rather than a career. This group of cottage Homes housed more than a hundred children, two thirds of whom were described as problem cases or subnormal. The Homes were managed at arm's length by a local authority committee,[63] and although receiving a generally positive report from the Ministry of Health inspector in 1942, they were plagued by recurring staffing problems through the 1940s. Their problems were probably more acute than those of the NCH because staff were not part of a religious community with a wider vision, and because house mothers were trained on the job, pay was low and there was no obvious career structure. A response from the Ministry of Labour to an appeal for help during their worst crisis in 1945 offered no redress, but does show the poor working conditions and low esteem in which this kind of work was generally held:

> You will appreciate that in filling vacancies of this kind there is, apart from the general shortage of women available for domestic work, the added difficulty of finding women who are suitable for these posts, which require women with a real liking and aptitude for the work. A further difficulty in this particular case is that women available for domestic employment of some kind consider the hours to be rather long and the rate of pay not sufficiently attractive.[64]

The Bristol children's committee minutes during the 1940s are much more revealing than those of the NCH sisterhood council about the difficulties experienced by unmarried women staff in children's Homes during this period, and show the desperation of a matron who eventually resigned though ill-health. These difficulties included vacancies for seven foster mothers at one time, relief staff leaving after only a week, an abusive house mother who had to be dismissed, and the refusal of a local elementary school (against the recommendations of the Curtis Report) to take children from the Homes, who were described as 'sub-normal, their behaviour very bad, their habits, filthy, and their language foul'.[65]

While I have no direct testimony from unmarried women staff at that time about the impact these situations had on their relationships with children, an interview with Sylvia, who was a relief house mother at a local authority children's Home during the 1950s, offers some interesting parallel evidence. A former local beauty queen, Sylvia said she had taken the job at the Home to avoid the jealousy of workmates who had called her names. Perhaps partly in order to refute any negative associations attached to beauty queens, Sylvia represented her position in the Home as being like that of a natural mother, adored by the children, bringing peace, discipline and order (much like Mary Poppins), and she offered photographic evidence as proof. She contrasted this picture with descriptions of the permanent house mothers from upper middle-class backgrounds, who hadn't been able to control their charges properly and whose children had no organisation: 'They didn't clean their shoes and they didn't know how to lay the tables and everything was in a chaotic mess, you see.' And the house mother in the sick bay, a qualified nurse, was described as a 'frustrated spinster' (even though she had a child and a man friend who visited her in the home) and 'very moody'.

Bachelors were much less likely to be employed as house parents, since the job of a father was not to provide hands-on care for children, but they did sometimes become voluntary 'uncles' who would bring presents and talk to the children. Sylvia described an unmarried man in his late thirties, who had offered his services in this capacity:

> And we used to have all sorts of feedback – we're not happy with the man who was there coming to visit. And even though he was supposed to be a volunteer carer, Mrs M would have us together and say I'm not very happy about this person ... I remember one particular man, and ... there was a mutual discussion and I don't think he was allowed. I don't know anything about the man's name, though strangely enough I would know his face, but I didn't think he was very trustworthy.

This story shows the suspicion attached to single men and the continuing difficulties for them to be trusted with children. This gender divide becomes clearer if we consider my interviewee Fred's answer to a question about children.

> KH: *Did you ever look after them [children] or have them around much?*

F: Yeah, when I were young … I used to take them out in the fields,
    they used to love animals.

KH: *Whose children were they?*

F: Strangers. Kids loves me. They calls me Daddy. (laughed) I like
    kids, I always did like kids, even some strangers. Kids always talks,
    likes talking to me no matter who they are, they were no relation.
    That's why I ought to have got married I suppose.

For Fred, the access to love and intimacy children offered when they
called him 'Daddy' was of supreme importance, rather than any working
or caring relationship. The doubts raised in my mind about his answer
were partly to do with his designation of some of the children as 'strangers', a label which would probably not have been applied by a woman.

Fred's image of a father's role had little connection with the hands-
on child care Sylvia had offered her charges. Yet as a paid employee,
her relationship with them also had its limits. Although she described
giving favourite children 'unconditional love', she knew she had to keep
a distance and not allow them to become too dependent on her because
they were not her children.

Child-care practitioners: governesses and nannies

Sylvia left the Homes in the late 1950s, and took a job as a nanny. While
the numbers of nannies were much lower in this decade, this was the
commonest child-related occupation undertaken by unmarried women
throughout the period. Until the Second World War nannies, nursery
nurses and nursery governesses (who often spent more time with children
than did their parents) were routinely employed in upper- and upper
middle-class homes, while less affluent families still often recruited general
servants combining domestic work and child care. The great majority
were untrained, or trained on the job, having gained the necessary experience through caring for younger siblings, or having had the experience
assumed because of their gender and supposed interest in children. For
many women in this situation a job was a necessity but could be short-
term, low paid and insecure.[66] The domestic situations vacant columns in
The Times carried lists of private and agency advertisements for children's
nurses, which show the high demand for and turnover of nannies both in
Britain and abroad during the 1920s and 1930s, and their decline after the
Second World War.[67]

Rising standards in girls' education and a wider range of employment
opportunities for middle-class women meant that the numbers of governesses decreased after the First World War, with most advertisements in

The Times asking for nursery governesses who combined teaching with elements of physical care and control.[68] During the interwar years, governesses remained especially popular with the more reactionary elements of the aristocracy and upper middle classes, worried that secluding their daughters in the all-female environments of boarding schools and colleges might decrease their marriage chances.[69] However, changes in work opportunities and educational standards after the Second World War saw the virtual disappearance of the governess, although some older women moved into other personal service employment, for example, as housekeepers or companions.

Women employed as nurses and governesses in private homes to care for children were faced with some particularly difficult splits and tensions, which can be related to class as well as to marital status and motherhood. Class tensions are suggested by the terms used in the domestic situations vacant and wanted columns of *The Times*. During the interwar years, nursery governesses were sometimes equated with 'Mother's Helps', perhaps to broaden the range of work they would be expected to undertake, but also indicating status anxieties which relate to these women's rather uncertain position in the home, midway between servant and teacher. In addition to child care and basic education, this work often included sewing and music lessons and occasionally also cooking or unspecified 'help in the house'; it could also at times involve taking entire charge of the children and/or household.

Similar concerns can be read in advertisements which used the terms 'lady help', 'lady nurse' or 'lady housekeeper' as opposed to 'help', 'nurse' or 'housekeeper'. These were not gender markers, but rather can be linked to class or racialised prejudices. Like the terms 'superior' and 'gentlewoman', they sought or offered an assurance that the carer came from the right background and would not expose children to the kinds of undesirable influences that employees from 'rough', working-class English or Irish families would bring with them. Yet it is unclear from these advertisements what the real differences between the work of a 'mother's help' or a 'lady's nurse' and that of a 'nurse', 'nanny' or indeed a 'children's useful maid' actually was, or indeed how far it overlapped with that of a nursery governess.

Oral testimony from Amelia (born 1905) throws some light on this subject. Her father's business had failed after the 1926 general strike and she had been removed from her private school and compelled to take daily jobs looking after children. The discomfort she and her employer felt about her status was reflected in the fact that she had no name for her occupation: 'No, no, I wasn't a nanny really. I was officially Miss Wilson who took them out for walks and things like that you see, more like a governess in a way'. Yet this did not in fact encompass all her work, which was in reality quite similar to that of a nanny and included putting her charges to bed.

The fluidity of these categories is also suggested by Penelope Lively's colonial childhood in Egypt. As she grew older, her nanny became her governess, even though the woman had no educational training.[70] One of Gathorne-Hardy's informants in *The Rise and Fall of the British Nanny* suggested the variation in the kinds of work nannies might be expected to perform during the 1930s at a time of high unemployment, when the supply of nannies appears to have exceeded the demand. She described the queue of 'desperate lonely women [which] stretched right around the block in response to an advertisement that promised five shillings a week more than the going rate for untrained Nannies (25 shillings) and promised no housework and no teaching'.

This account also shows the emotional costs of such an employment system for a child who had eleven nannies in eleven years. Aware that the successful applicant would have to 'sleep in the day nursery without even a dressing table of their own', she was genuinely puzzled why so many women would want to look after her. Yet she had still needed to keep in her mind the succession of nannies who had been her primary carers, some of whom had been dishonest, cruel or uncaring and only two of whom she ever saw or heard from afterward, and named them all individually in her prayers.[71]

Two enduringly popular children's books first published in the 1930s directly address the issue of attachment and loss in the lives of unmarried nannies and children. In Streatfield's *Ballet Shoes*, Nana, who has adopted the values and standards of a middle-class mother, represents the fantasy that a nanny will never leave because she has no other life or interests. She continued to look after her first charge, Sylvia, into adulthood and then took care of Sylvia's foster children, becoming the equivalent of a grandmother, while still doing all the physical work of caring. So important was Nana's presence that, although Sylvia became the children's guardian, she was never portrayed as being like their mother, since the work of mothering is still retained by her nanny. By contrast, in *Mary Poppins*, by P. L. Travers, a nanny arrives unexpectedly and takes control of the Banks family, whose previous nursemaid had left without giving notice. Mary is a much more complex and enigmatic figure than Nana, representing the contradictions many children experienced in their actual relationships with nannies: order, security, magic and adventure, but also fear, sadness and loss. Most significantly, the children were comforted after Mary's sudden and unexpected departure by her parting message to them that she would return (which she did in each new book in the series).[72]

It is clear that only a minority of households could have afforded to keep a nanny who was no longer needed to give physical care. But since this was a period when dominant theories of child care were influenced by the behaviourist ideas of John Watson and Truby King, emphasising order and routine and discouraging strong emotional attachments between parents and children,[73] it is unlikely that many parents would have recognised the departure of a nanny as potentially damaging or considered the pain felt by the nanny. Yet this is not the whole story. Perhaps the most important reason why the emotional costs of unmarried women's paid labour in bringing up other people's children has been insufficiently acknowledged is because of the difficulty for all parties concerned in reconciling a relationship based, as Davidoff has shown, partly upon financial gain and the workings of the labour market with its situation in the private sphere within the family.[74] This was an emotional as well as a financial economy where, despite the brisk, detached tone of interwar child-care manuals, children and their primary carers often did become closely attached. And, while the anxieties and conflicts mothers may have felt through these arrangements could be aired and displaced by referral to the 'servant problem', the interests and needs of the children and the women employed in these capacities were rarely articulated. Relationships had to be negotiated in which affection might be invested on each side, but whose beginnings and endings often depended on the financial position of employers or employees, or on other external circumstances such as the children reaching school age.

Oral testimony from Bridget (born 1906) shows the personal costs of being a nanny and the conflicts that could arise. As a youngest daughter, she had no experience of children when she started as a daily nurse to two-year-old twin boys, whom she looked after for four years, but had been unable to prevent their mother from spoiling them and eventually left her job in order to care for her sick father. There were, however, long-term consequences in her decision to leave her job both for herself and for the children. Her feelings of guilt that perhaps she hadn't been any good as a nanny remained with her and were only assuaged many years later when she met one of her charges again, who started to visit her regularly. Hearing of his subsequent 'tragic life' after she had left the family,[75] Bridget started to realise, though still could not explain, her value to him:

> He recognised me and spoke to me and he got in touch and he comes and visits me now, so I couldn't have been such a bad nanny as all that could I? … Strange after all these years he wanted to get in touch again.

> He wanted to know more what I could remember than he could. He
> seemed to like coming to see me … He used to say 'I'm going to marry
> Nanny': that's the only proposal I've had.[76]

This child's Oedipal desires had been directed away from his mother and
show the strength of his attachment to his nanny. However, Bridget's own
parents' needs for care made it difficult for her to maintain her primary
position in the twins' life, particularly when rivalry with the birth mother,
who was also her employer, became too strong. Unsure of her position
and unable to assert her authority over that of the mother, she quickly lost
touch with her charges without knowing how important she had been to
them.

Sylvia, who later married and had children of her own, was able to
see her position as daily nanny in less competitive terms. She described
herself as 'a surrogate mother', but once her day had finished at 6 p.m. she
acknowledged that 'they were their mother's you know and you wouldn't
dream of trying to alter that special relationship'. Emily (born 1903), who
remained unmarried, felt very differently. She had cared for a succession
of families from the 1920s to the 1960s, but insisted that there was no
resemblance between a mother and a nanny and objected to the word
'substitute':

> Oh the children looked on their parents, not later, mostly in the first
> place, as somebody, a lady who was beautifully dressed and came in,
> they saw this beautiful lady coming in, they loved her coming in, but
> there was no rushing up 'mummy, mummy' and tears and arms round
> there necks, not like nanny. They just knew that they belonged to them,
> but there was nothing between them. If they were ill or anything else,
> they might come and say goodnight to them but not always … 'cos you
> see they've got you night and day whatever happens.

Some of this envy and veiled hostility towards her charges' mothers
could be interpreted in terms of 'splitting'. For Emily, whose own mother
had been admitted to an asylum when she was fourteen, the term 'nanny'
embodied all the care and nurturing which were absent in her experience
of being mothered. Mothers were not there for their children in the way
that a nanny was. Gathorne-Hardy has shown that where mothers were
dependent upon nannies' services, the nanny often held the whip hand,
and equally that upper-class children could torment nannies, whose class
position they believed was inferior to their own. The confusion such
status inversions caused to children is shown by Lively, who remembered
hearing her nanny and mother arguing and was puzzled by the contemp-
tuous note in her nanny's voice and her mother's shrill and defensive

tones. Yet in retrospect Lively recognised that, although her nanny was her entire emotional world and her parents only satellite figures, there was something wrong with 'a maternal woman condemned like all her kind to be a surrogate mother to other people's children', and felt grateful for the security she offered.[78]

Emily's position was even less satisfactory. Her subservient status made it hard for her to be openly critical of her employer. She could not always be there for the children she looked after and had faced the pain of frequent partings. Yet like the child who listed her nannies in her prayers, she continued to hold the children in her mind, putting their photos together into one frame, a strange family whose changing styles of clothing spanned the forty years of her working life.

This chapter makes little mention of unmarried people who did not have any connection with children, or any desire to work with them. Objections to being associated with children have often been expressed in financial terms, particularly in relation to taxation and the obligation placed on single people to pay for state education and family allowances, from which it was argued they gained no benefit. Yet the very fact that this argument could be made illustrates the invisibility of unmarried people's working relationships with children and the mutual benefits they did gain. The implications of this and other divisions by marital status will be addressed in my conclusion.

Notes

1 A. P. Herbert, *Ballads for Broadbrows* (London: Ernest Benn, 1930).
2 For an account of the development of social maternalism among middle-class single women, see Eileen Yeo, *The Contest for Social Science: Relations and Representations of Gender and Class* (London: Rivers Oram Press, 1996), ch. 5.
3 *Ibid.*, p. 247.
4 With the gradual demise of the pupil-teacher system after the First World War. David Wardle, *English Popular Education 1780–1970* (Cambridge: Cambridge University Press, 1970), p. 104.
5 MSP, PP/MCS/A132. MCS to WJH, 1920.
6 W. E. Sargent, *The Psychology of Marriage and the Family Life* (London: Independent Press, 1940).
7 Eyles, *Unmarried but Happy*, p. 47.
8 *Ibid.*, pp. 44–7.
9 See Judy Giles, 'Help for Housewives: Domestic Service and the Reconstruction of Domesticity in Britain', *Women's History Review*, 10:2 (2001), for a useful discussion of domesticity and domestic service in the 1940s.
10 Vicinus, *Independent Women*; Ellen Ross, *Love and Toil: Motherhood in Outcast*

London, 1870–1918 (Oxford: Oxford University Press, 1993); Lewis, *The Politics of Motherhood*; Yeo, *The Contest for Social Science*.

11   Elizabeth Morrison, *Babies: Advice by Letter from Elizabeth Morrison of Nursery World* (London: Ernest Benn, 1949). Morrison was by trained by Mabel Liddiard, matron of the Mothercare training society in Highgate, whose *Mothercraft Manual* went through twelve editions between 1923 and 1956.

12   M. Truby King, *Mothercraft* (London: Whitcombe and Tombs/Simkin, Marshall, second edition, 1934).

13   Lewis, *The Politics of Motherhood*.

14   Truby King, *Mothercraft*, pp. 4–5, 67, 168 and 191.

15   Morrison, *Babies*, pp. 8–11, 122 and 201–2.

16   Dianne Richardson, *Women, Motherhood and Childrearing* (London: Macmillan, 1993), pp. 35–6.

17   See also Elizabeth Peretz, 'The Professionalisation of Childcare', *Oral History Journal*, 17:1 (1989).

18   Leap and Hunter in *The Midwife's Tale* encountered similar stories of resistance to midwives' authority by older married women.

19   Steedman, *Landscape for a Good Woman*, p. 2.

20   See John Welshman, 'In Search of the "Problem Family": Public Health and Social Work in England and Wales, 1940–1970', *Social History of Medicine*, 9:3 (1996).

21   *Our Towns: A Close-Up: A Study Made in 1939–42* (Oxford: Oxford University Press, 1943), p. 43.

22   Eleanor Graham, *The Children who lived in a Barn*, 1938 (Harmondsworth: Penguin, 1965), p. 54. The book's popularity is suggested by the fact that it was reprinted in the 1950s and 1960s.

23   *Our Towns*, p. 139.

24   Oram, *Women Teachers*, ch. 6.

25   Kay Whitehead, 'Postwar Headteachers' Perspectives of "Good" Teachers', *Journal of Administration and History*, 35:1 (2003), p. 33.

26   Imperial War Museum, London, UKY235, *Village School*, documentary film produced by Strand Film for the Ministry of Information. Miss Read's novel *Village School* (1955), published a decade later, showed unmarried teachers to be similarly involved in village life and watching over their socially disadvantaged pupils.

27   Cynthia Walton with Pauline Hodder, *A Grounding for Life: A History of Maltman's Green School* (Solihull: Barn Books, 2004), p. 24.

28   Clarke, *A Short Life*.

29   Interview with Gwen, 9 February 1994.

30   Janet Hitchman, *King of the Barbareens*, 1960 (Harmondsworth: Penguin, 1981), p. 116.

31   P. D. James, *Time to be in Earnest: A Fragment of Autobiography* (London: Faber and Faber, 1999), p. 48.

32   Penny Summerfield, 'Cultural Reproduction in the Education of Girls: A Study of Girls' Secondary Schooling in Two Lancashire Towns, 1900–1950' in Felicity Hunt (ed.), *Lessons for Life: The Schooling of Girls and Women 1850–1950* (Oxford: Blackwell, 1987), pp. 166–9.

33   *Ibid.*, p. 160.

34   Personal communication from Elizabeth.

35   The education historian Stephanie Spencer found evidence of this antagonism in

minutes of the headmistresses' conference in the 1950s (records held at the Modern Record Office in Warwick). Personal communication from Stephanie Spencer.

36 Personal communication from Elizabeth and Linda.

37 *Ibid.* Letter from H. G. Mullens, *The Times*, 19 April 1950, p. 9.

38 John Bridcut, *Britten's Children* (London: Faber and Faber, 2006), p. 5.

39 The census shows that of paid social welfare workers, 10 per cent in 1931 and 14 per cent in 1951 were unmarried, but unlike most other occupations, most were older men; for example, 59 per cent of bachelor social welfare workers in 1931 were over thirty. Many others undertook this kind of work voluntarily.

40 *Boy Scouts' Association Headquarters Gazette*, 15:1 (14 January 1921).

41 *Ibid.*

42 *Ibid.*, 15:2 (14 February 1921).

43 Wilmott, *A Singular Woman*, p. 124.

44 Cicely McCall, *They Always Come Back* (London: Methuen, 1938); Gloria Wood and Paul Thomson, *The Nineties: Personal Recollections of the Twentieth Century* (London: BBC Books, 1993), pp. 69–70.

45 Martin Page, *Crimefighters of London: A History of the Origins and Development of the London Probation Service, 1876–1965* (London: Inner London Probation Service Benevolent and Educational Trust, 1992), pp. 127–8.

46 H. M. Holden, *Hoxton Café Project* (1972), quoted in *ibid.*

47 This was the case for three of my interviewees, only one of whom actually went abroad.

48 Mary Heath-Stubbs, *Friendship's Highway* (London: GFS Central Office, 1935), p. 85.

49 Barbara Walsh, *Roman Catholic Nuns in England and Wales 1800–1937: A Social History* (Dublin: Irish Academic Press, 2002), p. 156.

50 *Ibid.*

51 Julie Grier, 'A Spirit of Friendly Rivalry: Voluntary Societies and the Formation of Post-War Child Welfare Legislation in Britain' in Jon Lawrence and Pat Starkey (eds), *Child Welfare and Social Action* (Liverpool: Liverpool University Press, 2001).

52 University of Liverpool, NCH archive (hereafter NCH), *Sisters of the Children: The Story of the National Children's Home* (1985), D541/E6/3. All names and identifying details from this archive have been omitted in order to protect the anonymity of the individuals concerned. NCH Action for Children bears no responsibility for the publication.

53 Susan Isaacs (ed.), *The Cambridge Evacuation Survey* (London: Methuen, 1941); Anna Freud and Dorothy Burlingham, *Infants without Families: The Case For and Against Residential Nurseries* (London: Allen and Unwin, 1944); M. Cole and R. Padley, *Evacuation Survey* (London: Routledge, 1940); Grier, 'A Spirit of Friendly Rivalry', p. 236. See also Denise Riley, *War in the Nursery: Theories of the Child and Mother* (London: Virago, 1983).

54 *Report of the Care of Children Committee*, para. 1, 478 and 485. It was estimated that there were 124,900 deprived children under the jurisdiction of various government departments (including 3,600 war orphans and 5,200 homeless evacuees) and 200,000 more in voluntary institutions or private foster homes.

55 The name of this home has been changed to protect the anonymity of staff and children.

56 NCH, E 1/1 and J38/8–9, sisterhood council minutes, 1938.

57 NCH, E7/5, Leaflet, 'Home-Making: A Vocation and a Career in the National Children's Home', January 1952, p. 4.

58 NCH J38/8–9.

59 NCH D541/D61/4, Comments by Mr H. C. Roycroft, *Child Care: The Quarterly Review of the National Council of Associated Children's Homes*, 1959, p. 27.

60 John H. Litten, *The Seven Lamps: Yearbook of the National Children's Home and Orphanage*, October 1934.

61 This was an isolated instance which indicates that some kind of problem may have arisen in the Homes at this time.

62 NCH, D541/E2/7, Sisters' Record of Progress, 1899–1940.

63 The committee rarely visited the Homes, relying on a monthly report by the matron.

64 Bristol Record Office (hereafter BRO), Bristol City Council Social Welfare Committee Minutes 1940–6, 67021/1. Letter from R. A. B. Butler from the Ministry of Labour to Sir Stafford Cripps, 26 June 1945.

65 *Ibid.*, Report of Children's Sub-Committee 'Star' Homes – educational facilities, January 1946.

66 Gathorne-Hardy estimated only 5,000 nannies passed through training colleges between 1892 and 1939 but that the number of nannies in any given year between 1850 and 1939 lay somewhere between a quarter and half a million. Jonathan Gathorne-Hardy, *The Rise and Fall of the British Nanny* (London: Weidenfeld and Nicolson, 1993), pp. 179–81.

67 One agency advertisement in 1929 offered jobs for nannies in South America, Turkey, Ceylon, Paris, Africa and other locations throughout the UK, with salaries of between £60 and £100 (exclusive of board and keep), although in private advertisements the rate was considerably lower, usually between £30 and £50 in the decade after the First World War.

68 Advertisements in *The Times* in 1919, 1925 and 1929 show this to have been the case.

69 Alice Renton, *Tyrant or Victim? A History of the British Governess* (London: Weidenfeld and Nicolson, 1991), pp. 139–41.

70 Lively, *Oleander Jacaranda*.

71 Gathorne-Hardy, *The Rise and Fall*, p. 182.

72 P. L. Travers, *Mary Poppins*, 1934 (London: Collins, 1995).

73 Christina Hardyment, *Dream Babies: Child Care from Locke to Spock* (London: Jonathan Cape, 1983).

74 Davidoff, *Worlds Between*, chs 1 and 4.

75 His twin had died at fifteen, both his parents were now also dead and he had later had a nervous breakdown while he was teaching.

76 Unmarried nurse maids and servants could often awaken a child's early sexual and emotional feelings through the physical care they gave. Davidoff, 'Class and Gender in Victorian England', in *Worlds Between*, p. 109.

77 Lively, *Oleander*, pp. 24–5.

9

Conclusion: 'other' lives

'Have you found your missing Maslin person yet Mummy?' ...
'No ... But if I do finally manage to track him down and he turns
out to be some boring old spinster guy who just lived here alone in
this house for all those years and has no interesting story at all then
I'm going to ...'
'What Mummy? What are you going to do?'
'I'm going to kill him.'[1]

THE MURDEROUS FEELINGS WRITER Julie Myerson expressed towards
an imaginary bachelor who had once lived in her house (who
turned out in the end to be a married man with children) deny
that excitement might be attached to the life of a single person. Rather
it reconfigures the missing Maslin as a dull, lonely, childless, 'spinsterish'
man with no life, no descendants and therefore no interesting story to
tell. Myerson's project was to tell the story of all the people who had ever
lived in her Clapham house, but despite this diatribe, she had in fact
already discovered much interesting information about a real spinster
who had lived there.

When Myerson discovered that Lucy Spawton, who had occupied
her house from 1893 until her death in 1944, was a spinster, she stared
with dismay at 'that horrid little word written in black ink'. But Spawton
had never lived there alone. A buyer at the department store Derry and
Tom's, she had shared the house with her mother and sister until their
deaths, and later with a married couple (who stayed there for thirty years)
and their two sons and two foster daughters. She also had a live-in housekeeper who may also have been a nurse or companion (to whom she left
£50 in her will), and an unmarried friend, Beatrice Haig, who lived in the
house for eighteen years and who received a legacy of £250. Myerson and
her daughter speculated that this legacy and Beatrice's death two months

later might have meant that they were lesbians and that Beatrice 'had died of grief'.[2]

This story illustrates how a belief system which situates unmarried people as sad, sterile, lonely and uninteresting could influence a researcher to ignore other evidence and to place a lower value on lives led at the periphery of marriage than those at its centre. This book has given those single lives a shape and a voice and demonstrated their value and need to be heard. This final chapter will show how these beliefs have influenced my own relationship to being single, both as a way of drawing the themes of the book together and to link them to current concerns. In a book of this length, it would be impossible to do justice to the very significant changes in the nature of singleness that have taken place since 1960, therefore my concluding remarks will focus mainly on continuities.

I reached adulthood in the early 1970s, at a time when the connections between marriage, sex and procreation were under unprecedented strain. Divorce rates were soaring, gay men and lesbians were asserting their rights to sexual freedom and for their relationships to be recognised in the same way as those of heterosexual couples, and a reinvigorated feminist movement was once again campaigning against the abuses and oppression women suffered within marriage and denouncing it as a patriarchal institution. Illegitimacy was no longer stigmatised and so effectively disappeared as a category after the 1989 Children's Act gave unmarried men parental responsibility and the right to legal fatherhood.

Since then, marriage as an institution has become increasingly fragile and the frequency of divorce and remarriage has created more complicated non-nuclear family structures, now commonly termed 'blended'. Yet in the twenty-first century, elaborate and expensive weddings are increasing in popularity, and same-sex partnerships are now recognised in a law giving similar rights and obligations to those of civil marriage.[3] Thus, despite very significant changes in social and economic relationships which make defining singleness today even more problematic than in the mid-twentieth century, the couple still reigns supreme.

It was the effects of the continuing dominance of the couple, whether married or cohabiting (although now no longer necessarily heterosexual), on my own life that led me in 1990 to start my research on single women. At that time, I was a single mature student and house owner with a male lodger. Yet when we both claimed unemployment benefit during university vacations (still possible in those days), we struggled to prove to a social security visitor that we were not a couple. This experience was not new to me. During the 1970s when I was genuinely living with a man, I had been classified as a common-law wife, my social security benefit was reduced and (unlike my 'husband') I was left with a smaller pension entitlement.[4] When in the early 1990s I bought a house with a close woman friend, once again I was in an anomalous position. While in the mid-twentieth century such arrangements were unremarkable, it has been more difficult to establish ourselves unambiguously as friends sharing a home and a life than if we had had been a lesbian couple. Our friendship is often treated as less important than married or cohabiting partnerships.

While, like Lucy Spawton's, my legal status is that of a spinster, in none of these living situations nor in other homes inhabited during my twenties and thirties was I single in the sense of being alone. These situations included: rented house shared with other childless women; two communal households containing a mixture of families with young children and other single people; lodging variously with an aunt and uncle, with married friends and their children, and with married strangers; two periods as a live-in mother's help looking after a baby and very young children; and a term as a resident matron in a boarding school.

This variety of living situations enriched my life and led me to question the equation of singleness with loneliness. More significantly, it exposed the hierarchy which places the married couple and their children above friendships and other relationships (important for married and single people alike), which have been consistently undervalued. It is these 'other' relationships and the ways in which they were experienced by unmarried people in mid-twentieth-century England that have formed the core of this book. And it is because this book has been primarily about relationships that I have placed less emphasis on single people's experience of living alone, but rather shown the variety of connections which unmarried men and women formed and the range of lifestyles they embraced.

The aspects of singleness most central to my analysis have been the personal benefits and pleasures unmarried men and women gained by living outside marriage and the costs and conflicts of being caught within its shadow. For example, being single for both women and men could mean dedication to a career, a creative project, or socially valuable unpaid work offering job satisfaction and a sense of identity, but it could also mean low-paid, monotonous work with limited promotion prospects. Single men in employment benefited financially from their lack of a family, but if unemployed, they were at greater risk of drifting into homelessness. This is still the case today, as is the disproportionate number of elderly single women and men in institutions. Women now have a greater choice of careers and no longer have to choose between career and marriage, but the glass ceiling remains in place and high-achieving women are still often single and/or childless. The frequent dismissal of pregnant women[5] suggests that changes in work culture are limited and that the choice between career and family is still a live issue for many women.

The range of housing possibilities for men and women in this study also reflects my own variety of experiences in the late twentieth and early twenty-first centuries. Single people lived in rooms, flats or houses of their own, but they also shared accommodation with parents, siblings or friends, or with other single people in clubs, communities and institutions, or stayed in other people's households as domestic servants, nannies, companions or lodgers. I have shown how each of these living situations offered the possibility for single people to form significant relationships and friendships which, because they did not conform to the model of a nuclear family, have been largely invisible. While sociologists have called for new and more inclusive definitions of family and intimacy which recognise the diverse and unique web of relationships in which individuals are embedded, there is still much work to be done to bring them out of the shadows, in both the past and the present.[6]

One very significant set of relationships for single people examined in this book is those with parents. Caring for parents in old age offered mid-twentieth-century unmarried women well-recognised roles and a sense of vocation, while men's roles as parental carers were much less visible. The need for women to be supported in caring responsibilities was finally acknowledged in 1965 when the Rev. Mary Webster set up the National Council for the Single Woman and her Dependants,[7] but no support was offered to single men in similar positions. The change of name in the 1980s to the National Council of Carers may have reflected the reduction in numbers of single women willing or available to give care and the higher value women now placed on careers and on individual personal fulfilment. But as Simpson has argued, families still often expect single women to be the primary carers even when they are in employment, and the current 'citizen worker' model of the welfare state fails to address the 'care' side of the breadwinner/caregiver dichotomy.[8] The extent to which this is also an issue for unmarried men, who still often remain in the parental home well into adulthood, is rarely mentioned, nor has their interdependent role as both recipients and providers of care been given much consideration.[9]

Perhaps the greatest shift has been in the social acceptability of heterosexual and homosexual relationships for unmarried women and homosexual relationships for men. I have explored the difficulties single people faced in the very recent past over the denigration of sexual relationships outside marriage, the denial of sexual feelings and the perceived necessity of sublimating them. Older unmarried women writing for MO in 1990 noted the 'intense pleasure and satisfaction' of sexual relationships openly undertaken in later life which had been much more difficult to achieve when they were younger, and the possibility of now having an equal partnership with a man.[10] But while the 1960s and 1970s may also have 'liberated' many gay people, it is still more difficult for unmarried gay men and lesbian women born before the Second World War to 'come out'. The continuing belief that sex is essential for health and happiness also makes celibacy appear even more problematic than it did fifty years ago, and explains why the 'mother's boy' and 'frustrated spinster' stereotypes are still alive and kicking in the twenty-first century.

Unmarried women are no longer shamed by having children, and men are allowed more involvement in and responsibility for childrearing. Yet concern about childlessness has reached new heights,[11] as women feel compelled to put off having children in order to pursue careers. Single women can now either adopt children or make use of assisted conception in the absence of a male partner. But the demonisation of teenage pregnancy, the association of single men with sexual abuse, and the failure of the (now defunct) Child Support Agency during the 1990s and early 2000s to compel men to contribute to their children's support show the continuing equation of parenthood with marriage, and the difficulty of persuading men not living with their child's mother to take responsibility for children.

The use of psychoanalytic theory in the last two chapters, particularly the concepts of projection and splitting, has been helpful in understanding the complexity of relationships between parents, children and other non-parental figures in their lives. My recognition of this issue was prompted partly by my own conflicted feelings and expectations about other people's children both in my paid work and in my private life, and also by expectations held of me by friends, family and their children. Single people's involvement with children stemmed from mutual needs which could not always be answered, and the rights and responsibilities that these relationships brought with them have often been ambiguous and unclear. Worries about being considered self-centred and putting their own creative or career projects before the needs of their families seem to be experienced more strongly by single women than men. Yet the identification that many of my male interviewees showed with the 'selfish' and 'loner' aspects of the bachelor stereotype often hid their own web of significant relationships and responsibilities.

The difficulty many of us have in making clear boundaries between paid and unpaid emotional and caring work is also still a live issue. The absence of social policies to support working parents has intensified the deep anxieties many parents feel about paying another person to care for their children. A report in the *Daily Telegraph* in April 2006 indicated that nannies were once again in great demand, with over 100,000 in the UK, and could command high salaries.[12] But the installation of 'nanny watch' cameras, like the demonisation of the British nanny Louise Woodward, believed to have murdered a baby in the US in 1997, suggests that both parents and single women carers still often idealise their own relationships with children by splitting off their negative feelings and projecting them into others. This is also apparent in the TV programme *Supernanny*, broadcast in forty-five countries, in which an unmarried career nanny in her thirties, who bears a striking resemblance to Mary Poppins, exposes the failings of parents and tames their children. This programme displays parents' uncertainty and continued willingness to accept professional single women's expertise in child care, yet it has also been severely criticised. Decca Aitkenhead's demolition of the nanny's methods in the *Guardian* mocked and demeaned her by drawing attention to her lack of education and limited vocabulary.[13]

One absence in this book has been any sustained discussion of friendship. My own friendships have at times been sources of anxiety but also of great value. Indeed, friends have sustained and supported me throughout this project and throughout my life. Yet friends were not discussed in depth by many of my interviewees. This does not necessarily mean that past friendships were unimportant but, in cases where they were not continued into the present, they may have been harder to recall than family, particularly if there was no one else still living who remembered them. Friendship was also an underresearched and undervalued category in the 1990s, at the time of the interviews.[14] The priority I gave to familial relationships, childhood, education, work and marital prospects meant that friendship was introduced at the end when interviewees were often tired.

Since then a brief visit to the archives of the GFS has shown the web of relationships surrounding women in this organisation both in England and in missionary work abroad. It is clear from one of the log books that GFS members in different roles and capacities in the organisation maintained their allegiances to one another and to the organisation over time through meetings, activities and exchanges of gifts and letters.[15] Some of my male interviewees described their time in the armed forces or in boarding schools as similarly enabling them to make long-term friends. Yet none of my sources showed the uncertainties, jealousy and rivalry which are as integral to friendship as they are to work and family. Catherine Clay, in her study of women writers and journalists associated with the feminist journal *Time and Tide*, gives important insights into this area. She discusses not simply the professional and personal value of these women's networks but also their conflicts and anxieties, which she argues 'unsettle more celebratory accounts of women's friendship'.[16]

Finally, both anxieties about being valued and a desire to be remembered can be read in the personal legacies left by women and men who lived in the shadow of marriage. Muriel had many friends during her professional life, yet an assumption that families take priority meant that she ended up leaving all her money to a cousin with whom she had little in common. Mildred's need to be loved and remembered led her to entrust a younger friend with a list of personal possessions to be distributed to specific friends when she died. David's lifelong interest in children and his attachment to his 400-year-old house came together in the trust he created, making it into a museum for their educational benefit. And lastly, Meg, alone in the world with few possessions, gave me her poems, letters, papers and books after our second interview because I had taken an interest in her life. This book is partly a product of my own need to be remembered. It is my legacy to the men and women who trusted me with their stories, and is dedicated to their memory.

Notes

1 Julie Myerson, *Home: The Story of Everyone Who Ever Lived in Our House* (London: Harper Perennial, 2004), pp. 67 and 389.

2 *Ibid.*, p. 288.

3 Women and Equality Unit, Civil Partnership Fact sheet, Department of Trade and Industry, June 2004, www.womenandequalityunit.gov.uk/research/lgb_cp7622_factsheet.pdf, accessed 28 August 2006,

4 He was credited with national insurance contributions but I was not.

5 See Clare McGlynn, 'Pregnancy Dismissals and the Webb Litigation', *Feminist Legal Studies*, 4:2 (1996), pp. 229–42.

6 See for example Elizabeth Silva and Carol Smart, *The New Family* (London: Sage, 1999); Lynn Jamieson, *Intimacy: Personal Relationships in Modern Society* (Cambridge: Polity, 1999).

7 Mary Stott (ed.), *Women Talking: An Anthology from the Guardian Women's Page, 1922–35, 1957–71* (London: Pandora, 1987), pp. 230–1.

8 Roona Simpson, 'Contemporary Spinsters in the New Millennium: Changing Notions of Family and Kinship', Gender Institute Working Papers, London School of Economics, 10 July 2003.

9 Fay Wright does include men in 'Single Carers: Employment, Housework and Caring' in Janet Finch and Dulcie Groves (eds), *A Labour of Love: Women, Work and Caring* (London: Routledge and Kegan Paul, 1983), p. 89.

10 MO, C2214, H2161, B2153, and H670 Close Relationships File, 1990.

11 See for example Sylvia Ann Hewlett, *Baby Hunger: The New Battle for Motherhood*

(London: Atlantic Books, 2002).

12　*Daily Telegraph*, 18 April 2006.

13　Decca Aitkenhead, 'You've Been Very, Very Naughty', *Guardian*, 22 July 2006, Family section, p. 6.

14　See Pat O'Connor, *Friendships between Women: A Critical Review* (London: Harvester Wheatsheaf, 1992), p. 2.

15　Women's Library, London, GFS, Log book of St Paul's GFS, Herne Hill, 1927–31 and 1935–6. This archive has been recatalogued since these records were accessed.

16　Clay, *British Women Writers*, p. 32.

Appendices

Appendix 1

NSLLL: working-class households in survey sample

Borough	Working-class households (no.)	Total persons in working-class households
Chelsea	212	753
Deptford	529	1,849
Hampstead	289	900
Total	*1,030*	*3,502*

Source: NSLLL vol. 3, pp. 375, 376, 421 and 425.

Appendix 2

NSLLL: lifestyles of working-class single men and women over the age of 30 in survey sample

	Total over 30	Living with relatives	Living apart from relatives
Men:			
Chelsea	6	5 (83%)	1 (17%)
Deptford	41	27 (66%)	14 (34%)
Hampstead	10	3 (30%)	7 (70%)
Total	*57*	*35 (61%)*	*22 (39%)*
Women			
Chelsea	20	9 (45%)	11 (55%)
Deptford	50	29 (58%)	21 (42%)
Hampstead	25	9 (36%)*	16 (64%)*
Total	*95*	*47 (49%)*	*48 (51%)*
Total single over 30	*152*	*82 (54%)*	*70 (46%)*

* Four men and three women living alone in Hampstead who have been included in this analysis did not have marital status recorded. However, a further nine households with lodgers whose sex, age and marital status are not recorded have been excluded from the analysis. Some of these lodgers were likely to have been single and over thirty.

Source: Household record cards for NSLLL held at the London School of Economics.

Appendix 3

The Hygiene Committee of the Women's Group on Public Welfare and witnesses interviewed for their report *Our Towns* (1943, pp. viii and 114)

Committee

Chairman: Miss Amy Sayle, MBE, MA, LCC; Women Public Health Officers Association

Secretary: Miss M. L. Harford, chief woman officer, National Council of Social Service

Members: Mrs John Barclay, BA, FSI, Society of Women Housing Managers

Miss E. Fabian Brackenbury, BA, (served to 1940), lecturer in health education, Avery Hill Training College: Ling Physical Education Society

Miss P. Spafford (served from 1940), organising secretary, Ling Physical Education Association

Miss Elizabeth Denby, Hon. ARIBA, housing consultant

Miss D. Ibberson, civil servant

Mrs Henry Haldane, (served to 1940), National Federation of Women's Institutes

Miss Cicely McCall, (served from 1940), National Federation of Women's Institutes

Witnesses interviewed

1 Miss Winny, headmistress of Daubeny Road, LCC infants school, Hackney
2 Miss Walsh, headmistress of Scawfell Street Senior Girls' School, Shoreditch
3 Miss Morrell, superintendent health visitor, Shoreditch
4 Miss J. Clarke, assistant organiser of children's care in St Pancras, Hampstead and Holburn
5 Miss L. M. O'Kell, chief billetting officer of Abbots Langley (formerly sanitory inspector and health visitor in the Paddington Area)
6 Mr R. A. Bishop, sanitary inspector and health visitor in the Paddington area
7 Miss D. C. Keeling, assistant secretary, National Council of Social Service, (formerly secretary, Liverpool Social Service Society)
8 Mrs Barclay, chartered surveyor, woman housing manager
9 Miss I. N. Hill, organising secretary, South St Pancras Charity Organisation Society
10 Miss Purdon, Central Council for Women's Training and Employment
11 Miss K. M. Walls, Ministry of Labour and National Service, London and SE Region
12 Mrs Chalk, voluntary helper in a reception area from St Pancras
13 Mrs Sheppard, voluntary helper in a reception area from St Pancras
14 Miss E. A. Sheppard, Ranyard worker in Paddington*

---

* Ranyard workers were district visitors from the domestic mission founded by Ellen Ranyard in London during the 1850s.

15 Miss F. Brackenbury, Ling Physical Education Association
16 Miss Locket, hon. organising secretary, East Lewisham Charity Association
17 Miss N. March, secretary, Health and Cleanliness Council
18 Miss W. M. Crossman, LMH Settlement worker, Cowley Estate, Lambeth
19 Miss I. Heather, until outbreak of war head of Cathedral Play House, Lambeth (formerly superintendent, Trinity Welfare Centre, Stratford East)
20 Miss Tann, HMI, Board of Education
21 Mrs Kent Parsons, MBE, superintendent, Maternity and Child Welfare, Tottenham
22 Mr R. Higdon, headmaster, Hutton, LCC residential school
23 Miss M. Veitch, formerly health visitor, Middlesborough and Stockton-on-Tees
24 Miss J. P. Young, queen's nurse, Metropolitan District
25 Mrs Rhees, psychiatric social worker, Metropolitan Emergency Child Guidance Service
26 Sister E. A. Thomas, LCC school nursing sister
27 Sister B. M. Sticklan, LCC school nursing sister

Appendix 4

Institutions caring for children supervised or staffed by nuns listed within Roman Catholic dioceses, 1897–1937

	1897	1917	1937
Orphanages	39	57	48
Homes for children (various)	6	8	10
Homes for women/girls	2	8	14
Homes for mother and babies	-	1	3
Homes for girls in business	4	9	15
Night Homes for girls	1	3	4
Total	52	86	94

Note: Figures for reform and industrial schools are not included.

Source: Walsh, *Roman Catholic Nuns in England and Wales*, table 10 (statistics derived from Catholic Directories 1857–1937)

Appendix 5 Profiles of interviewees

Most names have been changed to protect anonymity. Tapes are in the author's possession.

Unmarried women

Some women were unmarried for most or all of our period but subsequently married in late middle or old age.

Amelia, interviewed 26 January 1994
How contacted: Advertisement in her local library
Year of birth: 1905
Place of birth: Bristol
Mother's occupation(s): Married at twenty; no paid employment before marriage
Father's occupation(s): Corn importer; own business; went bankrupt in 1926
Number and position of siblings: One brother, eighteen months older
Education: Privately educated at a girls' high school; left at sixteen
Occupation(s): Daily child care; book-keeping for bakery; own handicraft business and shop

Betty, interviewed 18 January 1999
How contacted: Friend of friend
Year of birth: 1921
Place of birth: Westbury on Trym, near Bristol
Brought up by grandmother
Grandmother's occupation(s): Ran pub until her husband died; no paid work afterwards
Grandfather's occupation(s): Policeman – died when she was two
Number and position of siblings: Two uncles still living at home, one fourteen years older and one ten years older – thought of them as her brothers
Education: Elementary school; left at fourteen
Occupation(s): Ledger clerk in laundry; joined Wrens in 1942; worked for electricity board after the war

Bridget, interviewed 16 December 1993
How contacted: Friend of university librarian
Year of birth: 1906
Place of birth: Colchester
Mother's occupation(s): Cook general; no paid work after marriage
Father's occupation(s): Builder – had a previous wife
Number and position of siblings: Ten siblings: one brother, nine older half-brothers and half-sisters
Education: Elementary school; central school; left at sixteen
Occupation(s): Domestic servant; nanny; shop assistant

Charlotte, interviewed 21 February 1994
How contacted: Advertisement in Soroptimist Society newsletter

Year of birth: 1905
Place of birth: Midlands
Mother's occupation(s): No paid employment; came from a military family
Father's occupation(s): Vicar
Number and position of siblings: Six siblings: four brothers and two sisters, roughly two years between each child; she was the second child and eldest daughter
Education: Several governesses, all trained at Ampleside (qualified in Parents' National Education); girls' public school; Froebel training at London College; church missionary training
Occupation(s): Teacher; missionary
Married aged eighty

Daisy, interviewed 4 October 1993
How contacted: Volunteered after seeing advertisement in local library
Year of birth: 1908
Place of birth: Bristol
Mother's occupation(s): Parlour maid (before marriage); fostered children after marriage
Father's occupation(s): Butler (before marriage); own vegetable business; odd jobs (mainly building trade); in army during war – invalided out with TB
Number and position of siblings: Three siblings: brother eleven years older, sister (May) eight years older, adopted brother (George) ten years younger
Education: Elementary school; left at fourteen
Occupation(s): Domestic service, mainly as cook

Dora, interviewed 21 February 1994
How contacted: Member of the Soroptimist Society who knew her answered my advertisement in their newsletter
Year of birth: 1903
Place of birth: Sussex
Mother's occupation(s): In service as cook and house parlour maid (before marriage); part-time cooking (after marriage)
Father's occupation(s): Railway signalman
Number and position of siblings: Youngest of six children: two elder brothers, two elder sisters, twin brother; siblings spaced two years apart – twin brother never married
Education: Elementary school
Occupation(s): Office worker; housekeeper for her parents

Doreen, interviewed 7 October 1993
How contacted: Friend of my uncle
Year of birth: 1911
Place of birth: Surrey
Mother's occupation(s): Farmer (owner)
Father's occupation(s): Farmer (tenant and manager)
Number and position of siblings: Two siblings: one younger sister, one brother

Education: Secondary school; agriculture college
Occupation(s): Farm worker; farm secretary

Dorothy, interviewed 22 October 1993
How contacted: Friend of friend
Year of birth: 1906
Place of birth: Southwest England
Mother's occupation(s): No paid employment
Father's occupation(s): Manager of small branch of bank
Number and position of siblings: Four siblings: brother eighteen months older, younger brother, twin sister, sister five years younger
Education: Girls' public school; Royal College of Art; teacher training
Occupation(s): Art teacher; art college administrator; school inspector

Ellen, interviewed 22 September 1993
How contacted: Friend of friend
Year of birth: 1909
Place of birth: Wiltshire
Mother's occupation(s): Tailor (before marriage); no paid employment (after marriage)
Father's occupation(s): Railway worker
Number and position of siblings: Two siblings: sister four years older, brother five years younger
Education: Elementary school; left at fourteen
Occupation(s): Nanny; sewing-room attendant in workhouse; nurse; midwife, health visitor

Elsie, interviewed 22 February 1994
How contacted: Advertisement in Soroptimist Society newsletter
Year of birth: 1903
Place of birth: Guildford
Mother's occupation(s): Nurse (before marriage)
Father's occupation(s): Compositor in printing trade
Number and position of siblings: Four siblings (mother had five miscarriages): one sister a year younger (unmarried), three younger brothers
Education: Church school; left at fourteen; brief period at night school
Occupation(s): Messenger at War Office; worked for firm of lighting and heating engineers for forty-two years – progressed from office junior to head of office and showroom with four girls under her
Married aged fifty

Emily, interviewed 18 November 1993
How contacted: Via BBC producer
Year of birth: 1903
Place of birth: Kent
Mother's occupation(s): War work in brewery – sent to a mental hospital when Emily was fourteen

Father's occupation(s): Farm labourer – died aged thirty-five when she was thirteen
Number and position of siblings: Two siblings: one elder sister (married), one younger brother (died aged fourteen)
Education: Elementary school; left at fourteen
Occupation(s): Domestic service; nanny

Ethel, interviewed 9 October 1993
How contacted: Neighbour of cousin
Year of birth: 1902
Place of birth: Eastbourne
Mother's occupation(s): Cook and companion to a lady (before marriage); administration for family business (after marriage) – second wife
Father's occupation(s): Landau driver and later private car hire
Number and position of siblings: One half-brother thirteen years older
Education: Private school; left at fourteen or fifteen
Occupation(s): Home-based dressmaker
Married aged seventy

Gertrude, interviewed 2 November 1993
How contacted: Through day centre
Year of birth: 1892
Place of birth: London
Mother's occupation(s): Dressmaker before marriage; no paid employment after marriage
Father's occupation(s): Reporter on *Daily Telegraph*
Number and position of siblings: Only child; a brother had died before she was born
Education: Higher grade school; took Oxford local; left at sixteen; went to Pitman's College but never worked as a secretary
Occupation(s): Milliner all her working life

Gwen, interviewed 9 February 1994
How contacted: Neighbour of another interviewee
Year of birth: 1907
Place of birth: London
Mother's occupation(s): Teacher (before marriage); no paid employment after marriage
Father's occupation(s): Compositor for *The Times*
Number and position of siblings: One sister, five years younger
Education: Girls' high school; taught by progressive methods; domestic science training at London college
Occupation(s): Domestic science teacher and lecturer

Jane, interviewed 19 November 1990
How contacted: I was her cleaner
Year of birth: 1907

Place of birth: Bristol
Mother's occupation(s): Teacher (before marriage); no paid employment (after marriage)
Father's occupation(s): Leather merchant; smallholder
Number and position of siblings: One brother two years older
Education: Girls' secondary school; secretarial school
Occupation(s): Smallholding; secretary in various companies - lots of job changes
Married in her fifties

Joan, interviewed 28 October 1993
How contacted: Through warden of sheltered accommodation
Year of birth: 1906
Place of birth: Glasgow
Mother's occupation(s): Teacher (not certain) before marriage; no paid employment after marriage
Father's occupation(s): Business management (unsure what kind)
Number and position of siblings: One sister, identical twin
Education: High school; secretarial college
Occupation(s): Typist; secretary for Ministry of Labour

Margot, interviewed 3 November 1993
How contacted: Friend of my aunt
Year of birth: 1905
Place of birth: London
Mother's occupation(s): No paid employment – married young
Father's occupation(s): Solicitor; broker; accountant
Number and position of siblings: Two siblings: one brother seven years older, one sister four years older
Education: Small private school; secretarial training
Occupation(s): Chicken farmer; secretary
Married in her fifties

Martha, interviewed 17 December 1993
How contacted: Through my brother
Year of birth: 1908
Place of birth: South of England
Father's occupation(s): Yeomanry in war; landowner
Mother's occupation(s): Nursing; VAD
Number and position of siblings: Two siblings: one brother four years younger, one sister ten years younger
Education: Governess; girls' boarding school
Occupation(s): Secretary; organic farmer

Mary, interviewed 1 December 1993
How contacted: Through warden of residential home
Year of birth: 1908

Place of birth: Sunderland
Mother's occupation(s): Before marriage unknown; after marriage ran the local Conservative Club
Father's occupation(s): Butcher – blinded in the war
Number and position of siblings: Four siblings: two elder sisters, two younger brothers; one brother died in childhood, one ten years younger; all married
Education: Elementary school, half days only during the war; left at fourteen
Occupations: Shop assistant; nursing aid; nanny; gas-board worker
Had a son born 1940

Maud, interviewed 4 January 1991
How contacted: Ex-headmistress of friend
Year of birth: 1907
Place of birth: unknown
Mother's occupation(s): School teacher; headmistress – died when Maud was thirteen
Father's occupation(s): Schoolteacher; headmaster
Number and position of siblings: Four siblings: one elder brother, one elder sister (died at twenty-three), two younger brothers (middle brother died at nineteen)
Education: University degree
Occupation(s): Teacher; headmistress

Mavis, interviewed 9 February 1994
How contacted: Advertisement in Soroptimist Society newsletter
Year of birth: 1906
Place of birth: North London
Mother's occupation(s): Artist before marriage; worked in unknown occupation during First World War
Father's occupation(s): Own retail business (uncertain what kind) - died 1930
Number and position of siblings: One brother two years younger
Education: Elementary school; high school; evening classes in engineering; qualified in engineering at a polytechnic
Occupations: Job at a firm of instrument makers; trained at a power station as an apprentice engineer; demonstrator of electrical appliances for electricity board; factory inspector (Civil Service); member of Women's Engineering Society; chief inspector of factories in Palestine

Meg, interviewed 4 February 1991
How contacted: Through warden of residential home
Year of birth: 1902
Place of birth: Bristol
Mother's occupation(s): Court dressmaker; domestic service; helped in her mother's shop before marriage; no paid work after marriage
Father's occupation(s): General shopkeeper
Number and position of siblings: Two sisters: one eighteen months younger, one six years younger

Education: Elementary school (girls only); left at fourteen; night school; private shorthand lessons
Occupation(s): Laundry worker; cashier at grocer's shop; drapery warehouse worker; secretary and later officer for TocH

Millicent, interviewed 15 December 1993
How contacted: Aunt of an acquaintance
Year of birth: 1906
Place of birth: Essex
Mother's occupation(s): Married at nineteen; no paid employment before marriage; helped on farm during First World War
Father's occupation(s): Farmer
Number and position of siblings: Four siblings: brother two and a half years older, sister sixteen months younger, brother two and a half years younger, brother twenty-four years younger
Education: Girls' high school; domestic science training college
Occupation(s): Domestic science teacher and college lecturer

Molly, interviewed 28 September 1993
How contacted: Through Age Concern
Year of birth: 1899
Place of birth: Bath
Mother's occupation(s): Daughter of jeweller
Father's occupation(s): Printer; in army during First World War
Number and position of siblings: Nine younger siblings (two died in infancy)
Education: Council elementary school; left at fourteen
Occupation(s): Printing; munitions; hotel work, mainly as still-room maid

Muriel, interviewed 1 December 1990 and 29 April 1995
How contacted: Friend of friend
Year of birth: 1906
Place of birth: Bedfordshire
Mother's occupation(s): No paid work; did 'good works'
Father's occupation(s): Surveyor
Number and position of siblings: Two brothers a lot older; a third brother died in infancy
Education: Girls' boarding school; nurse training at St Mary's Hospital in London (SRN); midwifery at East End maternity hospital; passed examination in public health at the University of London in the late 1930s
Occupation(s): Nurse; midwife; nursing administration

Nellie, interviewed 7 December 1993
How contacted: Through warden of residential home
Year of birth: 1904
Place of birth: County Durham
Mother's occupation(s): Laundress before marriage; no paid employment after marriage

Father's occupation(s): Blacksmith
Number and position of siblings: One brother twelve years younger
Education: Elementary school – unclear when she left, but no secondary education
Occupation(s): Varied – included shop and factory work
Had a daughter

Patience, interviewed 14 October 1993
How contacted: Answered advertisement on notice board
Year of birth: 1907
Place of birth: London
Mother's occupation(s): Worked with children before married (vague)
Father's occupation(s): Company secretary (didn't know what kind of company)
Number and position of siblings: One younger brother
Education: Girls' high school
Occupation(s): Kindergarten teacher; church army (moral welfare and visiting)

Pearl, interviewed 23 September 1993
How contacted: Through warden of day centre
Year of birth: 1910
Place of birth: Bristol
Mother's occupation(s): In service (before marriage); no paid employment after marriage
Father's occupation(s): Brick-layer
Number and position of siblings: Two brothers: one four years older, one two years younger
Education: Elementary school; left at fourteen
Occupation(s): Packer in wholesale grocery business

Rona, interviewed 18 November 2005
How contacted: Friend of friend
Year of birth: 1930
Place of birth: Waterford, Ireland
Mother's occupation(s): No paid work
Father's occupation(s): Pharmacist
Number and position of siblings: Two older sisters
Education: Elementary school; left at 14; evening classes at Chelsea Polytechnic
– qualified in chiropody
Occupation(s): Office work; worker in children's day nursery; chiropodist

Ruby, interviewed 31 January 1991
How contacted: Through warden of sheltered accommodation
Year of birth: 1907
Place of birth: Bristol
Mother's occupation(s): Dressmaker
Father's occupation(s): Baker
Number and position of siblings: Three brothers, one sister who died aged six

Education: Elementary school; left at fourteen
Occupation(s): Chocolate factory worker

Violet, interviewed 29 November 1990
How contacted: Through another interviewee - fellow resident in retirement home
Year of birth: 1906
Place of birth: London area
Mother's occupation(s): Worked as a tobacconist at uncle's shop; married at 28; no paid employment after marriage
Father's occupation(s): Teacher and author of books on science
Number and position of siblings: Three siblings: two older brothers, one older sister
Education: London University degree in modern languages; hospital nursing training
Occupation(s): Nurse; lecturer in nursing
Main areas of residence between wars: Village somewhere near London; London; France

Winifred, interviewed 23 March 1994
How contacted: Friend of university secretary
Year of birth: 1903
Place of birth: Cambridgeshire
Mother's occupation(s): From a farming family; no paid employment before marriage
Father's occupation(s): Lawyer; owner of a brick manufacturing company
Number and position of siblings: Two siblings: one elder brother, one elder sister
Education: Private day school; girls' public school; Oxford University
Occupation(s): No paid work; bred dogs for show
Died 1995

   Unmarried men
Bert, interviewed 16 January 1999
How contacted: Employee of friend
Year of birth: 1930
Place of birth: Farm near Weymouth, Dorset
Mother's occupation(s): Invalid for most of her married life
Father's occupation(s): Farmer
Number and position of siblings: One older brother
Education: Elementary school; left at 14
Occupation(s): Farm labourer

Bob, interviewed 15 September 1998
How contacted: Friend of friend of relative
Year of birth: 1933
Place of birth: Sunderland
Mother's occupation(s): Not known

Father's occupation(s): Boilermaker
Number and position of siblings: Seven siblings: two older sisters, two older brothers, twin brother, younger twin brothers
Education: Elementary school; left at 14
Occupation (s): Laundry worker; National Service in army; building trade; later worked for council – sometimes unemployed

Charlie, interviewed 14 August 1998
How contacted: Through warden of retirement home
Year of birth: 1918
Place of birth: Sunderland
Mother's occupation(s): Not known – mother died when he was twelve or thirteen
Father's occupation(s): Tailor
Number and position of siblings: Five siblings: one older and three younger brothers; one much younger sister
Education: Elementary school; left at 14
Occupation(s): Errand boy; then unskilled jobs in factories and hotels

David, interviewed 24 April 1994
How contacted: Father's friend
Year of birth: 1910
Place of birth: Unknown to him
Mother's occupation(s): Private secretary, teacher – unmarried
Father's occupation(s): Veterinary surgeon – unmarried
Number and position of siblings: None known
Education: Prep school; public school; university degree in history
Occupation(s): Worked in several different departments of a gas, coal and coke company; probation officer

Dennis, interviewed 6 July 1999
How contacted: Acquaintance of a relative
Year of birth: 1923
Place of birth: Salisbury
Mother's occupation(s): Dressmaker
Father's occupation(s): Sergeant in army, chef
Number and position of siblings: Four siblings: one older half-brother and one older half-sister from father's first marriage (he was a widower); one older full brother and one younger full brother
Education: Elementary church school; left at 14
Occupation (s): Office work for firm of solicitors before and after the war; army dental corps during the war

Fred, interviewed 1 December 1993
How contacted: Through warden of sheltered accommodation
Year of birth: 1903
Place of birth: Devon

Mother's occupation(s): Cook (before marriage); no paid employment after marriage
Father's occupation(s): Worked on boats; farm labourer
Number and position of siblings: Twelve siblings: seven brothers and five sisters; he was the fourth child
Education: Elementary school; left at twelve
Occupation(s): Groom; farm labourer; hotel work; railway worker; other short-term or casual labour

Ian, interviewed 22 August 1998
How contacted: Advertisement in *Oldie* magazine
Year of birth: 1927
Place of birth: London
Mother's occupation(s): Took in lodgers
Father's occupation(s): Car salesman
Number and position of siblings: One sister, ten years older
Education: Elementary school; day boy at prep school; day boy at public school; left at 18
Occupations: RAF for ten years; filing clerk in surveyor's office; county surveyor

Jim, interviewed 13 August 1998
How contacted: Through warden of retirement home
Year of birth: 1921
Place of birth: Village in County Durham
Mother's occupation(s): No paid work
Father's occupation(s): Coal miner; boot mender; after pit closed, worked for local council mending roads; retired early on health grounds
Number and position of siblings: Three siblings: one sister five years older, one brother three years younger, one sister eight years younger
Education: Elementary school; left at fourteen
Occupation(s): Itinerant worker in building trade

Lionel, interviewed 4 September, 16 October and 21 October 1998
How contacted: Friend of friend
Year of birth: 1929
Place of birth: Westport, Somerset
Mother's occupation(s): Glover
Father's occupation(s): Great Western Railway guard
Number and position of siblings: Twin sisters, four years older
Education: Grammar school; English language degree at university
Occupation(s): National Service in RAF; secondary school teacher

Peter, interviewed 21 August 1998
How contacted: Friend of a cousin
Year of birth: 1928
Place of birth: Oxford
Mother's occupation(s): Land girl in First World War; receptionist in husband's

practice and later for a local firm
Father's occupation(s): Optician – died 1946
Number and position of siblings: One sister, five years older
Education: Grammar school; university; certificate of education after doing National Service
Occupation(s): Secondary school teacher

Roger, interviewed 13 November 1998
How contacted: Friend of friend
Year of birth: 1924
Place of birth: Carlyle
Mother's occupation(s): School teacher before marriage; lifelong invalid
Father's occupation(s): Lithographic proofer and artist
Number and position of siblings: Only child
Education: Grammar school; teacher training college
Occupations: Army during Second World War; teacher

Sid, interviewed 13 August 1999
How contacted: Through warden of retirement home
Year of birth: 1925
Place of birth: Village in County Durham
Mother's occupation(s): Not known - not married to his father - left to marry another man
Father's occupation(s): Worked in a foundry
Brought up by grandparents from two years old – grandfather was a gun maker
Number and position of siblings: Eldest – five younger brothers and sisters
Education: Elementary school; left at 13
Occupation(s): Shepherd; joined army at sixteen; prisoner of war; coal miner

Other interviews
Annette, interviewed 10 April 1993
How contacted: Friend of friend
Year of birth: 1923

Elizabeth, interviewed 30th November 2000
How contacted: Friend
Year of birth: 1947
Pupil of Maud (see above)

Joan E., interviewed 23 December 1990
Year of birth: 1919
How contacted: My mother

Lesley, interviewed 28 December 1990
Year of birth: 1928
How contacted: My aunt

Susan, interviewed 27 October 1993
How contacted: Friend of friend
Year of birth: c. late 1940s

Sylvia, interviewed 4 March 2002
How contacted: Advertisement in Regional Historian newsletter
Year of birth: 1932
Occupation(s): House parent, nanny

Select Bibliography of Secondary Published Sources

Adams, Margaret, *Single Blessedness: Observations on the Single Status in Married Society* (London: Heinemann, 1977).

Alberti, Joanna, *Eleanor Rathbone* (London: Sage, 1996).

Allan, Katherine, R., *Single Women, Family Ties: Life Histories of Older Women* (Sage, 1989).

Anderson, Michael, 'The Impact on the Family of the Elderly of Changes since Victorian Times in Governmental Income-Maintenance Provision' in Ethel Shanas and Marvin B. Sussman (eds), *Family, Bureaucracy and the Elderly* (Durham, NC: Duke University Press, 1977).

—— 'The Social Implications of Demographic Change', in F. M. L. Thompson (ed.), *The Cambridge Social History of Britain*, II (Cambridge: Cambridge University Press, 1990).

Auchmuty, Rosemary, *A World of Girls* (London: Women's Press, 1992).

Baker, Niamh, *Happily Ever After: Women's Fiction in Postwar Britain 1945–1960* (London: Macmillan, 1989).

Barber, Dulan, *Unmarried Fathers* (London: Hutchinson, 1975).

Barham, Peter, *Forgotten Lunatics of the Great War* (London: Yale University Press, 2004).

Beauman, Nicola, *A Very Great Profession: The Woman's Novel 1914–1939* (London: Virago, 1983).

Behlmer, George K., *Friends of the Family: The English Home and its Guardians, 1850–1940* (Stanford, CA: Stanford University Press, 1998).

Bennett, Alan, *Untold Stories* (London: Faber and Faber, 2005).

Bennett, Judith M., and Amy M. Froide (eds), *Singlewomen in the European Past* (Philadelphia, PA: University of Pennsylvania Press, 1999).

Bingham, Adrian, *Gender, Modernity and the Popular Press in Interwar Britain* (Oxford: Oxford University Press, 2004).

Birkett, Dea, *Spinsters Abroad: Victorian Lady Explorers* (London: Gollancz, 1991).

Bourke, Joanna, *Dismembering the Male: Men's Bodies, Britain and the Great War* (London: Reaktion Books, 1996).

Bourne, Stephen, *Brief Encounters: Lesbians and Gays in British Cinema, 1930–1971* (London: Cassell, 1996).

Boyd, Kelly, 'Knowing Your Place: The Tensions of Masculinity in Boys' Story Papers, 1918–39' in Michael Roper and John Tosh (eds), *Manful Assertions: Masculinities in Britain since 1800* (London: Routledge, 1991).

Braybon, Gail, *Women Workers in World War One* (London: Croom Helm, 1981).

—— 'Winners or Losers: Women's Role in the War Story' in Gail Braybon (ed.),

Evidence, History and the Great War (Oxford: Berghahn Books, 2003).

Braybon, Gail, and Penny Summerfield, *Out of the Cage: Women's Experiences in Two World Wars* (London: Routledge and Kegan Paul, 1987).

Bridcut, John, *Britten's Children* (London: Faber and Faber, 2006).

Bristow, Joseph, 'Symonds' History, Ellis's Heredity', in Lucy Bland and Laura Doan (eds), *Sexology in Culture: Labelling Bodies and Desires* (Chicago: University of Chicago Press/Cambridge: Polity, 1998).

Brittain, Vera, *Chronicle of Youth: Great War Diary 1913–1917*, ed. Alan Bishop (London: Phoenix Press, 1981).

—— *Chronicle of Friendship: Vera Brittain's Diary of the Thirties*, ed. Alan Bishop (London: Gollancz, 1986).

Brogan, Hugh, *The Life of Arthur Ransome* (London: Jonathan Cape, 1984).

—— (ed.), *Signalling from Mars: The Letters of Arthur Ransome* (London: Pimlico, 1988).

Bruley, Sue, 'A New Perspective on Women Workers in the Second World War: The Industrial Diary of Kathleen Church-Bliss and Elsie Whiteman', *Labour History Review*, 68:2 (2003).

Buettner, Elizabeth, *Empire Families: Britons and Late Imperial India* (Oxford: Oxford University Press, 2004).

Bulmer, M., K. Bales and K. Kish Sklar, 'The Social Survey in Historical Perspective' in M. Bulmer (ed.), *Essays on the History of British Sociological Research* (Cambridge: Cambridge University Press, 1985).

Burnett, John, *Idle Hands: The Experience of Unemployment, 1790–1990* (London: Routledge, 1994).

Cadogan, M. and P. Craig, *You're a Brick, Angela!: A New Look at Girls' Fiction from 1839 to 1975* (London: Gollancz, 1976).

Calder, Angus, and Dorothy Sheridan, *Speak for Yourself: A Mass Observation Anthology* (Oxford: Oxford University Press, 1984).

Chambers, Deborah, *Representing the Family*, (London: Sage, 2001).

Chudacoff, Howard, *The Age of the Bachelor: Creating an American Subculture* (Princeton, NJ: Princeton University Press, 1999).

Clarke, David (ed.), 'Marriage, Domestic Life and Social Change' in David Clarke (ed.), *Marriage, Domestic Life and Social Change: Writings for Jacqueline Burgoyne, 1944–88* (London: Routledge, 1991).

Clarke, Mary G., *A Short life of Ninety Years* (Edinburgh: privately published by Astrid and Martin Hughes, 1973).

Clay, Catherine, *British Women Writers, 1914–1945: Professional Work and Friendship* (London: Ashgate, 2006).

Coles, Gladys Mary, *Mary Webb* (Bridgend: Seren Books, 1990).

Cook, Hera, *The Long Sexual Revolution: English Women, Sex and Contraception 1800–1973* (Oxford: Oxford University Press, 2004).

Crang, Jeremy A., *The British Army and the People's War, 1939–1945* (Manchester: Manchester University Press, 2000).

Dale, Pamela, 'Training for Work: Domestic Service as a Route Out of Long-Stay Institutions before 1959', *Women's History Review*, 13:3 (2004).

David, Hugh, *On Queer Street: A Social History of Homosexuality, 1895–1995* (London: HarperCollins, 1997).

Davidoff, Leonore, "'Adam Spoke First and Named the Orders of the World": Masculine and Feminine Domains in History and Sociology' in Helen Corr and Lynn Jamieson (eds), *The Politics of Everyday Life: Continuity and Change in Politics, Work and the Family* (London: Macmillan, 1990).

—— *Worlds Between: Historical Perspectives on Gender and Class* (Cambridge: Polity, 1995).

Davidoff, Leonore and Catherine Hall, *Family Fortunes: Men and Women of the English Middle Class, 1780–1850* (London: Hutchinson Education, 1987).

Davidoff, Leonore, Megan Doolittle, Janet Fink and Katherine Holden, *The Family Story: Blood Contract and Intimacy, 1830–1960* (London: Longman, 1999).

Dawson, Graham, 'The Blonde Bedouin: Lawrence of Arabia, Imperial Adventure and the Imaginings of English-British Masculinity' in Michael Roper and John Tosh (eds), *Manful Assertions: Masculinities in Britain since 1800* (London: Routledge, 1991).

Deacon, Alan, *In Search of the Scrounger: The Administration of Unemployment Insurance in Britain, 1920–1931*, Occasional Papers in Social Administration No. 60 (London: G. Bell and Sons, 1976).

Derrick, Deborah (ed.), *Illegitimate: The Experience of People Born Outside Marriage* (London: One Parent Families, 1986).

Dixon, jay, *The Romantic Fiction of Mills and Boon, 1909–1990s* (London: UCL Press, 1999).

Doan, Laura (ed.), *Old Maids to Radical Spinsters: Unmarried Women in the Twentieth Century Novel* (Urbana, IL: University of Illinois Press, 1991).

Doan, Laura, *Fashioning Sapphism: The Origins of a Modern English Lesbian Culture* (New York: Columbia University Press, 2000).

Dyhouse, Carol, *No Distinction of Sex? Women in British Universities, 1870–1939* (London: UCL Press, 1995).

Edwards, Elizabeth, *Women in Teacher Training Colleges, 1900–1960: A Culture of Femininity* (London: Routledge, 2001).

Elder, Catriona, 'The Question of the Unmarried: Some Meanings of being Single in Australia in the 1920s and 1930s', *Australian Feminist Studies*, 18:2 (1993).

Essex, Rosamund, *Woman in a Man's World* (London: Sheldon Press, 1977).

Evans, Mary, *Missing Persons: The Impossibility of Auto/Biography* (London: Routledge, 1999).

Ferguson, Sheila and Hilde Fitzgerald, *Studies in the Social Services* (London: HMSO and Longmans, Green, 1954).

Finch, Janet, *Family Obligations and Social Change* (Cambridge: Polity, 1989).

Finch, Janet and Penny Summerfield, 'Social Reconstruction and the Emergence of Companionate Marriage, 1945–59' in David Clarke (ed.), *Marriage, Domestic Life and Social Change: Writings for Jacqueline Burgoyne, 1944–88* (London: Routledge, 1991).

Fink, Janet, 'Natural Mothers, Putative Fathers, and Innocent Children: The Definition and Regulation of Parental Relationships Outside Marriage in England, 1945–1959', *Journal of Family History*, 25:2 (2000).

Fink, Janet, 'Private Lives, Public Issues: Moral Panics and "the Family" in Twentieth Century Britain', *Journal for the Study of British Cultures*, 9:2 (2002).

Fink, Janet and Julie Charlesworth, 'Historians and Social-Science Research Data: The Peter Townsend Collection', *History Workshop Journal*, 51 (2001).

Fink, Janet and Katherine Holden, 'Pictures from the Margins of Marriage: Representations of Spinsters and Single Mothers in the Mid-Victorian Novel, Interwar Hollywood Melodrama and British Film of the 1950s and 1960s', *Gender and History*, 11:2 (1999).

Franzen, Trisha, *Spinsters and Lesbians: Independent Womanhood in the United States* (New York: New York University Press, 1996).

Froide, Amy M., *Never Married: Singlewomen in Early Modern England* (Oxford: Oxford University Press, 2005).

Frost, Ginger, '"The Black Lamb of the Black Sheep": Illegitimacy in the English Working Class, 1850–1939", *Journal of Social History*, 37:2 (2003).

Garfield, Simon (ed.), *Our Hidden Lives: The Remarkable Diaries of Post-War Britain*, 2004 (London: Ebury Press, 2005).

—— *We Are at War: The Diaries of Five Ordinary People in Extraordinary Times* (London: Ebury Press, 2005).

Gathorne-Hardy, Jonathan, *The Rise and Fall of the British Nanny* (London: Weidenfeld and Nicolson, 1993).

Giles, Judy, *Women, Identity and Private Life in Britain, 1900–50* (London: Macmillan, 1995).

—— 'Help for Housewives: Domestic Service and the Reconstruction of Domesticity in Britain', *Women's History Review*, 10:2 (2001).

Gillis, John, *For Better, for Worse: British Marriages 1600 to the Present* (Oxford: Oxford University Press, 1985).

—— 'Marginalization of Fatherhood in Western Countries', *Childhood*, 7:2 (2000).

Gittins, Diana, 'Marital Status, Work and Kinship 1850–1930' in Jane Lewis (ed.), *Labour and Love: Women's Experience of Home and Family, 1850–1940* (Oxford: Blackwell, 1986).

Glucksmann, Miriam, *Women Assemble: Women Workers and the New Industries in Interwar Britain* (London: Routledge, 1990).

—— 'Some Do, Some Don't (But in Fact They All Do Really); Some Will, Some Won't; Some Have, Some Haven't: Women, Men, Work, and Washing Machines', *Gender and History*, 7:2 (1995).

Grier, Julie, 'A Spirit of Friendly Rivalry: Voluntary Societies and the Formation of Post-War Child Welfare Legislation in Britain' in Jon Lawrence and Pat Starkey (eds), *Child Welfare and Social Action* (Liverpool: Liverpool University Press, 2001).

Hall, Andreas, '"May the Doctor Advise Extramarital Intercourse?": Medical Debates on Sexual Abstinence in Germany, c. 1900' in Roy Porter and Mikuláš Teich (eds), *Sexual Knowledge, Sexual Science: The History of Attitudes to Sexuality* (Cambridge: Cambridge University Press, 1994).

Hall, Lesley, *Hidden Anxieties: Male Sexuality 1900–1950* (Cambridge: Polity, 1991).

Hall, M. P. and I. V. Howes, *The Church in Social Work: A Study of Moral Wefare Work undertaken by the Church of England* (London: Routledge and Kegan Paul, 1965).

Haste, Cate, *Rules of Desire: Sex in Britain: World War I to the Present* (London: Chatto and Windus, 1992).

Hewlett, Sylvia Ann, *Baby Hunger: The New Battle for Motherhood* (London: Atlantic Books, 2002).

Hill, Bridget, *Women Alone: Spinsters in England* (London: Yale University Press, 2002).

Hodgson, John, *The Search for Self: Childhood in Autobiography and Fiction since 1940* (Sheffield: Sheffield Academic Press, 1993).

Holden, Katherine, 'Family, Caring and Unpaid Work', in Ina Zweiniger Bargielowska (ed.), *Women in Twentieth Century Britain* (London: Pearson, 2001).

—— '"Nature takes no notice of Morality": Singleness and *Married Love* in Interwar Britain', *Women's History Review*, 11:3 (2002). (Bristol: Policy Press, 2004).

—— 'Personal Costs and Personal Pleasures: Care and the Unmarried Woman' in Janet Fink (ed.), *Care: Personal Lives and Social Policy* (Bristol: Policy Press, 2004).

—— 'Imaginary Widows: Spinsters, Marriage and the Lost Generation in Britain after the Great War', *Journal of Family History*, 30:4 (2005).

Holloway, Gerry, *Women and Work in Britain since 1840* (London: Routledge, 2005).

Hooper, Walter, *C. S. Lewis: A Companion and Guide* (London: HarperCollins, 1997).

Hooper, Walter and Roger Lancelyn Green, *C. S. Lewis: A Biography* (London: William Collins, 1974).

Houlbrook, Matt, *Queer London: Space, Identities and Male Practices, 1918–1957* (Chicago: University of Chicago Press, 2005).

Humble, Nicola, *The Feminine Middlebrow Novel, 1920s to 1950s* (Oxford: Oxford University Press, 2001).

Hunt, Peter, *Arthur Ransome* (Boston, MA: Twayne, 1991).

Jackson, Margaret, *The Real Facts of Life: Feminism and the Politics of Sexuality 1850–1940* (London: Taylor and Francis, 1994).

Jamieson, Lynn, *Intimacy: Personal Relationships in Modern Society* (Cambridge: Polity, 1999).

Jeffreys, Sheila, *The Spinster and her Enemies: Feminism and Sexuality 1880–1930* (London: Pandora, 1985).

Johnson, Pam, '"The Best Friend that Life has Given Me": Does Winifred Holtby have a Place in Lesbian History?' in Lesbian History Group (eds), *Not a Passing Phase: Recovering Lesbians in History 1840–1985* (London: Women's Press, 1985).

Kennard, Jean E., *Vera Brittain and Winifred Holtby: A Working Partnership* (London: University Press of New England, 1989).

Kent, Susan Kingsley, *Making Peace: The Reconstruction of Gender in Interwar Britain* (Princeton, NJ: Princeton University Press, 1993).

Kessler-Harris, Alice, *In Pursuit of Equity: Women, Men and the Quest for Economic Citizenship in Twentieth Century America* (Oxford: Oxford University Press, 2001).

Kiernan, Kathleen, Hilary Land and Jane Lewis, *Lone Motherhood in Twentieth Century Britain: From Footnote to Front Page* (Oxford: Clarendon Press, 1998).

Kingsley Kent, Susan, *Sex and Suffrage in Britain 1860–1914* (Princeton, NJ: Princeton University Press, 1987).

Kirk, David and Susan McDaniel, 'Adoption Policy in Great Britain', *Journal of Social Policy*, 13:1 (1984).

Kuhn, Annette, *Cinema, Censorship and Sexuality, 1909–1925* (London: Routledge, 1989).

Kunzel, Regina, *Fallen Women, Problem Girls: Unmarried Mothers and the Professionalization of Social Work, 1890–1945* (New Haven, CT: Yale University Press, 1993).

Laqueur, Thomas, *Solitary Sex: A Cultural History of Masturbation* (New York: Zone Books, 2003).

Lawson, Valerie, *Mary Poppins, She Wrote: The Life of P. L. Travers* (London: Aurum Press, 1999).

Leap, Nicky, and Billie Hunter, *The Midwife's Tale: An Oral History from Handywoman to Professional Midwife* (London: Scarlet Press, 1993).

Lewis, Jane, *The Politics of Motherhood* (London: Croom Helm, 1980).

—— 'Dealing with Dependency: State Practices and Social Realities, 1870–1945' in Jane Lewis (ed.), *Women's Welfare, Women's Rights* (London: Croom Helm, 1983).

—— *Women in England: Sexual Divisions and Social Change 1870–1950* (Brighton: Wheatsheaf, 1984).

Lewis, Jane and Barbara Meredith, *Daughters who Care: Daughters Caring for Mothers at Home* (London: Routledge, 1988).

Linsley, Colin A. and Christine L. Linsley, 'Booth, Rowntree, and Llewelyn Smith: A Reassessment of Interwar Poverty', *Economic History Review*, 46:1 (1993).

Lively, Penelope, *Oleander Jacaranda: A Childhood Perceived* (Harmondsworth: Penguin, 1995).

Loftus, Donna, 'The Self in Society: Middle Class Men and Autobiography' in David Amigoni (ed.), *Life Writing, Gender, and Class Identity Formation in Victorian Culture* (Aldershot: Ashgate, 2004).

London School of Economics and Political Science, *The New Survey of London Life and Labour*, 9 vols (London: P. S. King and Son, 1930–5).

Mackinnon, Alison, *Love and Freedom: Professional Women and the Reshaping of Personal Life* (Cambridge: Cambridge University Press, 1997).

Matthews, Jill Julius, '"They Had Such a Lot of Fun": the Women's League of Health and Beauty', *History Workshop Journal*, 30 (1990).

Melman, Billie, *Women and the Popular Imagination in the 1920s: Flappers and Nymphs* (London: Macmillan, 1988).

Mitchell, Juliet, *Psychoanalysis and Feminism* (Harmondsworth: Penguin, 1975).

—— (ed.), *The Selected Melanie Klein* (Harmondsworth: Penguin, 1986).

Moore, Katherine, *Cordial Relations: The Maiden Aunt in Fact and Fiction* (London: Heinemann, 1966).

Myerson, Julie, *Home: The Story of Everyone Who Ever Lived in Our House* (London: Harper Perennial, 2004).

O'Connor, Pat, *Friendships between Women: A Critical Review* (London: Harvester Wheatsheaf, 1992).

Oldfield, Sybil, *Spinsters of this Parish: The Life and Times of F. M. Mayor and Mary Sheepshanks* (London: Virago, 1984).

Oram, Alison, 'Repressed and Thwarted, or Bearer of the New World? The Spinster in Interwar Discourses', *Women's History Review*, 1:3 (1992).

—— *Women Teachers and Feminist Politics, 1900–39* (Manchester: Manchester University Press, 1996).

Oram, Alison and Annmarie Turnbull, *The Lesbian History Sourcebook: Love and Sex between Women in Britain from 1780 to 1970* (London: Routledge, 2001).

O'Rourke, Rachel, *Reflecting on The Well of Loneliness* (London: Routledge, 1989).

Osgerby, Bill, '"Bachelors in Paradise": Masculinity, Lifestyle and Men's Magazines in Post-War America' in John Horne (ed.), *Masculinities: Leisure Cultures, Identities and Consumption*, LSA Publication 69 (Eastbourne: LSA Publications, 2000).

Page, Martin, *Crimefighters of London: A History of the Origins and Development of the London Probation Service, 1876–1965* (London: Inner London Probation Service Benevolent and Educational Trust, 1992).

Pateman, Carol, *The Sexual Contract* (Cambridge: Polity, 1988).

Pederson, Susan, *Eleanor Rathbone and the Politics of Conscience* (London: Yale University Press, 2004).

Peretz, Elizabeth, 'The Professionalisation of Childcare', *Oral History Journal*, 17:1 (1989).

Philips, Deborah and Ian Haywood, *Brave New Causes: Women in British Postwar Fiction* (Leicester: Leicester University Press, 1998).

Porter, Kevin and Jeffrey Weeks, *Between the Acts: Lives of Homosexual Men 1885–1967* (London: Routledge, 1991).

Porter, Roy and Lesley Hall, *The Facts of Life: The Creation of Sexual Knowledge in Britain, 1650–1950* (London: Yale University Press, 1995).

Pugh, Martin, *Women and the Women's Movement, 1900–1950* (London: Macmillan, 1992).

Rapp, Dean, 'The Early Discovery of Freud by the British General Educated Public, 1912–1919', *Social History of Medicine*, 3:2 (1990).

Renton, Alice, *Tyrant or Victim? A History of the British Governess* (London: Weidenfeld and Nicolson, 1991).

Reynolds, Barbara, *Dorothy Sayers: Her Life and Soul* (London: Hodder and Stoughton, 1993).

Richards, Margaret, *Adoption* (Bristol: Jordan and Sons, 1989).

Richardson, Dianne, *Women, Motherhood and Childrearing* (London: Macmillan, 1993).

Riley, Denise, *War in the Nursery: Theories of the Child and Mother* (London: Virago, 1983).

Roper, Lyndall, *Oedipus and the Devil: Witchcraft, Sexuality and Religion in Early Modern Europe* (London: Routledge, 1994).

Roper, Michael, *Masculinity and the British Organisational Man since 1945* (Oxford: Oxford University Press, 1994).

Rose, June, *Marie Stopes and the Sexual Revolution* (London: Faber and Faber, 1992).

Ross, Ellen, *Love and Toil: Motherhood in Outcast London, 1870–1918* (Oxford: Oxford University Press, 1993).

Scott, Joan, *Gender and the Politics of History* (New York: Columbia Press, 1988).

Sedgwick, Eve Kosofsky, 'Tales of the Avunculate: The Importance of Being Earnest', in Eve Kosofsky Sedgwick, *Tendencies* (London: Routledge, 1994).

Segal, Lynne, *Slow Motion: Changing Masculinities, Changing Men* (London: Virago, second edition, 1997).

Shaw, Marion, *The Clear Stream: A Life of Winifred Holtby* (London: Virago, 1999).

Shelley, Hugh, *Arthur Ransome* (London: Bodley Head, 1960).

Silva, Elizabeth B. and Carol Smart, *The New Family* (London: Sage, 1999).

Smith, H., 'Gender and the Welfare State: The Old Age and Widows' Pensions Act', *History*, 80 (1995).

Solinger, Rickie, 'Race and "Value": Black and White Illegitimate Babies in the USA, 1945–1965', *Gender and History* 4:3 (1992).

Stanley, Liz, *Sex Surveyed, 1949–1994: From Mass Observation's 'Little Kinsey' to the National Survey and Hite Reports* (London: Taylor and Francis, 1995).

Steedman, Carolyn, *Landscape for a Good Woman: A Story of Two Lives* (London: Virago, 1985).

Stocks, Mary, *Eleanor Rathbone* (London: Gollancz, 1949).

Summerfield, Penny, 'Cultural Reproduction in the Education of Girls: A Study of Girls' Secondary Schooling in Two Lancashire Towns, 1900–1950' in Felicity Hunt (ed.), *Lessons for Life: The Schooling of Girls and Women, 1850–1950* (Oxford: Blackwell, 1987).

—— *Reconstructing Women's Wartime Lives: Discourses and Subjectivity in Oral Histories of the Second World War* (Manchester: Manchester University Press, 1998).

Taylor, Pam, 'Daughters and Mistresses – Mothers and Maids: Domestic Service between the Wars' in J. Clarke, C. Critcher and R. Johnson (eds), *Working Class Culture: Studies in History and Theory* (London: Hutchinson, 1979).

Tincknell, Estella, 'Jane or Prudence? Barbara Pym's Single Women, Female Fulfilment and Career Choices in the "age of marriage"', *Critical Survey*, 18:1

(2006).

Tinkler, Penny, *Constructing Girlhood: Popular Magazines for Girls Growing Up in England, 1920–1950* (London: Taylor and Francis, 1995).

Todd, Selina, *Young Women, Work and Family in England 1918–1950* (Oxford: Oxford University Press, 2005).

Tosh, John, 'Domesticity and Manliness in the Victorian Middle Class: The Family of Edward Benson' in Michael Roper and John Tosh (eds), *Manful Assertions: Masculinities in Britain since 1800* (London: Routledge, 1991).

Townsend, Peter, *The Family Life of Old People*, 1957 (Harmondsworth: Penguin, 1963).

Tucker, Nicholas, 'Finding the Right Voice: The Search for the Ideal Companion in Adventure Stories', in Charlotte F. Otten and Gary D. Schmidt (eds), *The Voice of the Narrator in Children's Literature* (Westport, CI: Greenwood Press, 1989).

Vicinus, Martha, *Independent Women: Work and Community for Single Women 1850–1920* (London: Virago, 1985).

—— *Intimate Friends: Women who Loved Women 1778–1928* (London: University of Chicago Press, 2004).

Walsh, Barbara, *Roman Catholic Nuns in England and Wales 1800–1937: A Social History* (Dublin: Irish Academic Press, 2002).

Walton, Cynthia with Pauline Hodder, *A Grounding for Life: A History of Maltman's Green' School* (London: Barn Books, 2004).

Weeks, Jeffrey, *Coming Out: Homosexual Politics from the Nineteenth Century to the Present* (London: Quartet Books, 1977).

—— *Sex, Politics and Society: The Regulation of Sexuality since 1800* (London: Longman, second edition, 1989).

Whitehead, Kay, 'Postwar Headteachers' Perspectives of "good" Teachers, *Journal of Administration and History*, 35:1 (2003).

Wilmott, Phyllis, *A Singular Woman: The Life of Geraldine Aves* (London: Whiting and Birch, 1992).

Wilson, A. N., *C. S. Lewis: A Biography* (London: Flamingo, 1991).

Wimperis, Virginia, *The Unmarried Mother and her Child*, (London: George Allen and Unwin, 1960).

Winter, J. M., *The Great War and the British People* (London: Macmillan, 1985).

Worsnop, J., 'A Reevaluation of "the Problem of Surplus Women" in Nineteenth-Century England: The Case of the 1851 Census', *Women's Studies International Forum*, 13:1/2 (1990).

Wright, Fay, 'Single Carers: Employment, Housework and Caring' in Janet Finch and Dulcie Groves (eds), *A Labour of Love: Women, Work and Caring* (London: Routledge and Kegan Paul: 1983).

Yeo, Eileen, *The Contest for Social Science: Relations and Representations of Gender and Class* (London: Rivers Oram Press, 1996).

Young, Michael, and Peter Willmott, *The Family and Kinship in East London*, 1957 (Harmondsworth: Penguin, 1962).

Index